KW-223-011

Volume 15, Number 4   Autumn 1999

Editor-in-chief: E. Thomas Glasow
Book Review Editor: Joe K. Law

Oxford University Press, Cary, North Carolina

Reader information

The Opera Quarterly (ISSN 0736-0053) is published quarterly by Oxford University Press, 2001 Evans Road, Cary, NC 27513-2009. Periodicals Postage Paid at Cary, NC, and additional mailing offices. Postmaster: Send address changes to *The Opera Quarterly*, Journals Customer Service Department, Oxford University Press, 2001 Evans Road, Cary, NC 27513-2009.

Oxford University is a department of the University of Oxford. It furthers the University's objective of excellence in research, scholarship, and education by publishing worldwide.

Subscriptions

Subscriptions are available on a calendar-year basis. The annual rates (Volume 15, 1999—4 issues) are US$42 (£30 in UK and Europe) for individuals; US$25 (£19 in UK and Europe) for students (please include copy of current ID); US$110 (£80 in UK and Europe) for institutions. Single issues are available for US$12 (£10 in UK and Europe) for individuals and students; US$33 (£24 in UK and Europe) for institutions. All prices include postage. Individual rates are only applicable when a sub-scription is for individual use and are not available if delivery is made to a corporate address. All requests for subscriptions, single issues, back issues, changes of address, and claims for missing issues should be sent to: NORTH AMERICA: Oxford University Press, Journals Subscriptions Depart-ment, 2001 Evans Road, Cary, NC 27513, USA. Toll-free in the USA and Canada 800-852-7323 or 919-677-0977. Fax 919-677-1714. E-mail: jnlorders@oup-usa.org. ELSEWHERE: Oxford University Press, Journals Subscriptions Depart-ment, Great Clarendon Street, Oxford OX2 6DP, UK. Tel: +44 1865 267907. Fax: +44 1865 267485. E-mail: jnl.orders@oup.co.uk.

Editorial correspondence should be sent to

Editor
The Opera Quarterly
197 Oaklawn Drive
Rochester, NY 14617-1813

Books to be considered for review should be sent to

Book Review Editor
The Opera Quarterly
805 Warrington Place
Dayton, OH 45419

Compact-disc and videocassette recordings to be considered for review should be sent to

Editor
The Opera Quarterly
197 Oaklawn Drive
Rochester, NY 14617-1813

Advertising

Helen Pearson, Oxford Journals Advertising, P.O. Box 347, Abingdon SO OX14 5XX, UK. Tel/Fax: +44 1235 201904. E-mail: oxfordads@helenp. demon.co.uk.

U.S. newsstand distribution by

Eastern News Distributors, Inc.
111 Eighth Ave.
New York, NY 10011

The Opera Quarterly is indexed in *Arts & Humanities Citation Index*, *Current Contents*, *Humanities Index*, *IBR* (*International Bibliography of Book Reviews*), *IBZ* (*International Bibliography of Periodical Literature Covering All Fields of Knowledge*), *Music Article Guide*, *Music Index*, and *UnCover*.

The journal is printed on acid-free paper that meets the minimum requirements of ANSI Standard Z39.48—1984 (Permanence of Paper).

Cover illustration: Jacques Fromental Halévy (drawing by Janet Langs, based on a photograph by MM. L. Cremière et Comp., as published in *L'Illustration, Journal universel*, 29 March 1862). (Courtesy of Andrew S. Pope.)

Contents

Please visit the journal's World Wide Web site at
www.oup.co.uk/operaq

For more information about Oxford University Press,
please visit us at
www.oup-usa.org

Quarter Notes

OUR autumn issue, the fourth and last of 1999 (but, I hasten to add, *not* of the millennium, which doesn't officially end until 31 December 2000), contains what I believe to be an interesting assortment of feature articles and reviews. Although this year marks the centenary of the birth of Francis Poulenc (whose *Dialogues des Carmélites* ranks in my opinion as one of the great operas of the twentieth century), we have chosen instead to honor the *bi*centennial of the birth of another, lesser-known composer, Jacques Fromental Halévy (1799–1864). Those who have ever heard of Halévy will know that he wrote *La Juive*, that grand Meyerbeerian opera whose tenor role of Eléazar became a specialty of both Caruso and Tucker. TOM KAUFMAN, in an overview of the man and his work, reminds us that Halévy wrote more than *La Juive* and that revivals of at least a few of his other thirty-some operas are beginning to occur with some regularity. The article concludes with a catalog of Halévy's operatic works, including the names of roles and (when possible) the singers who created them.

The year 1999 has witnessed somewhat of a resurgence of interest in Halévy. In New York last April, I attended a symposium titled "Meyerbeer, Halévy, and Their Contemporaries" at the kind invitation of the Meyerbeer Fan Club, an internet-based organization established two years ago to promote a renewal of interest in neglected nineteenth-century French *grand opéra*. The event included some opening remarks by club co-founder Stephen A. Agus, musical selections performed by members of the St. Jude Opera Workshop, speeches by Tom Kaufman and Robert Ignatius Letellier (editor of the English version of the *Meyerbeer Diaries*), and a panel discussion enlisting the expertise of the aforementioned gentlemen and other distinguished academicians, including Dr. Diana Hallman of the University of Kentucky, author of a forthcoming book on Halévy. Two days later a rare concert performance of *La Juive* was given in Carnegie Hall by the Opera Orchestra of New York and the Dallas Symphony Chorus, under the direction of the adventurous Eve Queler. Amazingly, it was the first time in over six decades that the work had been heard in New York City (it was last done at the Metropolitan in 1936). The performance made me wonder why this imposing work, once a favorite vehicle of tenors as illustrious as

Enrico Caruso and Richard Tucker, seems in recent years to have all but disappeared from the American opera stage. Has this "apotheosis of Judaism," apparently the only opera in the history of the lyric stage to confront the theme of anti-Semitism head-on, fallen victim to a post-Holocaust dread of political incorrectness? (Scribe's libretto is pretty strong stuff: the Christian-Jewish conflict dominates the action of the plot, and the title-role character is executed by being hurled into a cauldron of boiling oil.) Queler, who was brave enough to tackle the score in the concert hall, has gone on record as being reluctant to see the work fully staged, feeling that "a Jewish audience is going to have trouble with [the ending]," which hits "a little too close to home."[1]

Ironically, Halévy's masterpiece appears to have received the lion's share of post-war attention from the Germans, who have mounted it in Bielefeld (1988), Nürnberg (1993), Dortmund (1995), and Ludwigshafen (1997). This fall a new staging was unveiled at the Vienna Staatsoper, in a co-production with the New Israel Opera, Tel Aviv. And the German publishing firm of Bärenreiter is overseeing the brand-new edition of the complete full score of *La Juive* edited by Karl Leich-Galland (coproduction Alkor-Edition Kassel / Musik-Edition Lucie Galland, Heilbronn).

CHRISTOPHER HEPPNER's in-depth analysis of *Le nozze di Figaro* demonstrates how concepts of monetary exchange and economics in general determine the nature and development of so many of the opera's character relationships—an approach that should speak loudly to us in this age of volatile markets, mutual funds, and capital gains. (My only apprehension is that this fascinating article might inspire some innovative stage director to relocate the Almaviva residence, from Fifth Avenue to Wall Street.)

Long-term subscribers to *OQ* may recall two articles chronicling the early history of opera production in the United States: "Grand Opera in St. Louis in 1886: A Champion Season?" (vol. 10, no. 3) and "Grand Opera in Nebraska in the 1890s" (vol. 11, no. 2). Their author, HARLAN JENNINGS, returns in this issue to offer another in his series of panoramas of operatic activity in the nineteenth-century American heartland, this time centering on Kansas City, Missouri.

A lively and uninhibited yet solidly reasoned and technically informative appraisal of the art of Beniamino Gigli constitutes the rich offering from JACQUES CHUILON, author of *Opéra Opinion* and *Battistini, le dernier divo*. Written exclusively for *OQ* in the author's native French, the text (which includes a critical survey of many of the famous Italian lyric tenor's recordings) is published here, for the first time ever, in your editor's translation.

In closing, I cannot allow the successful completion of this volume of *OQ* to pass into publication history without expressing my sincere appreciation to the staff of Oxford University Press for their uncanny efficiency, solid support, and inspiring work. Subscribers present and future can rest assured that this unique journal has found the most congenial of homes.

NOTE

1. Eve Queler, quoted in George Robinson, "Reimagining *The Jewess*," *The New York Jewish Week*, 9 April 1999, p. 33.

CALL FOR ARTICLES

The 2001 commemorative issue of *The Opera Quarterly* will mark the two hundredth anniversary of the birth of Vincenzo Bellini. The editor welcomes the submission of articles on Bellini-related topics. Manuscripts should be submitted by 15 September 2000. Please refer to "Submission of Articles and Instructions to Authors" in the back of this journal for guidelines in the preparation of manuscripts.

"L'ho perduta": Barbarina, Cherubino, and the Economics of Love in *Le nozze di Figaro*

CHRISTOPHER HEPPNER

I

Early in Mozart's opera, Marcellina remarks that "nothing better can be expected: money is everything" in response to the discovery that her beloved Figaro is hoping to marry Susanna, and that the Count is offering a dowry to pay off the lien she holds on Figaro, in exchange for time with Susanna's person.[1] Marcellina assumes the latter's willingness to go through with the transaction as a way of purchasing a husband: "We must / Frighten Susanna; we must cunningly / Persuade her to reject the Count" (1.3). Her words reflect a poor opinion of all around her: she assumes that Figaro can be bought for cash, that Susanna is ready to purchase a husband at the price of her body, and that these acts would be normal, given the way of the world as she has experienced it: *"l'argent fait tout."* The phrase focuses the economics of exchange in *Le nozze di Figaro*, in which money and love have become alarmingly convertible — two thousand crowns seems to be the current exchange rate.[2]

The action begins in a feudal world in which protection and privilege are granted in exchange for service in an economy governed by something like the system of the gift as described by Mauss: "a gift [is] generously offered; but the accompanying behaviour is formal pretence and social deception, while the transaction itself is based on obligation and economic self-interest."[3] The potlatch, as commonly interpreted (or misinterpreted — the real thing was a social event of considerable complexity), will be used here as a shorthand form of reference to a display of apparent generosity that only half conceals a strong expectation of return. A dark version of the potlatch might be called the poisoned gift, exemplified in Bartolo's words: "Oh, how I'd relish / Giving my old servant in marriage / To the one who stole my sweet-heart from me" (1.3); vengeful punishment forms the substance of such a "gift."

One large step above such interactions lies a wished-for world of bourgeois contract, in which individuals would negotiate freely their own self-interest without having to work through a maze of covert designs pretending to generosity, a world in which marriage as a contractual arrangement between free and equal individuals would become part of the "gradual dissolution of family dependency and the growth of individual obligation in its place."[4] A world governed by individual contract implies that the parties involved are "legal if not social equals"[5] and thus offers a halfway house toward a possible community of personal and sexual freedom glimpsed in the cooperation between the women in the story, a community in which love and money have been successfully uncoupled, and class boundaries and the exchange systems controlled by men have been bypassed in favor of freely exchanged mutual help.

The establishment of a changed and less oppressive society is a frequent aim of comic structures, but comedy also often includes one or more characters who repeat gestures with an almost mechanical compulsion and are excluded, or exclude themselves, from the renewed society created by the happy conclusion; Jacques in *As You Like It* and Malvolio in *Twelfth Night* are examples.[6] Comedy has to negotiate between the celebration of claimed radical change and the sober realization that the world will for the most part probably continue in its customary ways. Change is imminent throughout *Le nozze*, but one should ask whether the "day of torment" ends in a state of "happiness and joy" based on substantial and lasting transformation, or whether real change has been displaced into the golden future promised in the finale, while the action itself has represented merely a "Folle Giornata," as the subtitle of the 1786 Prague libretto has it, following Beaumarchais.

Susanna and Figaro try to move from feudal servitude toward the relative freedom of a bourgeois economy, in which they can exchange clearly defined services for money on a basis that recognizes their right to a measure of privacy and independence. They are trying to set up the "all-subsuming, all-organizing, all-containing contract"[7] of a marriage between two individuals as defense against the power of the Count as head of a feudal extended family. Their wished-for bourgeois household is figured at the opening in Susanna's making of her wedding hat, and in the measurements for the bed that Figaro is counting out, within a still feudal palace that surrounds and threatens their enterprise; ominously, their bedroom is planned for the space between the chambers of the Count and Countess. The hat and the bed act as metonyms for the socially and sexually charming aspects of Susanna's body, over which the battle will be fought.

The Count intends a rather brutal exchange of money for goods, though he still wraps his offer/demand in the feudal language of a gift of protection in exchange for service rendered as if on a basis of affection. He has made his intent clear: "Oh, for this favor I'd pay" (1.6), as Susanna has to explain to a rather slow Figaro: "And you thought / That my dowry was / A reward for your handsome mug? . . . He's given it to me / So he can claim those half-hours of pleasure" (1.1). There is a sting in the "mezz'ore," which offer both insult and ironic flattery; the half-hours are clearly not to be wasted on reading, but the pay per hour for the use of her body is high.

The Count attempts to reduce Susanna to a desirable and purchasable body, in the process asserting his power over dependents like Figaro to whom he was once indebted. His bitterest feeling is aroused by the thought of such once-dependent people now moving toward independence and, worse, arousing feelings of dependence within him; his desires, which in his view ought to take immediate hold upon their objects, now threaten to subject him to the whims of those objects as they withhold satisfaction while continuing to arouse desire: "Shall I live to see a servant of mine / So happy, while I am left to sigh?" (3.4). The refusal to be bought is an insult to the Count's self-definition as one who can purchase and enjoy whatever he desires, and an unwelcome reminder both of the limits of feudal power in a changing world and of how desire can shift rapidly from being an agent of power to becoming an agent of self-abasement.

The Count is at the center of a society nominally dominated by males, many of them commercial dependents (Beaumarchais's Count refers to his at one point as "mes vassaux" [5.12]) who piece out a living from scraps dropped from his table in exchange for aid with his projects. They have adopted the pervasive language of exchange; Basilio as a pandering go-between comments, "That which I buy I sell," while Curzio, the Count's lawyer, bluntly advises Figaro to "pay [Marcellina] or marry her." Bartolo is only partially successful as a social climber; he attempted to win Rosina but lost her and has kept Marcellina, her former tutor, as his mistress, after forcing her to abandon their infant long ago. Bartolo is unmasked and disarmed by the revelation of his responsibility for Figaro's conception; none of these male followers survives the opera unscathed.

Marcellina represents the potential fate of women in such a male-dominated society. She is initially presented as a comic figure, Susanna's "Sibilla decrepita" (decrepit old hag—1.4), but as Wye J. Allanbrook observes, "when later she shows herself capable of maternal affection, her mannerisms become instantly lovable; she seems an eccentric but amiable old dear."[8] Her move toward bourgeois marriage is a major step forward from the state of being mistress, which represents a kind of parody of feudal protection given in exchange for service. Although she never totally frees herself from the comic mold in which her role was conceived, Marcellina, in overcoming the alienation from feminine solidarity caused by her dependency on Bartolo and her cross-generational jealousy of Susanna, substantially furthers the move toward female solidarity and resistance to male feudal power that becomes stronger as the opera progresses.

The women resist male domination as best they can, while necessarily accommodating themselves to the situation. The Countess's mixed feelings about taking Susanna into her confidence ("E Susanna non vien") mark her reluctance to collapse the space between social classes, but in practice she and Susanna act warmly together; the Countess's help with Susanna's marriage is answered by and interlinked with Susanna's assistance with the Countess's project to reclaim and reeducate the Count. Till writes that the "relationship between the Countess and Susanna, however affectionate, is one of expediency brought about by a common threat rather than genuine sisterly sentiment";[9] expediency, however, seems to have given birth both to warm sentiment and a genuinely free reciprocity. Gift is answered by gift without anxious thought of equivalence, and with a pleasure in cooperative action that finds expression in the structure of "Che soave zefiretto," which begins with Susanna echoing the Countess's spoken phrases as she writes — the servant hand subordinated to the inventing noble mind — but moves to voices playing together as they sing "Certo, certo: il capirà" in celebration of their shared understanding of the Count.[10] The two join to protect both themselves and the polymorphous perversity of Cherubino, keeping alive the potential power of Eros to restructure the world in the shape of mutual desire rather than of exchanges forced by monetary and other power.

The women are assisted by the complex relationships that underlie the action and bridge classes in the small world of the Count's palace. Susanna is Barbarina's cousin. Marcellina instructed the Countess while the latter was Bartolo's ward and discovers late in act 3 that she is also Figaro's mother, thus helping at a critical moment to dissolve the sword the Count has been holding over Susanna's head — his power to assist Marcellina in forcing Figaro to marry her. Marcellina by virtue of her previous relationships with both the Countess and Figaro helps bridge the gap between classes in the action, as does the Countess herself, who has moved from being courted (not in this opera) by Bartolo to being married to the Count. The Countess is also Cherubino's godmother, which should give her some rights in protecting him and furthering his education. Though placed in the background, these collateral and independent relationships, flesh-and-blood family ties, diminish the Count's total control over the action, even though all the lines of direct power still radiate from him.

Figaro joins with the women to combat this power; he crosses both sex and class lines, and has learned that with the help of Susanna he may yet control the tune to which the Count dances. This is no empty metaphor. Peasant song and dance are among Figaro's weapons, for clearly someone has shaped the celebration in act 3, praising the "Si saggio signore" who has renounced "a right / That insults and offends"; Figaro, doubtless with help, has sounded a tune to which the Count is at least forced to listen.[11]

These actions can be understood as forms of potlatching. The Count offers a wedding complete with dowry and fireworks, covertly (except to those in the know) expecting a return on his expenditure, while Figaro offers — or has had a strong hand in organizing — public thanks to the Count for having renounced an offensive right, covertly expecting that it will help shame the Count into sacrificing his willful desire to maintain that right.

All these motifs come to a focus and temporary conclusion in the throwing of money at Figaro after the discovery of his true parentage. In one moment, Figaro is released from the threat of marriage to a woman with proprietary ambitions over him, receives as dowry the canceled bond which had given the Count power over him and Susanna, and wins a new (old) name, Raffaello, which might have acted as a focal point for the recognition of his new status, though it is not used again in the opera. Figaro has been redeemed to the happy state of one whose marriage to his beloved is almost assured and whose dowry is in his hands twice over. When Bartolo reluctantly joins in the transformation, a bourgeois nuclear family is created on the instant within the Count's own retinue, taking the figures concerned out of his total control and giving them a new basis from which to reorganize their lives. Susanna joins in by giving Figaro her two thousand crowns (the libretto does not specify the source, but in Beaumarchais it is the Countess, and that is the likeliest implication here), announcing bravely, "I've come to pay for Figaro, / And set him free for good"; this is ransom, redemption, canceling debt and the power of a bond—Portia and the Leonore of *Fidelio* are somewhere in the wings. This act is the type of the Countess's final forgiveness of her erring Count; power relationships supported by money lent or promised—always with expectation of a return—are transformed into affectional relationships based on mutual connection. Susanna is now secure—or relatively so—in her expectation of marriage with her Figaro, and therefore free to aid the Countess in return as the latter tries to win back and transform her Count.

At the end of act 3 Figaro has won, or been won by, his Susanna and has gained newly found parents and a doubled dowry into the bargain. Bartolo and Marcellina have made honest people of each other. But the last act of *Le nozze* is not merely a coda; the Count still retains a great deal of power and has not given up hope of a tryst with Susanna. Fortunately, in the course of the first three acts, the Count's selfish pursuit of his desires has forced counterstrategies from clever people who know how to stage-manage actions before witnesses. He has lost several encounters already and will lose more. Two who figure in that ongoing process of loss are Cherubino and Barbarina, linked figures who flit between classes, sexes, and generations in their lighthearted way, each a "farfallone amoroso," a butterfly charged with erotic feeling. In a lighter key they mirror the maturer figures in the drama and have an impact on the unfolding events.

II

Cherubino is the Count's page, his understudy, and a wonderfully in-between figure. Beaumarchais specified that the role of Chérubin could be played only "by a young and very pretty woman," giving him an ambiguous sexual identity from the beginning. Jacques Seebacher expands that ambiguity in describing Chérubin: "undifferentiated between two stages of growth, two sexes, two classes, coming from no one knows where, present everywhere, disappearing from everywhere, promised a postponed happiness, provisionally condemned to death, the rival of all, loved by all, Chérubin can scarcely be said to have a substantial body."[12] Cherubino inherits this fluidity; he can aspire to love the Countess while winning kisses from Barbarina, with Susanna socially sandwiched in between as a marginally acceptable substitute for the Countess. These are the three women to whom the Count makes some claim, and in each case he encounters his page present as a kind of shadow, pressing his own claims: "It seems I'm condemned / To find that page every time I turn around" (2.8). Cherubino is a child, a "fanciullo," but is old enough to arouse the Count's jealousy, as we see in act 2 when the Count draws his sword and threatens to kill him.

As Susanna seconds, those who find Cherubino attractive "han certo il lor perchè." He is Da Ponte/Mozart's version of Shakespeare's Rosalind/Orlando, the figure who symbolizes and enacts the polymorphous and irresistible power of the ancient/young winged Eros to inspire human acts of folly and new creation. Cherubino is the representation of desire itself, and loves or desires (he does not yet know if there is a difference) all women. His naive energy moves them—desire is contagious.[13] Susanna is lightly touched, responding with a laughing affection released by the (relative and assumed) harmlessness that forms part of his attractiveness; she is free to respond precisely because she is confident that she will soon be united with Figaro. The discouraged Countess is amused and erotically touched by Cherubino, stirred by a memory of what had been her hopes, and perhaps her experience, when she and the Count were younger; it is her lack of hope for the fulfillment of her deeper desires that leaves her vulnerable to the absurd but touching love of Cherubino. Barbarina is touched too, but I shall discuss that relationship later.

Cherubino goes through the opera leading the charmed life of youth; he jumps out of windows without injury and spends time in women's chambers as if he were a eunuch who has managed to keep his sexuality because it has not yet been fully expressed or recognized. He embodies the ever-transgressive and fluid nature of desire before age, social position, and responsibility have ballasted it with the need for loyalty to a single partner: "Every woman makes my heart throb." As the representative of desire itself, his leitmotif is "Voi che sapete," an attempt to describe the phenomenology of this new and overpowering feeling, combined with an appeal to women to instruct him in its mysteries. Cherubino acts as a contagious fluid that interrupts, disturbs, arouses, catalyzes actions in others and reveals partially hidden fault lines in relationships.

The libretto of the first performance in Vienna in 1786 had the following entrance for Cherubino at the beginning of act 4, scene 11, although it has been lightly scored out:

> *Cher.* La la la la la la la la lera
>   Voi che intendete
>   Che cosa è amor,
>   Donne [v]edete
>   S'io l'ho nel cor.

The Count recognizes the voice and responds, "Il picciol paggio!" These words for Cherubino disappear thereafter, not being present in the 1786 Prague libretto. No setting for them has survived in any copyist's full score, but they are set as one would expect to the music of "Voi che sapete" in parts that Haydn obtained from Vienna for a production planned for Eszterháza in 1790. Alan Tyson speculates that the cut was made reluctantly by Mozart, and that the passage should be restored.[14] The lines imply that Cherubino's representative nature as the figure of pure desire was incorporated into the original structure of the opera; in effect, the repetition of the tune says "Here comes Signor Amor again."[15]

Cherubino sings of his yearnings as unfixed and unformed, but they have a center in his godmother, the Countess, toward whom he feels respect suffused with a desire limited so far to requests for a kiss. His movement toward desiring the love-object possessed by the Count, who stands in a quasi-paternal relationship to him, is in the process of producing an openly Oedipal rivalry. There is a suspicion that Cherubino's desire is triggered by women found desirable by others: "Why shouldn't I get / What the Count gets every day?" (4.11); desire is not only contagious, but perhaps itself the result of the kind of contagion traced by René Girard.[16] Cherubino's descends from the medieval courtly tradition of adoration of the wife of another from a distance, and though he freely offers songs and admiration to all, the Countess remains the focal point of his attentions.

Beaumarchais specifies that Chérubin is thirteen and will be very different at eighteen — by which age he is both father and dead in *La mère coupable*. Da Ponte/Mozart do not specify Cherubino's age but give the impression that he is close to the age given by Beaumarchais, maybe a year or so older. His lack of the power that comes with maturity almost guarantees his freedom from serious offense and punishment,[17] although the Count finds it possible to be angry. In this Da Ponte follows Beaumarchais's conception: "Young adept of nature, all that he sees has the power to disturb him; perhaps he is no longer a child, but he is not yet a man."[18] Cherubino mirrors the Count with a large difference that allows him to attract all the women who in one way or another flee from or complain of the Count. What has become in the Count a hardened assault on the freedom of others is in Cherubino still a playful and pleasing eagerness, forgiven almost without thought (except by the Count). Part of the joke of Cherubino's appearance as a soldier is that the soldier is conventionally a figure who seconds his sexual power with weapons: Don Giovanni owes much of his success to his perpetual readiness to fight fathers and rivals. This is not Cherubino's territory yet, though Beaumarchais's Chérubin pluckily half-draws his sword on the Count (5.19).

Cherubino enjoys the stir and excitement of desire —"I've come to enjoy/ My suffering" (2.3) — but, having little present power of his own, must plead with women to feed that desire a little. His posture is that of one who begs, not commands, although he is not above small thefts, as he shows when he snatches the Countess's ribbon from Susanna, offering his written song in exchange ("in ricompensa"). He deals in largely symbolic gifts and values: a ribbon made precious by its past contact with the Countess, a song that may touch the heart of women in the palace and win him a response he cannot command more directly. Having as yet no substantial erotic capital, such opportunism must for the time being limit his entry into the world of love, with the possible exception of Barbarina.

In the act 1 terzetto the Count refers to Cherubino as "il seduttor" and appears — or pretends — to view him as a dangerous rival as well as a nuisance. But the women whom Cherubino courts, though charmed, respond with a laughter that denies him any dangerous power to seduce. Susanna and the Countess even dress him in Susanna's clothes as bait to catch the Count, embarrass him into doing whatever they want, and are a little cavalier about the potential risk to Cherubino, who allows himself to play their game since it wins him further time with Susanna and the Countess. This episode ends with Cherubino in tears before the Countess, fantasizing death as the moment when his lips might dare a kiss — just as the Count knocks at the door. The dangerous seducer feared by the Count, and now to be hidden from his anger, has been dressed as a woman, imagines imminent death as the only circumstance that might embolden him to kiss the Countess, and has been affectionately teased by the two women whom he "loves." There is an air of sacrificial victim about him in this scene; he is about to be loosed to the Count in order to save Susanna, who laughs at him in the process. His chief weapon as a seducer is his vulnerability and openness to seduction by the desires of others.[19] Like the Count, he discovers that desire, while attempting to control its object, can result in the subjection of the desirer to that object.

Cherubino's relationship to Barbarina is both less intense and less ruled by fantasy than his relationships with the Countess and Susanna. In introducing "Non so più," Cherubino tells Susanna to read it "to my lady, . . . to yourself, . . . to Barbarina, and to Marcellina, [and] . . . to every woman in the palace!" (1.5). This places Barbarina third, whether in social ranking or in the intensity of his affections is not clear; with the addition of Marcellina the metrical scheme changes, and as Susanna observes, Cherubino seems to go mad. Cherubino holds the Countess in too much respect to feel truly comfortable with her. Susanna he addresses as "Susannetta" and "cor mio" with considerable freedom, while she teases him about the desertion of the Countess implied in his playful courting of herself; the relationship threatens neither of them with the potential consequences of taking his affections seriously. But Barbarina is in a different and more vulnerable category, and he has already spent time alone with her behind a locked door.

III

In many ways Barbarina is Cherubino's counterpart, though much less has been written about her. Fanchette, the original of Barbarina, is described by Beaumarchais in the "Préface" as twelve years old. In defending his play against attacks on its alleged immorality, Beaumarchais exonerates Chérubin, Figaro, and the Countess, and points at the Count and his agents as the guilty parties, emphasizing "*la corruption des jeunes personnes*" as the central issue in public morality. What Beaumarchais means by this is the subject of an impassioned dialogue originally placed in act 3, in which Marceline explains and defends the course of her life: "*But during the age of illusions, of inexperience and need, during which seductors lay siege to us, and while poverty stabs us in the back, what can a child oppose to so many gathered enemies?*" Beaumarchais was forced to cut this dialogue from the play, but so that the point would not be lost, moved it to his preface, where he comments editorially: "I showed the humiliation of this woman [Marceline], Bartholo's rejection of her, and Figaro, their common son, in order to direct the attention of the public toward the true instigators of the evils toward which all uneducated young girls endowed with a pretty face are pitilessly being dragged."[20] These comments link Marceline very closely with Fanchette, the visible exemplar of those "young girls" and "*jeunes personnes*," and another potential victim of the predatory lust of the powerful, a potential future Marceline.

Fanchette, however, is not a helpless ingenue, as such commentary as this attests: "naivete here is highly ambiguous, and the character incapable of suspecting vice (cf. act 4, scene 5) is always ready to yield to its seductions. Fanchette is fairly close to some of De Sade's heroines (another eighteenth-century libertine writer). . . . This part would therefore be closer to the role type of *perverse ingenu*."[21] Ambiguously both victim and (up to a point) willing seducee, Fanchette, despite the relative modesty of her role, is central to the thematic concerns of the play; I hope to show that Barbarina has an analogous role in the opera.

Da Ponte changes Fanchette's name, though he keeps the diminutive form. St. Barbara had a tyrannical father who first burned and then beheaded his daughter for having adopted the Christian religion. Barbarina's father, Antonio, is perpetually drunk and a bully as far as lies in his means. Da Ponte seems to have chosen Barbarina's name to evoke at a distance the martyr who chose the god of love in spite of a father's opposition.

As Cherubino feels desire for all women, so Barbarina stirs desire in those who meet her; the unnamed "brava gente" who claimed a kiss in exchange for a gift of food add their voices to those of Cherubino and the Count. We learn of Cherubino's attraction first from the Count; the latter is not a disinterested observer, but we can believe that Barbarina's extreme discomposure ("Paurosa fuor dell'uso"—1.7) was real and not merely invented by the Count to score a point.[22]

Despite this apparent vulnerability to Cherubino, we next see her managing him in a way analogous to Susanna's managing of Figaro—"Leave everything to your Barbarina" (3.7); she will disguise him as a girl, enabling him to present himself before the Countess. She is prepared to assist his unrealistic desires as part of her own campaign to win him for herself, and shows considerable self-confidence in the process; she refers to "casa mia" (my house) and assumes responsibility for the presentation to the Countess. In the libretto printed for the first Vienna performance, Barbarina's words are followed by an arietta for Cherubino:

Se così brami		If you so desire
Teco verrò:		I shall come with you;
So che tu m'ami,		I know that you love me,
Fidar mi vo:		I wish to trust [you].
Purchè il bel ciglio	*(a parte)*	Providing that her fair brow
Riveggia ancor,		I may see again,
Nessun periglio		no danger
Mi far timor.		makes me afraid.

As Tim Carter, whose translation I have given, points out, the first stanza is addressed to Barbarina and the second, marked *a parte* (aside), refers to the Countess.[23] Cherubino accepts Barbarina's offer of help in bad faith, as a way of coming once more into the presence of the Countess. Barbarina would seem to be at risk in this encounter, though how seriously we do not know, since she offers her assistance fully aware of the target of his desires.

Barbarina repeats her strategy with the Count. When Cherubino's disguise is penetrated by Antonio and the Count renews his threats to Cherubino, Barbarina turns the tables by claiming that the Count, while hugging and kissing her, promised that if she would love him, "I'll give you whatever you want" (3.12). The payment she now asks is Cherubino himself: "Oh master, if you give me / Cherubino for a husband, / I'll love you as much as my kitten." The comparison is richly ambiguous—did and does Barbarina really misunderstand what the Count had in mind when he said (if he said) "se m'ami," or does she understand very well, choosing to intensify his embarrassment by claiming innocence for herself while allowing the hearers to draw their own conclusions about the Count's motives? The episode is lightly comic, but that does not erase the economic nature of the transaction. Barbarina frees Cherubino from the immediate danger posed by the Count's jealousy and simultaneously asks to be credited with a large installment—allegedly paid for with the small change of minor sexual favors—toward the purchase of Cherubino for herself; she is mirroring Susanna's role, but with the difference that she has actually given up something (the Count and Basilio usurped Susanna's breast, but only while she was unconscious: "Come, oddio, le batte il cor!"—1.7). Barbarina specifies hugs and kisses as the payment ("m'abbracciate, / e mi baciate"); we can try to be fair to both by assuming that the Count has been softening her up for future conquest rather than pursuing immediate total possession, and that Barbarina has been at least partly in command, allowing light transgressions as a way of both controlling the Count's power and winning some of her own.

We hear neither explicit response to nor denial of this claim, and Cherubino is in no position to protest even if he wished to. The Countess tells the Count "now it's up to you," and Antonio (ironically?) congratulates his daughter on a smart play: "Good girl! / You've learned your lesson well." All seem to assume that Barbarina is not too young to be sexually attractive to the Count, and none questions the marriageable status of Cherubino, who might well be a good catch for the gardener's daughter. The Count is abashed and worsted by her claim: "I'd like to know what man or demon or god / Has turned everything against me." His guilt seems established by silence—defense would probably be self-defeating. Barbarina has nonplussed a usually formidable opponent and may just possibly have made headway toward winning a desired partner, but at a cost.

Barbarina has confessed her desire for Cherubino first directly to him and now to the whole company; her youth keeps the situation comic, but her claim involves an admission—or apparently naive boast—of those hugs and kisses allowed to the Count, which casts doubt on her innocence in the eyes of the company, as we see from Figaro's comments early in act 4. Cherubino's silence might mean anything, including a hope that a Barbarina in the hand would be worth two Susannas and Countesses among the bushes, although in act 4 he is still doing his best to fulfill those high-flying fantasies.

Barbarina and Cherubino are tied together by the complementarity of their erotic strategies. Barbarina plays the game of risk ventures by exposing part of her capital to trade, hoping—but without guarantee—that the goods she offers will be found desirable enough to be bought at a price that brings substantial profit. But her capital is limited, and she exposes herself to loss through accident or theft in the process. Cherubino also lacks substantial erotic capital, although his charm sometimes works as a substitute; he is on the lookout for inexpensive goods that he can bargain for at a cheap rate, or if necessary steal, hoping that the low value of the goods stolen, and his considerable charm, will fend off prosecution. He pleads for kisses or snatches ribbons; only with low-ranking prospects might he dare more. His strategy is precisely the one Barbarina must guard against; she cannot afford to sell too cheap, though she cannot ask too high a price, and must therefore negotiate toward a goal that is both desirable and within reach. Cherubino will be less fearful of prosecution for theft if the goods stolen have a low valuation. His erotic capital is on the increase—he shows promise and has some social stature as the Count's page. Barbarina's erotic capital is nearing its modest height; she will reach the point of maximal sexual attractiveness in a few years but is in danger of cheapening it by the aura of lightness that is beginning to surround her: "At such a tender age, / You're already learning" (4.2). If she succeeds in being awarded Cherubino, she wins; if Cherubino seduces her, she loses. In the meantime, they may be able to play the first stages of love's game for a while without either of them incurring serious consequences.

Beaumarchais, in defending Chérubin on the grounds of youth's innocence, writes ironically: "I should have difficulty in making credible the innocence of these impressions [i.e., those made by Chérubin on women] if we lived in a century less chaste, one of those centuries where all was selfish reckoning, in which, wishing for all things too soon, like their hothouse fruits, rich people married off their children at twelve years old, making nature, decency, and good taste yield to the most sordid considerations."[24] The words testify to the pressures that a corrupt society can bring to bear on the young, who may be forced to compromise their innocence in self-defense. Barbarina appears to have given to two men without as yet having won any certain return; she is, to use an old term, within the *daunger* of both Cherubino and the Count. She is at risk of losing in a potlatch game, of giving with no certainty of a return. However, she is not without resources of her own, and indeed it is unclear whether Barbarina is more in danger of seduction by Cherubino or Cherubino more at risk of finding himself bought by Barbarina at a fire sale forced by his own rash pursuit of the objects of his fantasizing desire.

IV

Act 4 opens with Barbarina mournfully searching for an unnamed something that she has lost. The libretto so far has given no clue as to what this might be, although Barbarina expresses anxiety over the possible reactions of both Susanna ("mia cugina") and the Count ("il padron"). With the arrival of Figaro and Marcellina we discover that Barbarina is lamenting the loss of a pin, "the seal of the pine-trees"— the sign of a contract for the delivery of the body of Susanna to the Count. The pin itself was given by the Countess, taken presumably from her own dress, and has the remarkable quality of being "stranger / Than the one on the commission" (3.10). It becomes part of the note that Susanna plants for the Count to pick up, whence it descends to Barbarina as she bears the Count's reply to Susanna. The pin is both a concrete symbol of the connections linking the women and a medium of their revenge, since it pricks the Count's finger as a reminder of how women exert their power everywhere—"Women have to stick their pins wherever possible" (3.14). The pin remains lost; Figaro removes another pin from Marcellina's dress to offer Barbarina in its place, and the substitution is not detected.

The loss is mourned in a touching cavatina, "L'ho perduta, me meschina," Barbarina's only solo in the opera, placed at the strong moment of the opening of act 4, just as the Countess's "Porgi Amor" opens act 2. The cavatina may have been a late addition;[25] the singer playing Barbarina may have demanded a solo— Da Ponte writes in a poem inscribed to Casti that in his experience singers always demand "a better part" or "a bravura aria to cut a better figure."[26] But it is equally possible that the cavatina was inserted for thematic and musical reasons, and, even under pressure from a singer, Da Ponte and Mozart would have stuck to their vision of the opera. Although much of the ensuing dialogue comes from Beaumarchais, the loss of the pin and the aria it prompts are invented by Da Ponte and Mozart; the incident is not strictly necessary to the plot and is thus free to carry thematic freight.

Responses to this number vary widely. One recent commentator observes that Mozart devotes "fewer than forty bars to her sorrow over the lost pin. There is nothing tragic or ominous about it; at the first Vienna production this piece, which raises the curtain on the fourth act, was sung by a twelve-year-old girl."[27] Ironically, Anna Gottlieb, the singer who created the part in 1786 and became the first Pamina five years later, has been romantically associated with Mozart, despite her youth.[28] From a different perspective Hildesheimer writes that the cavatina "opens up a delicate spectrum of other losses," and Mann that "we are kept guessing — perhaps deliberately — by the authors who enjoyed mild lewdness."[29] These last comments point in fruitful directions, but there is more to say.

Allanbrook deals sensitively with the musical action of the piece:

> Barbarina . . . in choosing pastoral rhythms for her cavatina . . . imitates the Countess and Susanna. Her little-girl anguish at losing the pin is caught by the F-minor tonality of the piece and by its frequent pathetic accents; it is an essay in the mock-tragic genre. Chords of the diminished seventh prevail, especially in the orchestral introduction. . . . The introduction closes with a four-measure half-cadence on the dominant featuring a regular [harmonic] alternation . . . as the figures in the treble spiral higher and higher in the purposeless circles of someone searching in vain. Barbarina shortens the introduction by omitting this phrase, making her move to the dominant instead by a fervid augmented sixth on the words "Ah, chi sa dove sarà?" She repeats this half-cadence — a typical *opera seria* model which she probably learned from the Countess, who moves into "Dove sono" from the preceding *recitativo accompagnato* by one very much like it — at the end of the aria, just before Figaro interrupts her. This would suggest that Barbarina had intended her cavatina to be a composite aria: here she would swing into a new section in A-flat major, perhaps cast in exalted-march style like the second part of "Dove sono." But other elements of the piece militate against grand passion: Barbarina's wavering child's voice, the thin texture of the reduced orchestration (strings only), the nursery-rhyme simplicity of the phrase structure. While aping the manners of the Countess and Susanna, Barbarina cannot assimilate them into her childish habit, and this makes for delicate comedy.[30]

This is excellent commentary, and I wish only to darken and complicate the picture a little.

Allanbrook's view of comedy has too little room for felt pain and feared damage; we have no serious doubt that the resolution will be happy, but the plot allows the exploration of dark corners before that happens, and disaster is a possibility hinted at though not indulged in this particular narrative. Da Ponte and

Mozart (like Shakespeare) afford glimpses into disturbing places in the rich fabric of their comedies, opening abysses that only the miraculous powers of forgiveness or divine intervention can close up again. In *Don Giovanni*, for instance, we are left wondering just how far the attempted rape of Donna Anna has gone, while Elvira's life has been darkened permanently. Here in *Le nozze* also we are left wondering for a deliberate moment.

Allanbrook's stress on the second-hand nature of the aria — it is "mock-tragic," Barbarina "apes" the manners of her betters — minimizes the genuine pathos of the piece. Barbarina is admittedly too young to have accumulated a weighty personal history, and so her cavatina lacks the felt personal experience conveyed in the Countess's arias, which both demonstrate a process of thought enacted in word and music. "Porgi Amor" moves between hope for restoration and a desire for death, "Dove sono" between pathetic lament and hope for change in the ungrateful heart of the Count; the drama of thought and choice is reflected in the interplay between sections of the orchestra, which in "Porgi" includes Mozart's favorite clarinets. However, Barbarina's number is the only one in the minor mode in the whole opera, set in what was for Mozart a tragic key.[31] The unaccompanied strings are not necessarily "thin" and "reduced"; Mozart used them for both Elettra's "Idol mio" and Elvira's "Ah! fuggi." There may be "conscious archaism" in such accompaniment, but Heartz, after discussing the question, summarizes that "strings alone bring a special color to a set piece precisely because they are so rarely heard without winds in Mozart's master operas."[32] As the only number in a minor mode, and distinguished from the Countess's laments by its reduced orchestration, Barbarina's cavatina strikes the ear with a different and touching air. The pathos of youth has a plangency that differs from the complex pain of maturity, but it can touch nonetheless, and the cavatina is heartfelt enough to have been used for the ending of the recent film *L'accompagnatrice*, in which another young girl is left alone to face an uncertain future.

In previous acts the libretto has given us a variety of credible threats emanating from the Count: an unwelcome marriage thrust on Figaro, pressure on Susanna to deliver her body to the Count's pleasure, a sword drawn with the declared intent of killing Cherubino, and an apparent willingness to drive bargains involving Barbarina's sexual being, if we assume at least a grain of truth in her version of their past interaction. Now we are presented with an actual, but for a drawn-out moment unspecified loss that apparently puts the loser at risk from the Count. To lose something that is evidently part of a "deal" puts one at risk of sudden foreclosure by a claim that cannot be honored and threatens an unspecified and uncontrollable penalty: "And the master, what will he say?" The suppression of the antecedent of the pronoun *la* enables Barbarina's cavatina to express the pathos of the generalized anxiety and fear of loss of young girls subjected to the almost arbitrary will of powerful males. Mozart's music articulates her fear of dark potential consequences; the solo does for the role of Barbarina something of what Beaumarchais did for that of Fanchette through Marceline's impassioned attack on those who exploit young girls. For an extended moment Barbarina has the power to represent all the victims and potential victims of the narrative.

This of course is a comedy, and the pathos is soon dissipated. What has been lost is concealed behind the nonspecific *L'* and *la*, whose referent is withheld until Figaro and Marcellina, with growing impatience, each ask "Cosa?" All that pathos for a pin, "la spilla"; Da Ponte and Mozart have played a musical shaggy dog story, have deliberately teased us just as Barbarina quite unconsciously teases Figaro and his mother. The object lost turns out to be anticlimactic, a little absurd, and, thanks to Figaro's quick wit, easily replaced. Barbarina is released from her fears and goes to look for Susanna and then Cherubino with restored cheerfulness.

This small but crucially placed and exquisite episode follows a sequence of indirect implications that have been woven into the fabric of the opera, following cues taken from Beaumarchais. In the play, the Count describes how he caught Fanchette with an embarrassed or disheveled look ("l'air empêtré" [1.9]); the act ends with Bazile giving Chérubin an insinuating warning to leave Barbarina alone: "Chérubin! vous lui causerez des chagrins! *Tant va la cruche à l'eau!* . . ." Figaro moves the proverbial tag toward the expected conclusion—breakage—by adding "*qu'à la fin . . .*" but Bazile shifts gears: "Elle s'emplit." The implications are obvious. The imagery is picked up again when Antonio enters in act 2, scene 21, holding "*un pot de giroflées écrasées*" and complaining that someone in jumping out of the window has damaged his flowers.

Whether or not Beaumarchais took his cues from contemporary painting—he refers to an engraving "*d'après Vanloo*" to convey the blocking ("*tableau*") he wants at one moment in act 2, scene 4—there is an eighteenth-century pictorial idiom behind these references that finds clearest expression in a number of well-known paintings by Greuze depicting young girls mourning the loss of various broken or dead objects. *Une jeune fille qui a cassé son miroir*, exhibited in the Salon of 1763, is one; *Une jeune fille qui pleure son oiseau mort*, exhibited in 1765 and engraved by Flipart, is another (fig.1), and *La cruche cassée*, engraved in 1773 though not exhibited until 1777, is a third. A closely related painting is *Une jeune fille qui envoie un baiser par la fenêtre, appuyée sur des fleurs, qu'elle brise*, exhibited in 1769 and engraved by Saint-Aubin.[33]

Around these paintings there played an air of sexual ambiguity, most fully articulated by Diderot—who had become a friend of Greuze in 1759—in describing *Une jeune fille qui pleure son oiseau mort* in his essay on the 1765 Salon:

> Come, little one, open up your heart to me, tell me truly, is it really the death of this bird that's caused you to withdraw so sadly, so completely into yourself? . . . You lower your eyes, you don't answer. . . . Well, well, I've figured it out, he loved you, and for such a long time, he swore to it! He suffered so much! How difficult to see an object of our love suffer! . . . On this morning, unfortunately, your mother was absent; he came, you were alone; he was so handsome, his expressions

Jean-Baptiste Greuze: Une jeune fille qui pleure son oiseau mort, *exhibited at the Paris Salon of 1765. (Courtesy of National Galleries of Scotland.)*

so truthful! He said things that went right to your soul! . . . Still your mother didn't return; it's not your fault, it's your mother's fault. . . . My goodness, how you're crying! . . . When one forgets oneself, does one remember one's bird?[34]

As Michael Fried writes, "Diderot finds in Greuze's canvas a scarcely veiled allegory of the young girl's loss of virginity, an interpretation he extends retrospectively to the *Jeune fille qui a cassé son miroir* in the previous Salon."[35]

Da Ponte and Mozart, taking cues from Beaumarchais, invoke this imagery in their characterization of Barbarina, beginning with the moment in the act 2 finale when Antonio enters carrying a pot of carnations ("garofani")[36] broken by Cherubino in his escape from the Countess's chamber, a moment that recalls Greuze's *La cruche cassée* as well as Beaumarchais's damaged flowers. The broken flowerpot and crushed flowers offer nicely transposed objects for Antonio's anger and fear that Cherubino may have trespassed too far with Barbarina. In the cavatina we have the insinuatingly concealed signified behind the repeated *L'* and *la*; lost maidenheads are not usually found by looking on the ground, but the despairing search for an unnamed object calls up the pictorial language of young girls with broken mirrors, dead birds, and crushed flowers exploited by Greuze.

It would be as wrong to push the implications of this moment too far as it would be not to see them at all. In the ambiguous tradition of Greuze's paintings, there are perfectly innocent portraits like that of *Une jeune enfant qui joue avec un chien*, and analogously Da Ponte gives Barbarina a kitten to soften her blackmail of the Count in act 3. Barbarina is still—relatively—innocent. But she has lost something, and for a deliberately, exquisitely prolonged moment, the audience is allowed, even encouraged, to suspect that Barbarina may have paid the price that Susanna was in danger of having to pay in order to accomplish her desires. The exposed and vulnerable situation that Barbarina was in at the end of act 3 in relation to Cherubino is still fresh in our memories, as is the page's willingness to toy with her feelings in his unreal pursuit of the Countess. The Count, too, remains potentially dangerous, although he has other game in his sights just now.

Stage tradition places the whole of act 4 in the garden. However, the libretto of the first Vienna production of 1786 gives the stage direction "*Gabinetto*" as the location of the first four scenes.[37] Da Ponte is here following Beaumarchais, in whose play the equivalent scenes form part of act 4 and take place within the Count's palace; act 5, which opens with Fanchette's entry with oranges and biscuits for her Chérubin (Da Ponte's act 4, scene 5) is set in "*une salle de marronniers, dans un parc; deux pavillons . . . sont à droite et à gauche.*" Though he compressed Beaumarchais's five acts into four, Da Ponte respected his predecessor's intentions by directing that Barbarina's cavatina and the aria for Marcellina that follows take place in a "*Gabinetto*" that is clearly within the Count's palace, where his rule is unchallenged; the set underlines the risks surrounding Barbarina. She skips off ("*parte saltendo*") at the end of the scene to find first Susanna and then Cherubino, which implies that she expects to find them off-scene, in the garden where they await her.

Barbarina's cavatina is a perfect introduction to the larger structure of act 4, which includes a whole series of misunderstandings, mistaken identities, and paranoid but largely unfounded suspicions; all of the women are finally shown to be both innocent and (for)giving, but all of them—except, ironically, Marcellina, the one "fallen" woman among them—have dark suspicions cast on them by men at some point during this final act.

The frequent cutting of Marcellina's and Basilio's arias, which follow shortly after Barbarina's number and extend its expression of vulnerability and loss, weakens these thematic aspects of the drama. Allanbrook comments on Marcellina's aria: "[da Ponte] adapts her feminist diatribe, originally delivered after the recognition scene to a sympathetic Figaro about the wrongs she suffered at Bartolo's hands . . . to a soliloquy occasioned by her concern about Figaro's own sudden abandonment of Susanna."[38] However, the adaptation in no way weakens the generalizing force of Marcellina's words; in the recitative preceding the aria, she says, "When personal interest / Doesn't harden our hearts, / Every woman's inclined / To come to the defense of her own poor sex, / So wrongly oppressed by these ungrateful men"; and the aria ends with a strong statement: "It's only us poor women, . . . Who are treated so very cruelly / And betrayed by all of them" (4.4). Marcellina's words reflect her own situation as one who has been seduced, forced to abandon her son, and made hard and cruel by desire and continued subordination to the lawyer who is both betrayer and protector; now, softened by satisfaction, she can protest in the name of her whole sex against the wrong that men in their misuse of power can do to women.

Marcellina is followed by Basilio, after a brief scene for Barbarina to be considered shortly. The key point of his aria is made explicit in the recitative, which speaks of the need to take cover when the powerful are at large: "It's always been dangerous / To clash with the powerful few." The fearsome beast of the aria is clearly an analog of the Count, since Basilio's aria springs from his opinion, expressed to Bartolo, that Figaro should simply grin and bear the pain of allowing the Count to have his will with Susanna: "Couldn't he bear / What so many do?" Basilio's aria is one expression of the loser's perspective, a reminder that in the power games of desire, in which some have inherited capital and others none, real suffering and damage are not only possible but likely. Basilio himself has become, to quote Susanna, a "vile agent / For someone else's lechery" (1.7); he seems to have given up his own desires in the process of serving his master. Allanbrook comments that "Basilio is . . . a spiteful lightweight, with his high tenor voice and his habit of giving every second measure of the *alla breve* a mincing feminine ending."[39] These musical indications imply that Basilio's masculinity is something he has had to give up in the service of a master, or perhaps that its lack made him especially suited to such service.

All the middle characters in the opera, Beaumarchais's "vassaux," testify to the distorting and destructive effects of having to come to terms with feudal power. Their own desires having been thwarted or deformed, they become in turn enemies of the truer desires of the servants. Once the desires of these middle characters are enabled to flow into more natural channels, they can become the friends and assistants of Figaro and Susanna, and support the bourgeois revolution waiting in the wings.

The arias of Marcellina and Basilio are key contexts for Barbarina's cavatina, exposing past outcomes for those subjected to abuses of power; Barbarina's innocence, too, has begun to be questioned as she implicates herself further in the economics of erotic exchange under pressure from fear of the Count's displeasure and proven sexual interest. Barbarina tells Figaro how the Count persuaded her to bear his message: "Come here, my girl, and take this pin / To my pretty little Susanna, and tell her: 'This / Is the seal of the pines'" (4.2); she adds that he also told her to "make sure that no one sees you," thereby implicating her in a guilty enterprise. Barbarina is participating in the selling of Susanna because she is still in the Count's *daunger*, and perhaps also because she hopes to accumulate further credits toward the purchase of Cherubino. Her defensive strategy mirrors Susanna's in showing an apparent willingness to make some payment—sexual or other—in exchange for the long-term possession of the object of her true desire. Figaro points to the ambiguity of Barbarina's motivation by wryly observing "At such a tender age, / You're already learning" (4.2). Like Fanchette, Barbarina seems willing to be seduced, although only up to a point and at her own price.

Immediately after Marcellina's aria, the set changes to "*Folto giardino, con due nicchie parallelle praticabili*"; Da Ponte follows Beaumarchais, who made a set change at this point in the action. Allanbrook discusses the pastoral elements in Barbarina's cavatina, but there she is heard within a stage set that reflects a threat heard again in Marcellina's aria about goats and ferocious beasts ("Le più feroci belve").[40] Barbarina now reenters cheerfully into a nocturnal pastoral erotically charged by the discussion in the preceding act of an impending tryst between Susanna and the Count due to occur "sotto i pini del boschetto." The atmosphere has moved closer to the sophisticated pastoral of Watteau's paintings, though such rough beasts as the donkey and "fiera orribile" of Basilio's aria, the screech-owls and vixens of Figaro's "Aprite un po' quegli occhi," and the Count's ungentle "Gente" still lurk behind Barbarina's cheerfulness and Susanna's invocation of the night's babbling brook, soft breezes, laughing flowers, and sheltering trees ("Deh, vieni").

Barbarina enters this freer pastoral world pursuing a love-tryst of her own with Cherubino: "'In the arbor on the left,' I think he said." But there are disturbing implications behind her gaiety: "Oh, what a generous lot! I could hardly get them to give me an orange, a pear and a pastry. 'Who's it for, my dear?' 'It's for someone I know, sir.' 'We know that.' Oh well, my master hates him, but I love him: it cost me a kiss, but what does it matter? Someone's bound to pay it back." Barbarina has been socialized to expect to pay her way with sexual favors and now assumes the normality of such transactions. She has bought food for Cherubino, still in hiding from the Count's displeasure, at the price of a kiss. No more than a kiss was demanded because she is still a "madamigella," but she recognizes the sexual nature of what she has given in payment and understands the kiss as an expenditure to be offset by the kiss she hopes to receive from Cherubino in return for her food parcel. She is living her love life as if it were a trading enterprise, assuming that the accomplishment of her desires depends on her willingness to satisfy the desires of others, as she hopes her gifts will bring their appropriate reward. The world is a market, in which her only capital is sexual attractiveness and a naive but quick wit; she accepts her fate with equanimity, hoping to have enough in hand to balance the liabilities of low birth and an unhelpful father. She has allowed hugging and kissing, but has wisely kept the rest of her capital intact.

Cherubino, still on the prowl, enters in act 4, scene 11, singing, according to the original libretto, "Voi che intendete / Che cosa è amor"—his theme song has not changed. Alerted by the sound of someone arriving, he seeks shelter in the arbor where he has apparently made an assignation to meet Barbarina. He then notices the Countess disguised as Susanna and decides to make a teasing attempt at blackmail by claiming to know why she (Susanna, as he supposes) is here, reminding her that he was behind the chair when the Count asked for an assignation; now Cherubino tries to extort a kiss as his cut in the deal. There is a mix of innocent bravado and insinuating demand in this episode that leaves one not displeased when his kiss lands on the Count, though Cherubino escapes the merited slap. He then slips into the arbor to join Barbarina in the dark, where they remain until the two are pulled out just in time to witness the Count's final humbling. Barbarina presumably wins the compensatory kiss she hoped for when she paid for the fruit, but she has again put herself at risk, and her trading economics may or may not bring home a winner for her.

Both lovers have only the thin currency of youth to offer in their pursuit of love-objects and remain only loosely connected by affection, modulated by Cherubino's willingness to exploit and Barbarina's willingness to be exploited while hoping to attach the exploiter to herself by creating indebtedness. So far the two have been protected by the magic of youth, by an innocence that enables Cherubino to jump and slip out of trouble, and Barbarina to allow the Count kisses and hugs without being sériously touched by his touching. Beneath the hairbreadth escapes made possible by their butterfly lightness of flight lurk such possible future outcomes as the Count's attempts to force himself on unwilling women, the unhappy servitude of Marcellina, and the Countess's long experience of betrayal. Cherubino and Barbarina are both poised on the verge of erotic power, at which point they will lose their relative invulnerability and become serious players in the game, capable of both inflicting and suffering damage and defeat.

V

Beaumarchais's fifth act shows the Count at his old tricks still; Figaro recalls that "as recompense [*prix*] for having won his wife with my help, he [the Count] now wishes to intercept my own!" (5.3). The insulting asymmetry is repeated when the Count meets his own wife (disguised as Suzanne): "Here is the gold promised for the repurchase of that right which I will possess no longer than the delicious moment that you favour me with. But since the grace you deign to accord is priceless [*sans prix*], I am adding this diamond, which you will wear for love of me" (5.7). A forced yielding is praised as if it were a free gift, while an allegedly free gift made in return is to be worn as a badge of ownership; the Count articulates the only lightly disguised brutality of feudal tyranny.

The play ends with the Countess's pardoning of the Count, echoed by Suzanne, Marceline, and Figaro in a communal act, and with the Countess, now a center of power in her own right, redistributing wealth according to justice: "Each will receive what belongs to him." She gives the dowry to Figaro and the diamond to Suzanne, since the Count intended it for her. Figaro presses a claim to an ambassadorship, and Chérubin snatches the ribbon that the Countess throws down in place of the traditional bride's garter. The Countess's generosity transforms all the players into winners.

In the final vaudeville characters speak from their own perspective at that concluding moment. The Countess considers the best strategy with which to handle a husband she no longer loves, the Count extols *"la femme aux bons airs"* who *"sert au bien de tous,"* and Chérubin laughs at women for chastising those they secretly desire, and at himself for allowing these mighty beings to arouse tormenting desires within him. Although Figaro and Suzanne have won freedom, most of the players continue their tragicomic repetitions; there have been more changes in fortune than in character. We hear nothing from Fanchette, who is not included in the distribution of rewards.

Mozart's opera ends a little differently. The Count gives his disguised wife a diamond ring, as in Beaumarchais, and threatens ironically in financial metaphors that show his continued attempts to enforce his power: "Madam, come on out! / And you'll be justly rewarded [Il premio or avrete] / For all your honesty" (4.12). But there are changes in the role of the Countess. Her final forgiveness is solo, without seconding voices to echo her generosity, and unaccompanied by any distribution of largesse; we assume that she keeps her diamond ring, perhaps in hope of a revitalized marriage. Her "si"—the libretto has made wonderful use of "si" and "no" in preparation for this moment—is sung to a melody of sublime simplicity and conclusiveness that gives an almost magical power to the gift inherent in her words, as if music had replaced Beaumarchais's money and jewel as the argument moves from a market economy— *l'argent fait tout*—to the healing power of love and beauty mediated through the Countess.

That "si" leads into a "hymnlike chorus"[41] that seems to confirm her transformation of the situation for all concerned: "Ah! tutti contenti / Saremo così" (Ah! And so we'll / All be content at last). The cast, no longer participants in forgiving the Count as in Beaumarchais, remain recipients of the Countess's general gift of happiness as she demonstrates "Che cosa è amor." The fireworks party, promised by the Count at the end of act 3, is taken over by the newly established community as a whole and promises to prelude a golden age of contentment and joy. The Countess's generosity has collapsed the ticktock of reciprocal and self-interested potlatching into the simultaneity of shared pleasure. Susanna and Figaro can now move into the world of freely given love, which rises above while still including that of bourgeois contract, while Basilio and Marcellina will, we hope, live decently hereafter, now that they are joined in successfully completed parenthood. The act has moved from loss ("L'ho perduta") to restitution, from fear of centralized power ("the master, what will he say") to free and communal rejoicing.

However, a wistfulness underlies these final moments. We intuit, after our initial delight at seeing the Count on his knees, that the Countess's victory may be over her own despair and potential bitterness rather than over the Count's selfish philandering. She has given him her pardon, exacting no promise in return; the gift, emanating from a nature "più docile," has brought to at least a temporary end the mercantile economics of the drama. In entering the realm of the truly free gift, however, the Countess risks the final exhaustion of her resources; the Elvira of *Don Giovanni* stands as the distant warning image of a woman who forgave once too often.

There is no conclusion to the stories of Cherubino and Barbarina. Early in act 4 they are looking for each other; Cherubino, after his flirtation with Susanna (as he thinks), enters the *nicchia* where Barbarina awaits him in the dark. There they remain, together but out of sight until the very end. The partial repetition of the circumstances of the encounter between them related to us by the Count in act 1 suggests that there has been little change; Cherubino is still the potential seducer on the prowl, while Barbarina, still willing to put herself at risk, remains the potential victim. Barbarina and Cherubino are too young to be fixed into stable postures; they remain unsettled energies that join the other disturbing eddies around the Count and Countess to make this long crazy day but a magical moment in the continuing flux of human desires wise and foolish, constructive and destructive. The silence of Da Ponte/Mozart about the final disposition of the two youngest lovers reflects the continuing power of desire to destabilize and reshape relationships. Barbarina began the act fearful of the consequences of a loss; the lost object was soon replaced, and she found — or was found by — her Cherubino. So far, her economic strategy in love has been the risky one of giving a little with intent to create indebtedness, attempting to use while preserving her capital, but the success of this depends on the response of a partner. Cherubino's strategy has been to use charm to support pleas for alms and to cover the potential offense of small thefts ("Just give me one little kiss"). If they continue to interact, possible future outcomes are mirrored in the stories of Elvira and Don Giovanni, or, with a more radical transformation, of Pamina and Tamino. More probably, however, Da Ponte and Mozart imagined their interaction simply as a stage on the way to quite other, and separate, conjunctions. For now, they join their elders in hastening toward the distantly heard march, a "modest soldierly one [that] belongs to Eros militant."[42] For Barbarina, that means pleasure modulated by continued risk, although her naive resourcefulness gives promise that she will find a way to transform "L'ho perduta, me meschina" into a happier song.

NOTES

1. For convenience and for its relative literalness, I have used the text, translation, and act and scene references in Paul Gruber, ed., *The Metropolitan Opera Book of Mozart Operas* (New York: Harper-Collins, 1991). Translations, except from the libretto or where otherwise credited, are my own.

2. See Suzanne R. Pucci, "The Currency of Exchange in Beaumarchais' *Mariage de Figaro: From the 'Master Trope' Synecdoche to*

Fetish," in *Eighteenth-Century Studies*, vol. 25, no. 1 (Fall 1991), pp. 57–84, for an account of related imagery in Beaumarchais, though the essay takes a quite different approach.

3. Marcel Mauss, *The Gift*, trans. Ian Cunnison (New York: Norton, 1967), p. 1.

4. Tony Tanner, *Adultery in the Novel: Contract and Transgression* (Baltimore: Johns Hopkins University Press, 1979), pp. 4–15.

5. Nicholas Till, *Mozart and the Enlightenment* (London: Faber and Faber, 1992), p. 145.

6. A classic account of comic structure is Northrop Frye, *The Anatomy of Criticism* (Princeton: Princeton University Press, 1957), pp. 163–86. Henri Bergson talks about comic rigidity in *Le Rire: Essai sur la Signification du Comique* (Paris: Presses Universitaires de France, 1964), pp. 7–13.

7. Tanner, *Adultery*, p. 15.

8. Wye Jamison Allanbrook, *Rhythmic Gesture in Mozart: "Le Nozze di Figaro" and "Don Giovanni"* (Chicago: University of Chicago Press, 1983), p. 135.

9. Till, *Mozart and the Enlightenment*, p. 145.

10. See Allanbrook, *Rhythmic Gesture*, pp. 145–48, for further commentary on this number.

11. Ibid., pp. 92–93.

12. Jacques Seebacher, "Chérubin, le temps, la mort, l'échange" in *Europe*, no. 528 (April 1973), p. 64.

13. Brigid Brophy, *Mozart the Dramatist* (New York: Da Capo, 1990), pp. 105–7.

14. Alan Tyson, *Mozart: Studies of the Autograph Scores* (Cambridge: Cambridge University Press, 1987), pp. 314–16.

15. Alan Tyson, on p. 20 of the booklet accompanying the complete recording conducted by Arnold Östman, L'Oiseau-Lyre CD 421 333-2, suggests that the tune was intended to "identify him disguised as a girl on the stage," though I am not clear why he assumes that Cherubino is still disguised as a girl in act 4; in Beaumarchais, Chérubin enters act 5, scene 6, singing and *"en habit d'officier."*

16. René Girard, *Deceit, Desire, and the Novel* (Baltimore: Johns Hopkins University Press, 1976).

17. Beaumarchais is very touchy on this point in the "Préface" to *Le mariage de Figaro*; see *Théâtre: Le Barbier de Séville, etc.* (Paris: Garnier-Flammarion, 1965), pp. 120–21.

18. Ibid., p. 120.

19. Brophy, *Mozart the Dramatist*, p. 105, writes that Cherubino "is as much seduced as seducer," but her meaning is that he is himself the victim of Eros working through him.

20. Beaumarchais, "Préface," pp. 122–24. Beaumarchais describes Fanchette as "a child twelve years old, very naive" (p. 136). Chérubin is "a child thirteen years old" (p. 120). Beaumarchais is defending himself against accusations of immorality and thus minimizes the sexuality of both these figures.

21. Anne and Guy Fontaine, Annick Dusausay-Benoit, and Marie-Claude Urban, "Regards de comédiens sur la distribution d'une comédie: personnages, emplois dans *Le Mariage de Figaro*," in *Analyses et Réflexions sur . . . Beaumarchais "Le Mariage de Figaro"* (Paris: Ellipses, 1985), p. 168.

22. In Beaumarchais, Fanchette is described by the Count as having "l'air empêtré" (1.9), which may imply that her clothes have become entangled or displaced; the implication may be reflected in Da Ponte's phrase.

23. Tim Carter, *Le Nozze di Figaro* (Cambridge: Cambridge University Press, 1987), p. 68. The arietta has been lightly excised in the libretto, although its presence is marked in the autograph score—see Tyson, *Mozart: Studies of the Autograph Scores*, pp. 117–22.

24. Beaumarchais, "Préface," p. 121.

25. Suggested by Tyson, *Mozart: Studies of the Autograph Scores*, p. 120.

26. Lorenzo Da Ponte, "The State of the Theatre Poet," reproduced in Daniel Heartz, *Mozart's Operas* (Berkeley: University of California Press, 1990), p. 100.

27. Georg Knepler, *Wolfgang Amadé Mozart*, trans. J. Bradford Robinson (Cambridge: Cambridge University Press, 1994), p. 266.

28. Maynard Solomon, *Mozart* (New York: Harper Perennial, 1995), p. 452; her age is given by Knepler, *Mozart*, p. 266.

29. Wolfgang Hildesheimer, *Mozart*, trans.

Marion Faber (New York: Vintage Books, 1982), p. 228; and William Mann, *The Operas of Mozart* (New York: Oxford University Press, 1977), p. 424. Both cited by Sandra Corse, *Opera and the Uses of Language* (London: Associated University Presses, 1987), pp. 43–44.

30. Allanbrook, *Rhythmic Gesture*, p. 158.

31. Sigmund Levarie, *Le Nozze di Figaro: A Critical Analysis* (New York: Da Capo, 1977), p. 185.

32. Heartz, *Mozart's Operas*, p. 209.

33. Compiled from Anita Brookner, *Greuze* (London: Elek, 1972); and Edgar Munhall, *Jean-Baptiste Greuze: 1725–1805*, trans. Evelyne Mornat (Dijon: Musée des Beaux-Arts, 1977).

34. Denis Diderot, *Diderot on Art:* Volume 1, *The Salon of 1765 and Notes on Painting*, ed. and trans. John Goodman (New Haven: Yale University Press, 1995), p. 98.

35. Michael Fried, *Absorption and Theatricality* (Berkeley: University of California, 1980), pp. 56–61.

36. Da Ponte has translated Beaumarchais's "giroflées" closely. The English equivalent is "gillyflower"; there is an old English tradition linking these plants with wantonness — see the note to 4.4.81–85 in J. H. P. Pafford, ed., *The Winter's Tale* (London: Methuen, Arden Shakespeare, 1963). The *OED* records "gillyflower" as meaning "a wanton woman" in dialect from 1797. I have found no record of such usage in French, but it is conceivable that Beaumarchais and Da Ponte knew the tradition.

37. See Ernest Warburton, ed., *The Librettos of Mozart's Operas, III: The Da Ponte Operas* (New York: Garland, 1992), p. 83.

38. Allanbrook, *Rhythmic Gesture*, p. 163.

39. Ibid., p. 89.

40. Ibid., pp. 158ff., and Wye J. Allanbrook, "Nature and Convention: *The Marriage of Figaro*," *Current Musicology*, vol. 51 (1993), p. 85.

41. Allanbrook, *Rhythmic Gesture*, p. 192.

42. Ibid., p. 193.

Jacques Fromental Halévy
More Than a One-Opera Composer

TOM KAUFMAN

THE term "one-opera composer" is often erroneously applied to composers who, despite their having written a substantial number of works for the theater, remain best known for a single towering masterpiece. Obvious examples are Mascagni (whose most famous work is, of course, *Cavalleria rusticana*), Flotow (*Martha*), and Ponchielli (*La Gioconda*). Even Giordano (*Andrea Chénier*) might have borne the misnomer, before his *Fedora* became such a hit in a recent season at the Met. The sad fact is that, although all these composers wrote many fine operas, the majority of them have more or less fallen into neglect.

In the case of the French composer Jacques Fromental Halévy, *La Juive* is the one work that has kept his name alive for the general public. In the mid-nineteenth century, however, during the heyday of French *grand opéra*, several of his creations—along with those of Giacomo Meyerbeer—figured in the standard repertory of houses throughout Europe and had a great influence on composers outside of France—including Verdi, Wagner, and Musorgsky.

As it happened, grand opéra took a relatively short time to lose its influence on the development of French lyric drama. By the turn of the century it was already a sign of good taste among Parisian composers to mock the "classics of yesteryear like Meyerbeer and Halévy."[1] In 1903 Debussy moaned that *Les Huguenots* was "one of the most miserable of the crosses we have to bear, together with such things as epidemics, the three percent devaluation, and the excavations for the Métro."[2] Inevitably, performances of such works became less and less frequent, although it is a mistake to believe—as one historian claims—that *La Juive* was not done in Paris "between its 544th performance in 1893 and a revival in 1933–34,"[3] since there were at least three revivals in the intervening years at the Gaîté Lyrique and, very probably, more theaters. The opera was mounted in Rouen as late as 1938–39, and perhaps later.

Although this might seem to imply that the major nineteenth-century grand operas survived in the French provinces longer than they did elsewhere, that was not necessarily the case. Performances of not only *La Juive* but also *Guil-*

laume Tell, Robert le diable, Les Huguenots, and *Le prophète* depended on the avail-ability of singers, especially tenors, who could meet the vocal challenges such works presented. It is not surprising that *La Juive*'s ill-fated goldsmith, Eléazar, is a role that, at least until the mid-twentieth century, attracted many of the world's greatest tenors, including Adolphe Nourrit, Gilbert-Louis Duprez, Enrico Tamberlik, Valentin Duc, Léon Escalaïs, and Paul Franz. Enrico Caruso and Giovanni Martinelli sang the role primarily in the United States, Leo Slezak in Austria and Germany, the Corsican César Vezzani in the French provinces and probably North Africa, and the legendary John O'Sullivan in Paris, East-ern Europe, and in French provincial theaters.[4] In more recent times, it has been revived for Tony Poncet and, most notably, for Richard Tucker. Although *La Juive* is generally regarded as a tenor's opera, many great sopranos and mez-zos have sung the role of Rachel, including Pauline Viardot, Antonietta Fricci, Abigaille Bruschi-Chiatti, and Félia Litvinne in the nineteenth century; and Marjorie Lawrence, Rosa Ponselle, Rosa Raisa, and Elisabeth Rethberg in the 1930s.

It seems safe to assume that *La Juive* was produced every year between 1901 and 1938 in one city or another. In Vienna, it was given every year between 1903 and 1933, with the exceptions of 1912 and 1913.[5] It was done in San Francisco with Rethberg, Martinelli, and Pinza for two consecutive seasons, in 1935 and 1936. Although productions of it on the American continent have dwindled since it was last heard at the Metropolitan Opera in 1936 and in Chicago in 1937, a number of recordings (most of them live) have been available off and on for years.[6]

The lighter repertory of the 1830s and 1840s, especially Halévy's *L'éclair*, pre-sents a totally different state of affairs for the opera historian, insofar as much less attention seems to have been paid to opéra comique than to grand opéra. To make things worse, the documentation of opera in French provincial cities and the lesser houses of Paris is far too fragmentary to draw any significant con-clusions about the performance frequency of many of these works. About all for certain that can be said of *L'éclair* is that there is no record of it being done in Paris after 1899, although it is known to have been revived in Berlin (Stadt Theater) as recently as 1927 and in Neuburg an der Donau in 1977. (In the twen-tieth century, Germany and Austria seem to have paid more attention to the works of Halévy and Meyerbeer than France has. *La Juive*, for instance, was performed in concert in Vienna in January 1981 and was presented again there in full production at the Staatsoper in autumn 1999.)

Nevertheless, three Halévy works besides *L'éclair* and *La Juive* are known to have survived into the twentieth century in France. The first, *Charles VI*, was given in Marseille in 1901. The other two were given at the Gaîté Lyrique in its 1917–18 season, which was apparently devoted to neglected nineteenth-century French repertory: *La reine de Chypre*, with O'Sullivan in the role of Gérard, and *Les mousquetaires de la reine*. It would not be surprising if there were other Halévy operas given in the lesser theaters of Paris or the French provinces during the early 1900s, although the previously mentioned lack of documentation (chronologies of French theaters) needed to carry out the research also makes it exceedingly difficult, if not impossible, to know for sure.

Since Halévy is no longer a very familiar name to the operagoing public of today, a brief sketch of his career might be in order here. He was born in Paris on 27 May 1799 to a German Jewish father and a French Jewish mother. In spite of the notorious Dreyfus case (which, of course, occurred much later), anti-Semitism may not have been as much of a problem in France as it was in neighboring countries, and it was quite possible for middle-class Jews to succeed. And that is exactly what Halévy did. In fact, he became one of the most successful French opera composers of his era. During his lifetime, his only serious rivals were Meyerbeer (a German), Daniel-François Auber (a fellow Frenchman, who, however, was at his best in lighter works), Ambroise Thomas, and Charles Gounod. Hector Berlioz should also be mentioned, but his operas failed dismally at their premieres and did not really come into their own until both he and Halévy were long dead.

Halévy entered the Paris Conservatoire in 1810, becoming a pupil and later a protégé of Luigi Cherubini. He won the Prix de Rome in 1819. His first opera to be performed was *L'artisan*, at the Opéra-Comique in 1827, but it, like his other early works, was a failure. He did, however, become *chef de chant* at the Théâtre Italien from 1826 to 1829, later (1829–45) holding the same post at the Opéra. While at the Théâtre Italien, he met Maria Malibran, for whom he wrote the semiseria *Clari*, the first of his two Italian works. After a triumphant premiere in 1828, *Clari* was deemed good enough to be revived in the ensuing season, after which it disappeared (it received six performances in its first season and four more during the second).[7] The fact that it was not given in London, as so many works created at the Théâtre Italien were, was probably due to the popularity in the British Isles of Henry Bishop's opera on the same subject. Another opéra comique, *La dilettante d'Avignon*, was relatively successful, and further recognition of Halévy's talent came in 1833 when he completed the score of *Ludovic*, an opéra comique left unfinished by the late Ferdinand Hérold (the composer of *Zampa*).

Two years later, Halévy achieved his first major, international triumph with *La Juive*, a work that was to become one of the cornerstones of the French repertory, given with great regularity all over the world for about a century. It is one of the grandest of grand operas, with a formal ballet, major choruses, a spectacular procession in act 1, and the most impressive of celebrations in act 3. It culminates with the heroine's being thrown into a vat of boiling oil in act 5 in another public "ceremony." Gustav Mahler admitted being "absolutely overwhelmed by this wonderful, majestic work," which he regarded as "one of the greatest operas ever created."[8] The tenor aria at the close of act 4, "Rachel, quand du Seigneur" (ex. 1), one of the gems of the tenor repertory, has been made famous by such outstanding recordings as those of Caruso, Vezzani, Martinelli, Slezak, Beniamino Gigli, Joseph Schmidt, and Georges Thill. Other

*Jacques Fromental Halévy (drawing by Janet Langs, based on a photograph by MM.
L. Cremière et Comp., as published in* L'Illustration, Journal universel, *29 March 1862).
(Courtesy of Andrew S. Pope.)*

highlights include the finale to the first act, the Passover scene, the final trio of
act 2, the Cardinal's curse in act 3, and the two central duets of act 4—first
between Rachel and Eudoxie, and then the major confrontation between
Eléazar and the cardinal ("Ta fille en ce moment").

L'éclair is, in many ways, the complete antithesis of its immediate predecessor. Whereas *La Juive* represents the epitome of grand opéra (it was perhaps the
most elaborate spectacle ever offered at the Paris Opéra until then), *L'éclair* has
no crowd scenes, no large-scale ensembles, and only four characters. Set in a

Example 1. Eléazar's aria in act 4 of Halévy's La Juive.

Ra - chel, quand du _ Sei - gneur la grâ - ce tu - té - lai - re à mes trem-blan - tes

modest bourgeois dwelling just outside of Boston, the plot involves only a pair of sisters—Henriette, very sentimental by nature, and the rather frivolous young widow Mme Darbel—and two young men: George, an Englishman from Oxford (who never lets you forget it), who must marry either of the sisters to get his inheritance, and Lionel, a sailor just passing through. During a sudden storm the sailor is blinded by a lightning flash and helped by Henriette. They fall in love, but in his sightless state Lionel has no idea what she looks like. He is miraculously cured, sees the sisters for the first time, and embraces the wrong one, breaking Henriette's heart. All is eventually resolved, and both men win their girls.

The work was a tremendous success in Paris, where it was warmly received by public and press alike, despite some criticism of the fact that there was no chorus. The opera quickly made the customary tour of the civilized world, being translated into German for a production in Berlin on 3 August 1836. Stagings in at least twenty other German-language theaters followed in Germany, Austria, and what is now the Czech Republic, while the original French version was given throughout France (with 311 performances in Paris by 1893), Belgium, and even as far away as New Orleans, where it was first heard as early as 1837. It stayed in the repertory of the American city for quite a few years, until the 1848–49 season; the company performed *L'éclair* in its entirety in New York and apparently in excerpted form in Philadelphia while on tour in the summer of 1843. But it was not given in Montreal. Strangely, in light of the opera's New England setting, there is no record of an English version, nor is there any indication that it was ever performed in Boston.

Now, finally, the release on CD of *L'éclair*—which had its premiere in 1835, hard on the heels of *La Juive*—offers record collectors an opportunity to become acquainted with another of this fairly prolific composer's stage works. A tape of a 1989 Freiburg production (sung in German) has now surfaced and been privately issued on CD, becoming only the second complete opera by Halévy on record.[9]

Musically, *L'éclair* is somewhat atypical of conventional opéras comiques, above all because it contains only four roles: two sopranos and two tenors— no mezzo, no bass. However, the parts are cleverly differentiated in that one couple (Henriette and Lionel) is serious and sentimental, while the other couple (Mme Darbel and George) is lighthearted, gay, and even comical. The uncle who cures Lionel's blindness (a perfect excuse for a bass role) does not appear on stage. The opera is a succession of many attractive arias and ensembles, but,

Example 2. Lionel's aria in act 3 of Halévy's L'éclair.

LIONEL

Quand de la nuit   l'é - pais nu - a - ge cou - vrait mes yeux ____ de son ban-deau,

Example 3. Guido's aria "Quand renaîtra la pâle aurore" from Halévy's Guido et Ginevra, ou La peste de Florence.

with the exception of Lionel's third-act aria, "Quand de la nuit l'épais nuage" (ex. 2), the score is virtually unknown to modern audiences.[10] Other outstanding numbers cited by the French press at the time of the premiere include the opening duet for the two sisters, the entrance arias of George and Lionel, the first finale, and George's buffo aria in act 2. The pivotal act 1 storm scene and the act 2 love duet ("Comme mon coeur bat et palpite") are equally noteworthy.

After Halévy's double triumph in 1835, he became one of the leading figures of Parisian operatic life, continuing to be very active and producing new operas at a much faster rate than Meyerbeer. *Guido et Ginevra, ou La peste de Florence* (Opéra, 1838) contains many beauties, including two fine tenor arias: "Pendant la fête une inconnue" and "Quand renaîtra la pâle aurore" (ex. 3). *Le guitarrero* (Opéra-Comique, January 1841) did fairly well, while *La reine de Chypre* (Opéra, December 1841) was probably the most successful opera by a native French composer produced between 1836 and 1852 (Berlioz's *Benvenuto Cellini*, which had its premiere in 1838, is much better known today, but in terms of performance frequency, it will be a long time before it catches up with *La reine de Chypre*).

The plot of *La reine de Chypre* is virtually identical to that of Donizetti's *Caterina Cornaro*, and, in fact, it was used for five different works between 1841 and 1846. Jules-Henri Vernoy de Saint-Georges, one of the librettists of *L'éclair*, sold the same libretto to both Franz Lachner and Halévy, and both of their operas premiered less than a month apart in 1841 — Lachner's in Munich on 3 December, and Halévy's in Paris on 22 December. Donizetti was also working on a version intended for Vienna, but it was offered to Naples when he learned that Lachner had beaten him to the punch in the Austrian capital. Later settings were by Michael Balfe (in English) and Giovanni Pacini (again in Italian). As fate would have it, Halévy's setting proved the most successful of the five versions during the nineteenth century, with 152 performances at the Opéra alone. Lachner's and Balfe's were also successful, but less so. Pacini's had only a limited number of stagings (about nineteen, many of them in Rio de Janeiro). On the other hand, Donizetti's attempt failed, for it was given in only two cities (Naples and Parma) in the 1840s, followed by more than a century of neglect. Ironically, Halévy's *La reine de Chypre* has not been heard (to the best of our knowledge) since 1917, while *Caterina Cornaro* staged a comeback after the war and has been available at one time or another in four or more different recordings on LP and CD.

Example 4. A famous passage from the Gérard/Lusignan duet in Halévy's
La reine de Chypre.

That *La reine de Chypre* has apparently not been given for over eighty years is hard to believe, especially in view of the many good things that have been written about it, including compliments by Richard Wagner, who remarked how the composer "continues to advance along the path he was pursuing in *La Juive*, as he is more and more concerned with simplifying his means. It is truly a beautiful spectacle to see how Halévy, while purposely keeping the reins on his inspiration . . . managed to achieve such a great variety of effects — not to mention that he thereby rendered his intentions all the more clear and intelligible."[11] Perhaps the most famous single number in *La reine de Chypre* is the middle portion of the grand duet between Gérard and Lusignan: "Triste exilé" (ex. 4). It has been recorded several times, and is currently available on CD.[12] Other numbers in the score worth mentioning include Catarina's first-act "Le gondolier dans sa pauvre nacelle" (ex. 5) and the last-act duet for Gérard and Catarina.

When Spontini was expelled from Berlin in 1842, Meyerbeer, then already at work on *Le prophète*, left Paris to take over as kapellmeister in Berlin, leaving the field of grand opéra open to Donizetti and Halévy (Auber by that time was devoting himself almost exclusively to the opéra comique genre). Donizetti's career in Paris, however, was tragically cut short by rapidly declining health. He more or less alternated between that city and Vienna before returning to his birthplace, Bergamo, where he died in 1848.

The year 1843 witnessed the premieres of both Donizetti's *Dom Sébastien, roi de Portugal* and Halévy's *Charles VI* at the Opéra. The latter was by far the more successful of the two, running up a grand total of sixty-one performances at the Opéra over six seasons, but, like *La reine de Chypre*, it has virtually disappeared not only from the repertory but even from the awareness of opera lovers. I heard excerpts from both on 78s many years ago (the duet "Triste exilé" sung by Henri Beyle and Hector Dufranne; and "Guerre aux tyrans" sung by Vigneau, both on the G&T label), was most impressed, and have always been fascinated at the prospect that they may some day be revived. Both operas survived into the

Example 5. Catarina's aria from act 1 of La reine de Chypre.

twentieth century. *La reine de Chypre* was revived in Paris (at the Gaîté Lyrique) in 1917 with O'Sullivan as Gérard. *Charles VI* was given in Marseille as late as 1901 but never achieved the fame it deserved in Paris, due probably to the political incorrectness of a piece that lauded French patriotism at the expense of the British at a time when the French government was trying to improve its relations with its northern neighbor.

The 1840s was a period of extreme nationalism in music, although relatively few of the operas premiered actually went so far as to celebrate the patriotic feelings of the host country. *Charles VI*, based on the fifteenth-century struggles between the French and their British invaders, was designed to rouse French patriotic feelings versus their longtime political arch-enemies, just as Meyerbeer's *Ein Feldlager in Schlesien* (Berlin, 1844) was intended to exploit Prussian patriotism or Verdi's *Attila* and *La battaglia di Legnano* were made to appeal to Italian patriotic sentiment. According to Clément, Halévy had intended his *Charles VI* to be the French national opera.[13] But it was not to be, since the attitudes of the French government did not reflect those of the man in the street, and the last thing that the powers that be wanted was to antagonize the British, especially with a state visit from Queen Victoria in the planning stages.

Example 6. The choral refrain, "Guerre aux tyrans!" from act 1 of Halévy's Charles VI.

In his memoirs Berlioz relates an amusing tale of how politics got mixed up in the arts in mid-nineteenth-century Paris. As Berlioz was preparing the program for a giant concert to be held in connection with the industrial exhibition of 1844, Halévy complained when he saw that none of his music had been included. Therefore, Berlioz added an excerpt from act 1 of *Charles VI*, in which Raymond exhorts the French to fight against the foreign troops who have occupied much of their country ("La France a l'horreur du servage"). When the number was performed during the concert, which Berlioz conducted, three-fourths of the audience joined the chorus in the refrain "Guerre aux tyrans! jamais en France, jamais l'Anglais ne règnera!" (War to the tyrants, never in France, never will the Englishman rule!) (ex. 6). In his memoirs Berlioz describes the unexpected occurrence as "a crudely nationalistic protest by the common man against the policy which Louis-Philippe was following at the time." Berlioz, called "on the carpet" by the Commissioner of Police, explained that it was merely a late addition to please Halévy, chosen because its scoring happened to suit the forces he had at his disposal for the concert. The explanation was accepted, but from that day on, censorship of concerts was established in Paris.[14]

The "Guerre aux tyrans" ensemble occurs at the very beginning of the opera, setting the stage for a typical historical plot dealing with a mad king of France (*Charles VI*); his traitorous queen, Isabelle de Bavière, who wants the British to occupy France; their patriotic son, the Dauphin; and the gentle peasant girl, Odette (Raymond's daughter), who helps the king in his distress. Another highlight of the score is Odette's act 4 Ballade ("Chaque soir, Jeanne sur la plage"), alternating with the king's "Avec la douce chansonette" (ex. 7a–b). The cast of the premiere of *Charles VI* included several of the Opéra's most established stars, the same singers who had first sung Donizetti's *Les martyrs* and *La favorite* and who were to create the latter's *Dom Sébastien* later that same year (see appendix). In cities such as New Orleans where no attempt had to be made to be nice to the British (one wonders if the opposite was the case), *Charles VI* actually survived much longer, staying in the repertory from the 1846–47 season to the

Example 7a. Odette's Ballade, from act 4 of Charles VI.

Example 7b. Charles VI's gentle interjection between the verses of Odette's Ballade.

KING   Moderato

a - vec la _ dou - ce chan - son net - te_____ qu'il ai - me tant

ber - ce, ber - ce, gen - tille O - det - te, ton vieil en - fant

1873–74 season, and getting revived several times in the 1880s and as late as the 1891–92 season.

A large number of additional works followed, the most successful of which were two in the light vein: *Les mousquetaires de la reine* (1846) and *Le val d'Andorre* (1848). The former racked up 294 performances at the Opéra-Comique by 1893, the latter trailing with 160. Halévy's second opera to an Italian text, *La tempesta* (London, 1850), after the Shakespeare play, boasted Luigi Lablache in the role of Caliban. Halévy's most important grand operas in his later years were undoubtedly *Le Juif errant* (Opéra, 1852), which had a respectable 49 performances during two seasons, and *La magicienne* (Opéra, 1858). The latter had a run of 42 performances during its first season, and another three the second, but, like *Le Juif errant*, was never revived. His last major triumph was the opéra comique *Jaguerita l'Indienne* (1855), which had a run of 124 performances at the Théâtre Lyrique over four seasons and was given as far away as New Orleans. It was revived at the Opéra-Comique in 1869, and at the Opéra Populaire in 1886.

A tally of performance totals at the Opéra of the leading grand operas of the day shows that Meyerbeer's works were the ones given most often (see table). Rossini comes in second, with Halévy third and Auber fourth. Amazingly, each of all six of Halévy's grand operas did better in Paris, in terms of performance frequency, than any of the three Verdi works premiered there. This cannot be ascribed to a dislike of Verdi on the part of the subscribers to the Opéra, since *Le trouvère* (the French version of *Il trovatore*) was performed over 200 times. Of course, the three Verdi operas made up for their lack of Parisian success outside France, while only three of Halévy's grand operas (*La Juive*, *La reine de Chypre*, *Charles VI*) had any significant international careers. I would hesitate, however, to draw any conclusions from these data.

Considering the unexpected beauties of the finally accessible *L'éclair* and the extent to which Halévy's other operas have been neglected by musicologists during the last fifty years, it would seem that these works should represent a gold mine for operatic archaeologists and record companies to explore and

TABLE. Performance totals of selected grands opéras at the Paris Opéra during the nineteenth century.

Meyerbeer: *Robert le diable* 751; *Les Huguenots* approx. 950; *Le prophète* approx. 520; *L'Africaine* 471

Halévy: *La Juive* 544; *Guido et Ginevra* 44; *La reine de Chypre* 152; *Charles VI* 61; *Le Juif errant* 49; *La magicienne* 45

Donizetti: *Les martyrs* 20; *La favorite* approx. 670; *Dom Sébastien, roi de Portugal* 33

Auber: *La muette de Portici* 489; *Gustave III* 168; *L'enfant prodigue* 44

Rossini: *Le siège de Corinthe* 105; *Moïse* 188; *Guillaume Tell* approx. 800

Verdi: *Jérusalem* 33; *Les vêpres siciliennes* 24; *Don Carlos* 43

bring back to life. Among the grand operas, a truly note-complete *La Juive* is still badly needed — the usual cuts, whether they be entire numbers or just internal cuts within numbers, ruin the majestic architecture of the opera and make it impossible to judge fairly. But *La reine de Chypre*, once so popular, and so highly praised by Wagner, seems equally deserving of attention, as does *Charles VI*, a work robbed of its erstwhile success in France because it was deemed "politically incorrect" by the government. Among the lighter works, we await a French version of *L'éclair*, while both *Les mousquetaires de la reine* and *Le val d'Andorre* merit consideration. Finally, with the current interest in operas dealing with conflicts not between neighboring countries but between cultures and civilizations, *Jaguerita l'Indienne* seems to be a natural. In it, a fascinatingly depicted American Indian queen in Guyana rescues a Dutch soldier she is in love with from her own warriors.

For now, *L'éclair* is the only complete recording of an opera that gives us a glimpse into the works of Halévy other than *La Juive*. May this "lightning bolt" serve as a wake-up call for other complete recordings, leading to a better appreciation of this underestimated composer and the removal of that "one-opera composer" stigma from his name.

Appendix: A Chronology of Halévy's Operatic Works

The gracious assistance of the following individuals and organizations is gratefully acknowledged for providing various cast details of the operas: Mr. Jack Belsom of New Orleans for checking numerous scores at his disposal and providing details on the registers of many of the roles; M. Eric Butruille of the Opéra de Lyon; Mr. Charles Sens of the Library of Congress for checking several libretti in their collection; Herr Clemens Risi of Munich for obtaining details on the premiere of *Noah* from Stuttgart; Mr. Jack Rokahr and the

Rokahr Family Library for checking numerous scores in their unbelievable collection and providing details on the registers of many of the roles.

Key to abbreviations: s = soprano; ms = mezzo-soprano or contralto; t = tenor; b = baritone; bf = buffo; bs = bass; bal = ballerina; oc = opéra comique; go = grand opéra.

Preliminary, unperformed works

A. *Les bohémiennes* (composed 1819–20).

B. *Marco Curzi* (finale only; composed 1822).

C. *Les deux pavillons* (Vial, composed circa 1824).

D. *Pygmalion* (opéra, 1 act, Arnoult, composed circa 1824).

E. *Erostrate* (opéra, 3 acts, Arnoult and Léon Halévy, composed circa 1825).

Later works (all premieres in Paris unless otherwise indicated)

1. *L'artisan* (oc, 1 act; Jules-Henri Vernoy de Saint-Georges; 30 Jan. 1827; Opéra-Comique). Cast: Louise (Alphonsine Virginie Casimir, s); Gustave (Jean-Baptiste Chollet, t); Justin (Louis-Augustin Lemonnier, b); Patron Jean (Tilly); Françoise (Desbrosses); Pierre (?); Ammandin (?).

2. *Le roi et le batelier* (oc, 1 act; Vernoy de Saint-Georges; 8 Nov. 1827; Opéra-Comique). Cast: unknown.

3. *Clari* (opera semiseria, 3 acts; Pietro Giannone; 9 Dec. 1828; Théâtre Italien). Cast: Clari (Maria Malibran, ms); Bettina (Marinoni, s); Il Duca (Domenico Donzelli, t); Germano (Carlo Zucchelli, bf); role unknown (Vincenzo Graziani, bs); Simonetta (?); Luca (?).

4. *Le dilettante d'Avignon* (oc, 1 act; François-Benoît Hoffmann and Léon Halévy; 7 Nov. 1829; Opéra-Comique). Cast: Marianne (Alphonsine Virginie Casimir, s); Elise (Monsel, s): Dubreuil (Louis-Antoine Ponchard, t); Maisonneuve (Fargueil); Poverino (Jamain); Valentin (Boulard); Ribomba (St. Ange); Zuccherini (Beinie).

5. *Attendre et courir* (oc, 1 act; Fulgence; 28 May 1830; Opéra-Comique). Cast: unknown.

6. *La langue musicale* (oc, 1 act; Saint-Yves; 11 Dec. 1830; Opéra-Comique). Cast: Eveline (?); Caroline (?); Gustave von Walldorf (?); Chevalier von Zart (?); Baron von Walldorf (?) Hermann (?).

7. *La tentation* (opéra-ballet, 5 acts; Hygin-Auguste Cavé and Charles-Edmond Duponchel; 20 June 1832; Opéra). Cast: Hélène (Julie Dorus-Gras, s); Mizael (Louise-Zulmé Dabadie, s); Asmondée (Alexis Dupont, t); Bélial (Jean-Etienne Massol, b).

8. *Yella* (oc, 2 acts; Moreau and Duport; unperformed).

9. *Les souvenirs de Lafleur* (oc, 1 act; Carmouche and de Courcy; 4 Mar. 1833; Opéra-Comique). Cast: Madame de Surville (Clara Margueron, s); Adrien (Etienne Thénard, t); Baron de Valbonne (Henry); Lafleur (Jean-Blaise Martin, b); Duchene (Léon); Labriche (Duchemin).

10. *Ludovic* (oc, 2 acts; [started by Hérold; finished by Halévy]; Vernoy de Saint-Georges; 16 May 1833; Opéra-Comique). Cast: Francesca (Felicité Pradher, s); Nice (Marie Hébert-Massy); Ludovic (Louis-Augustin Lemonnier, b); Gregorio (Louis Feréol, b); Scipion (Vizentini).

11. *La Juive* (go, 5 acts; Eugène Scribe; 23 Feb. 1835; Opéra). Cast: Rachel (Marie Cornélie Falcon, s); Eudoxie (Julie Dorus-Gras, s); Eléazar (Adolphe Nourrit, t); Léopold (Marcel Lafond, t); Cardinal Brogni (Nicolas Prosper Levasseur, bs); Ruggiero (Henri-Bernard Dabadie, b); Albert (Ferdinand Prévost, bs); Crieur (Prosper Dérivis, bs); Premier homme du peuple (Jean-Etienne Massol, b); Deuxième homme du peuple (Alexis Dupont, t); Garde du Conseil (Pouillet).

12. *L'éclair* (oc, 3 acts; Vernoy de Saint-Georges and F. A. Eugène de Planard; 16 Dec. 1835; Opéra-Comique). Cast: Henriette (Cécile Camoin, s); Madame Darbel (Felicité Pradher, s); Lionel (Jean-Baptiste Chollet, t); George (Joseph-Antoine Couderc, t).

13. *Guido et Ginevra* (go, 5 acts; Scribe; 5 Mar. 1838; Opéra). Cast: Ginevra (Julie Dorus-Gras, s); Ricciarda (Rosine Stoltz, ms); Guido (Gilbert-Louis Duprez, t); Forte-Braccio (Jean-Etienne Massol, b); Cosimo de Medicis (Nicolas Prosper Levasseur, bs); Léonore (Lebrun); Antonietta (Flécheux); Manfredi (Prosper Dérivis, bs); Téobaldo (Ferdinand Prévost, bs); Lorenzo (Molinier).

14. *Les treize* (oc, 3 acts; Scribe; 15 Apr. 1839; Opéra-Comique). Cast: Isella (Jenny Colon-Leplus, s); Hector de Fieramosca (Jean-Baptiste Chollet, t); Gennaio (Ernest Mocker, t); Marquis de Rosenthal (Henri, bs); Matteo (Fleury); Greffier de Barigel (?); Mazarin (?).

15. *Le shérif* (oc, 3 acts; Scribe; 2 Sept. 1839; Opéra-Comique). Cast: Camilla (Rossi, s); Keatt (Laure Cinti-Damoreau, s); Edgard Falsingham (Gustave Roger, t); Sir James Turner (Achille-Henri Deshayes, b); Amabel d'Invernesse (Théodore Moreau-Sainti, bs); Yorik (?); Trim (?); Un domestique (?).

16. *Le drapier* (opéra, 3 acts; Scribe; 6 Jan. 1840; Opéra). Cast: Jeanne Bazu (Maria Nau, s); Urbain (Mario, t); Gautier (Jean-Etienne Massol, b); Maitre Bazu (Nicolas Prosper Levasseur, bs); Frère Benoist (Adolphe Alizard, bs).

17. *Le guitarrero* (oc, 3 acts; Scribe; 21 Jan. 1841; Opéra-Comique). Cast: Manuela (Boulanger, s); Zarah (Capdeville); Riccardo (Gustave Roger, t); Lorenzo (Théodore Moreau-Sainti, bs); Ximena (Honoré Grignon).

18. *La reine de Chypre* (go, 5 acts; Vernoy de Saint-Georges; 22 Dec. 1841; Opéra). Cast: Catarina Cornaro (Rosine Stolz, ms); Gérard de Coucy (Gilbert-Louis Duprez, t); Jacques de Lusignan (Paul Barroilhet, b); Mocénigo (Jean Etienne Massol, b); Andréa Cornaro (Stefano Luciano Bouché, bs); Strozzi (Pierre-François Wartel, t); Héraut d'armes (Ferdinand Prévost, bs).

19. *Charles VI* (go, 5 acts; Casimir Delavigne and Germain Delavigne; 15 Mar. 1843; Opéra), Cast: Isabelle de Bavière (Julie Dorus-Gras, s); Odette (Rosine Stolz, ms); Dauphin (Gilbert-Louis Duprez, t); Charles VI (Paul Barroilhet,

b); Raymond (Nicolas Prosper Levasseur, bs); Gonran (Placide Poultier, b); Duc de Bedfort (Jean-Baptiste Canaple, t); Homme de la Forêt de Mans (Jean-Etienne Massol, b); Tanguy Deschatel (Ferdinand Prévost, bs); Lionel (Raguenot, t); Dunois (Jean-Baptiste Octave, t); Saintrailles (Saint-Denis, t); Lahire (Martin, b).

20. *Le lazzarone, ou Le bien vient en dormant* (opéra, 2 acts; Vernoy de Saint-Georges; 29 Mar. 1844; Opéra), Cast: Baptista (Julie Dorus-Gras, s); Beppo (Rosine Stolz, ms); Mirobolante (Paul Barroilhet, b); Josué Corvo (Nicolas Prosper Levasseur, bs).

21. *Les mousquetaires de la reine* (oc, 3 acts; Vernoy de Saint-Georges; 3 Feb. 1846; Opéra-Comique). Cast: Athénais de Solange (Louise Lavoye, s); Berthe de Simiane (Clémentine Darcier, s); Olivier de l'Entragues (Gustave Roger, t); Hector de Biron (Ernest Mocker, t); Roland de la Bretonnière (Léonard Hermann-Léon, bs); Grande maîtresse (Annette Blanchard); Demoiselle d'honneur (Martin-Charlet); Narbonne (Carlo); Rohan (Charles-François Duvernoy); Créqui (Garcin Brunet): Gontaud (Louis Palianti); Grand prévot (Victor).

22. *Les premiers pas* (collaborative opera with Adolphe Adam, Daniel-François Auber, Michele Carafa; Alphonse Royer and Gustave Vaëz; 15 Nov. 1847; Opéra National). Cast: unknown.

23. *Le val d'Andorre* (oc, 3 acts; Vernoy de Saint-Georges; 11 Nov. 1848; Opéra-Comique). Cast: Rose de Mai (Clémentine Darcier, s); Georgette (Louise Lavoye, s); Thérèse (Antoinette Révilly, ms); Stéphan (Marius-Pierre Audran, t); Lejoyeuz (Ernest Mocker, t); Saturnin (Pierre Marius Jourdan, t); Jacques Sincère (Charles Bataille, bs); L'endormi (Louis Palianti); Grand syndic (Henri, bs).

24. *La fée aux roses* (oc, 3 acts; Vernoy de Saint-Georges; 1 Oct. 1849; Opéra-Comique). Cast: Nerilha (Delphine Ugalde, s); Cadige (Meyer, s); Gulnare (Léocadie Lemercier, ms); Prince Adel Roudour (Marius-Pierre Audran, t); Xailoun (Pierre-Marius Jourdan, t); Atalmuc (Charles Bataille, bs); Aboul-faris (Charles Sainte-Foy).

25. *La tempesta* (opera, 3 acts; Scribe, trans. Pietro Giannone; 8 June 1850; Her Majesty's Theatre, London). Cast: Miranda (Henriette Sontag, s); Ariel (Carlotta Grisi, bal.); Stephano (Teresa Parodi, s); Spirit of the air (Esther Elisa Julian van Gelder, s); Syncorax (Ida Bertrand, ms); Fernando (Carlo Baucardé, t); Prospero (Filippo Coletti, b); Antonio (Federico Lablache, b); Alfonso, King of Naples (Signor Lorenzo, bs); Caliban (Luigi Lablache, bs).

26. *La dame de pique* (oc, 3 acts; Scribe; 28 Dec. 1850; Opéra-Comique). Cast: Princesse Poloska Dara Dolgorouski (Delphine Ugalde, s); Lisanka (Meyer, s); Prince Zizianov (Joseph-Antoine Couderc, t); Constantin Nelidoff (Jacques-Lucien Boulo, t); Klaremberg (Achille Ricquier, bs); André Roskaw (Charles Bataille, bs); Sowbakin (Léon Carvalho, b); Banquier de jeux (Bellecour).

27. *Le Juif errant* (go, 5 acts; Scribe and Vernoy de Saint-Georges; 11 Apr. 1852;

Opéra). Cast: Irène (Emmy La Grua, s); Théodora (Fortunato Tedesco, ms); Léon (Gustave Roger, t); Ashvérus (Jean-Etienne Massol, b); Nicéphore (Louis-Henri Obin, bs); L'ange exterminateur (Chapuis); Manoël (Jean-Baptiste Canaple); Andronique (Guigneau, b); Jean (Noir); Abas (Goyon); Guetteur de nuit (Merly); Officier (Lyon b); Seigneur (?); Autre seigneur (?).

28. *Le nabab* (oc, 3 acts; Scribe and Vernoy de Saint-Georges; 1 Sept. 1853; Opéra-Comique). Cast: Dora (Caroline Miolan-Carvalho, s); Corilla (Andrea Favel, s); Lord Evendale (Joseph-Antoine Couderc, t); Arthur (Charles-Marie Ponchard, t); John Cliffort (Ernest Mocker, t); Toby (Prosper-Alphonse Bussine); Domestique (Lejeune).

29. *Jaguarita l'Indienne* (oc, 3 acts; Vernoy de Saint-Georges and Adolphe de Leuven; 14 May 1855, Théâtre Lyrique). Cast: Jaguarita (Marie Cabel, s); La créole Héva (Marie Garnier, s); Capitaine Maurice (Jules-Sebastien Montjauze, t); Major Hector van Trump (Auguste-Alphonse Meillet, b); Sergeant Petermann (Colson, bs); Mama Jumbo (Marcel Junca, bs); Toby (Henry Adam).

30. *L'inconsolable* (oc, 1 act, Vernoy de Saint-Georges and de Leuven; 13 June 1855; Théâtre Lyrique). Cast: roles unknown (Chevalier, s); (Auguste Legrand, t); (Ernest Leroy, t); (Ribes, b).

31. *Valentine d'Aubigny* (oc, 3 acts; Jules Barbier and Michel Carré; 26 Apr. 1856; Opéra-Comique). Cast: Valentine (Caroline Duprez, s); Sylvia (Caroline Lefèbvre, s); Marion (Zoé Bélia, s); Chevalier de Boisrobert (Ernest Mocker, t); Gilbert de Mauléon (Charles Battaille, bs); Baron de Corisandre (Elias Nathan, bs); Julie (Laserre).

32. *La magicienne* (go, 5 acts; Vernoy de Saint-Georges; 17 Mar. 1858, Opéra), Cast: Blanche (Pauline Lauters-Guéymard, s); Méluzine (Adelaide Borghi-Mamo, ms); René de Thois (Louis Guéymard, t); Stello (Marc Bonnehée, b); Comte de Poitou (Jules Belval, bs); Alois (Delisle, s); Dame (Demgraf).

33. *Noé* (opéra, 3 acts — completed by Bizet as *Le déluge*; Vernoy de Saint-Georges; 5 Apr. 1885; Hoftheater, Karlsruhe, as *Noah*). Cast: Sara (Pauline Mailhac, s); Ebba (Fräulein Beles, s);[15] Japhet [Iaphet] (Elise Harlacher, s); Iturid (Alfred Oberländer, t); Sem (Hermann Rosenberg, t); Ham (Fritz Plank, b); Eléazar (Bösch, bs); Noah (Karl Speigler, bs); Diener (Götz).

34. *Vannina d'Ornano* (opéra, 3 acts; incomplete — never performed).

NOTES

1. Anselm Gerhard, *The Urbanization of Opera: Music Theater in Paris in the Nineteenth Century*, trans. Mary Whittall (Chicago: University of Chicago Press, 1998), p. 402.

2. "*Gil Blas*, 23 March 1903," in *Debussy on Music: The Critical Writings of the Great French Composer Claude Debussy*, collected and introduced by François Lesure, trans. and ed. Richard Langham Smith (New York: Alfred A. Knopf, 1977), pp. 152–53.

3. Gerhard, *The Urbanization of Opera*, p. 403. The three confirmed revivals at the Gaîté Lyrique were in 1903 (Alfred Loewen-

berg, *Annals of Opera* [Totowa, N.J.: Rowman and Littlefield, 1978], p. 766); in 1910 (Stéphane Wolff, *L'Opéra au Palais Garnier 1875–1962* [Paris: Slatkine, 1983], p. 130; and in 1917 (the writer's personal files, based on an examination of various Paris newspapers).

4. As an example, O'Sullivan first sang it in Paris at the Gaîté Lyrique in 1917–18; Budapest, Bucharest, Cluj, and Belgrade between 1927 and 1929; Algiers and Marseille in 1930; Perpignan, Marseille, and Toulon in 1931; Algiers again, Bordeaux, and Rouen in 1932; Paris, Angers, Marseille, and Avignon in 1933; Rouen, Lyon, and Bordeaux in 1934; and Nancy in 1936.

5. See Franz Hadamowsky, *Die Wiener Hoftheater*, vol. 2: *Die Wiener Hofoper (Staatsoper) 1811–1974* (Vienna: Brüder Hollinek, 1974), p. 232.

6. The 1988 studio recording on Philips 420 190-2 (currently out of print) is with José Carreras and Julia Varady, Antonio de Almeida conducting. Live recordings available at one time or another have included a 1981 performance with Carreras and Ilona Tokody, conducted by Gerd Albrecht (formerly Lyric Distribution LCD 224-2) and three performances with Richard Tucker (New York 1964—Lyric Distribution; New Orleans 1973—HRE; London 1973—OPR). Excerpts recordings include a 1962 Philips issue with Tony Poncet and Jane Rhodes, conducted by Marcel Couraud; and

a 1974 RCA disc with Tucker and Martina Arroyo, conducted by Antonio de Almeida. Highlights from a 1936 performance with Giovanni Martinelli and Elisabeth Rethberg were also issued on SRO 848-1 (apparently now out of print).

7. Félix Clément and Pierre Larousse, *Dictionnaire des Opéras*, vol. 1 (New York: Da Capo Press, 1969), p. 245.

8. Quoted in Hugh Macdonald's booklet notes accompanying the Philips complete recording of *La Juive*.

9. This recording was privately issued by the Meyerbeer Fan Club and is available to its members (for more information, visit the club's Website at *www.meyerbeer.com*).

10. Jerry Hadley sings Lionel's aria on his CD recital *The Age of Bel Canto* (RCA Victor 68030-2).

11. Wagner's commentary can be found in articles he wrote for the *Revue et Gazette musicale* in 1842. Extracts are reprinted in Didier Van Moere, comp. and ed., "Richard Wagner: Halévy, *La Juive* et *La reine de Chypre*," *L'Avant Scène Opéra*, no. 100 (July 1987), p. 16. (Editor's translation.)

12. Cyprès CYD 3603.

13. Clément and Larousse, *Dictionnaire des Opéras*, vol. 1, p. 222.

14. *Memoirs of Hector Berlioz*, trans. and ed. David Cairns (New York: Alfred A. Knopf, 1969), pp. 362–64.

15. The spelling is uncertain and could also be Belse or Belec.

The Early Days of Grand Opera in Kansas City, Missouri, 1860–1879

HARLAN JENNINGS

IN 1821 François Chouteau, an employee of John Jacob Astor's American Fur Company, established a trading post and warehouse in the remote wilderness of western Missouri. First known as Chouteau's Landing or Westport Landing, the site near the confluence of the Kansas and Missouri Rivers would eventually develop into a major center for trade, transportation, and manufacturing. By 1853, when the town was christened the City of Kansas,[1] the area, including nearby Westport and Independence, had already become the eastern terminus of the Santa Fe Trail as well as a major outfitting post for the Oregon Trail and the California gold mines. Here goods and people were transferred from steamboats to wagon trains and vice versa. Though now a bustling commercial center, the community had a large population of transients and lacked the requisite number of permanent residents to encourage cultural pursuits.

Late in the decade, however, an editorial appeared in the *Kansas City Journal of Commerce* signaling that area residents were ready to support so-called legitimate entertainment:

> We [have] received . . . a letter from one of the best theatrical managers in the West. . . . He desires to establish a theatre here, and will visit us in a few days. . . . We mention the matter thus early, that our citizens may reflect upon the matter, and be prepared to extend such encouragement as may be necessary, in aid of the enterprise.[2]

As a result, J. S. Langrishe, manager of a theatrical troupe trying to capitalize on the Colorado Gold Rush, brought his organization downriver from St. Joseph, Missouri, for two short summer engagements at the court house: 4–6 July and 1–12 August 1859 (a local band provided music between the acts). Once again the *Journal* expressed the fledgling community's eagerness to attract culture: "We feel an interest in the establishment of the drama in our young metropolis. The great object, is to start right. If our people will refuse to patronize any but a good company, and liberally support one when we have it, we will always have a legitimate performance."[3]

The Langrishe seasons paved the way for the arrival, the following summer, of Anna Bishop, the first of many famous divas to grace the Kansas City stage. Cultural inroads would take time, however. Kansas City was still a raw frontier community, as evidenced by the following notice, which appeared in the *Journal* a week after the first Langrishe season: "Should be stopped—This throwing of dead horses, dogs, mules, and other carrion into the river above the landing, when they are almost sure to be drawn into the eddy, and kept floating for some days. The Missouri [River] water is used by many for . . . drinking, and when a dead animal is seen just above the place from which it is dipped up, the sensation of nausea is very likely to result from an attempt to drink the water. Let the dead be thrown below town hereafter."[4]

The United States Census of 1860 showed an aggregate population of nearly 9,000 for greater Kansas City. The city proper contained only 4,418 people, 166 of whom were slaves. Nearby Westport counted 1,195 souls, including 134 slaves. Independence, in a mockery of its name, had an appalling 678 slaves out of a total population of 3,164.[5] That spring the *Journal* noted that daytime fistfights were not uncommon on the streets of the young metropolis. Stray dogs proved such a public nuisance that the city declared open season on them in April. A few days into the extermination program, the paper attempted to exert its civilizing influence by insisting that dogs shot by officers and others should be buried, adding: "There are many complaints made that the victims of the war upon dogs are left wherever they are shot or killed."[6]

Into this rough-and-tumble, slave-holding outpost of civilization came English soprano Anna Bishop (1810–84), who arrived in the dust and heavy heat of midsummer 1860 to give two concerts in Kansas City. Bishop, now at the advanced vocal age of fifty, was in the midst of a long and distinguished career in both concert and opera. Her touring days would last until age sixty-six, by which time she had appeared in Australia, Southeast Asia, India, South Africa, South America, and nearly all the major cities of Europe. Her final public appearance took place in New York City on 22 April 1883.[7]

The soprano first came to the United States in the summer of 1847. Writing of her public debut in his *Annals of the New York Stage*, C. D. Odell remarked: "Few who preceded her on the American stage had been her equals."[8] In his account of Bishop's first American appearance, Odell quoted the New York *Albion*, which stated that Bishop possessed "a very high soprano, neither powerful nor metallic . . . but sweet and pure"; her voice was even throughout its range and remarkably flexible.[9]

Bishop's 1860 appearances in Missouri were part of one of her extensive tours, this one encompassing the United States and Canada. Although newspaper accounts are sketchy or nonexistent, part of the soprano's progress across Missouri and northeast Kansas can be pieced together. She appeared in St. Louis on 25 and 26 June, then took the train to Jefferson City (one of the state's few existing rail lines had linked the two cities in 1855), where she sang on 28 and 29 June. Her whereabouts immediately thereafter are unknown, but two weeks later Bishop turned up in the Missouri River town of Lexington, where her advance agent had negotiated the abatement of a $100 tax so that she could give a concert on 13 July.[10] From there she took a steamboat to Kansas City (traveling at an average speed of five to six miles per hour), because no rail line existed west of Sedalia.

Accompanying Madame Bishop were F. Rudolphson, baritone, and Thomas Aug. Hogan, pianist. The concerts, originally scheduled for Lockridge Hall (the city's first public theater, erected in 1859 and situated at the southeast corner of Fifth and Main Streets), were moved to an unknown location referred to as Concert Hall. Frederic Schattner, a German immigrant and prominent Kansas City music teacher, loaned his piano for the performances. General admission sold for fifty cents; reserved seats were a dollar. Predictably the *Journal* urged the public to attend:

> We cannot do a greater favor to the lovers of music, than to call attention to the Concert of Madame Anna Bishop to-morrow night. It is the first time a Kansas City audience have had offered to them the privilege of hearing one of those who stand in the list of great artistes. . . . We shall look upon her audiences as a test of the musical tastes of our people, and . . . we expect to see the largest, most fashionable and brilliant audiences ever known here, to greet her during her short stay in this city.[11]

As one would expect, Kansas City received its first prima donna with open arms. Swept away by enthusiasm in the wake of Bishop's first concert, the *Journal* mistakenly claimed her as a native songbird:

> One of the largest and most appreciative audiences greeted Madame Anna Bishop's first appearance in our city last night. . . . No one, we presume, was there who did not come away satisfied that no such vocal talent had ever before visited the west. The gentlemen who accompany her are also artists of the highest order. . . .[12]
>
> While listening to her, we could but feel a just pride that we were hearing an American [?] woman who had delighted the most refined and critical audiences of Europe. . . . We are not competent to properly criticise either her musical powers or her . . . faultless execution. We can only say that her power and compass of voice and her complete and admirable management of it, far surpasses anything of the kind we have ever heard.[13]

The report mentions only three selections sung by Bishop: "Robin Redbreast," "Oft in the Stilly Night," and "Home, Sweet Home." The latter, written by her former husband, Sir Henry Rowley Bishop, thrilled the audience. Unfortunately there was no review of the second concert and no mention of its repertoire. From Kansas City the Bishop troupe traveled upriver to Leavenworth, Kansas, for concerts on 18–20 July, appeared at nearby Atchison, Kansas, on

21 July, and then surfaced in St. Joseph, Missouri, for two concerts on 24 and 25 July. In Hannibal, a day's journey by rail across northern Missouri, two more concerts were given (27 and 28 July). Here the local newspaper gallantly declared that Bishop "could easily pass for twenty by gas light."[14] On 30 July she sang in nearby Palmyra, Missouri, before disappearing from the regional historical record.

Bishop's early foray into western Missouri stands out as a cultural anomaly for the time. Events conspired to keep other ranking artists away from the area for nearly a decade. Within two weeks of Bishop's departure, local citizens had returned to a more familiar type of recreation, as the *Journal* noted in one of its columns: "Two of our oldest and most prominent citizens gave a bit of a sparring exhibition on Main Street yesterday morning."[15] Kansas City's rowdy frontier period was about to come to an end, however. The onset of the Civil War fostered an extended period of more lethal lawlessness and effectively put a damper on nearly all forms of entertainment. Not until the cessation of hostilities in 1865 were Kansas City residents able to turn their thoughts again to cultural matters:

> We are glad to learn that the Hall over the new block of Shannons', at the corner of Third and Main, is to be finished for a theatre. The room will . . . supply a deficiency that is felt . . . by our citizens. . . . We are greatly deficient in proper places of amusements. Next to commodious hotels, we need most such facilities for the disposal of leisure as will make our city an attraction to those who stop here. It is by such influences, far more than by mere business advantages, that our neighboring cities attract a large class whose wealth and influence go into the general capital of a city's growth. These appliances are no less essential to our general prosperity than business houses, churches and schools.[16]

The extension of the Missouri Pacific Railroad to Kansas City that same year made the community considerably more accessible to touring theatrical organizations. The completion of the line reduced travel time from St. Louis, 250 miles to the east, to just twelve hours.[17] Still, four more years elapsed before professional singers set foot again on Kansas City soil.

In the spring of 1869, Kansas City heard its first professional opera performance when the Brignoli Italian Opera Company, headed by tenor Pasquale Brignoli and managed by C. A. Chizzola, presented Donizetti's *Don Pasquale*, in Italian, on 1 June at Frank's Hall, located at the northwest corner of Fifth and Main Streets.[18] Traveling with the star tenor were Marie Louise Durand, soprano, a native of Charleston, South Carolina; Egisto Petrilli, baritone; Sarti, listed as a buffo; Domenico Locatelli, basso cantante; and Steffanone, musical director. The Kansas City appearance was part of a Midwestern tour that brought culture to the frontier settlements of St. Louis (24–26 May); Lawrence, Kansas (29 May, a mere six years after the savage Quantrill's Raid); Leavenworth, Kansas (31 May); and St. Joseph, Missouri (2 June). Earlier in

Pasquale Brignoli (carte de visite photo by Rockwood).
(Courtesy of the Harvard Theatre Collection.)

the spring the troupe had sung in Washington, D.C., Richmond, Norfolk, Raleigh, Charleston, Savannah, Atlanta, and New Orleans.[19]

Brignoli (1824–1884) had first come to the United States in 1855, making his New York City debut on 12 March as Edgardo in Donizetti's *Lucia di Lammermoor* at the Academy of Music.[20] For the next two decades, he reigned as the leading Italian tenor in the United States. Upon hearing the tenor as Gennaro in Donizetti's *Lucrezia Borgia*, the critic John Sullivan Dwight had this reaction:

> He is a youth of rather an elegant and distinguished presence, although his stage gait was awkward; his voice is sweet, fresh, flexible, sympathetic, and of good volume, sometimes *reminding* one of Mario's by a certain elasticity of tone, and capable of some strong, effective outbursts. He sings with taste and feeling, and (to his credit be it said) is given to a simple, faithful, unembellished rendering of the music of his author.[21]

Brignoli was never much of an actor. Dwight soon noticed his tendency to be listless on stage, except when singing. In an 1858 performance of Bellini's *La sonnambula*, the critic observed that the tenor sang "sweetly" and acted "only when it pleased his sovereign laziness."[22] Dwight, however, never grew tired of Brignoli's singing.[23] Walt Whitman also admired Brignoli and tried to capture and preserve his essence in a farewell poem, "The Dead Tenor":

> As down the stage again,
> With Spanish hat and plumes, and gait inimitable,
> Back from the fading lessons of the past, I'd call, I'd tell and own,
> How much from thee! the revelation of the singing voice from thee!
> (So firm — so liquid-soft — again that tremulous, manly timbre!
> The perfect singing voice — deepest of all to me the lesson — trial and
>   test of all:)
> How through those strains distill'd — how the rapt ears, the soul of me,
>   absorbing
> *Fernando's* heart, *Manrico's* passionate call, *Ernani's*, sweet *Gennaro's*,
> I fold thenceforth, or seek to fold, within my chants transmuting,
> Freedom's and Love's and Faith's unloos'd cantabile,
> (As perfume's, color's, sunlight's correlation:)
> From these, for these, with these, a hurried line, dead tenor,
> A wafted autumn leaf, dropt in the closing grave, the shovel'd earth,
> To memory of thee.[24]

Brignoli had begun his spring tour with a company of forty-five people, including, most likely, a chorus and orchestra.[25] By the time he arrived in Missouri, however, his forces apparently had been reduced to only the six artists listed above. No local newspaper mentions either a chorus or an orchestra. Since Brignoli lacked an ensemble, the performance of *Don Pasquale* must have been truncated. An abbreviated version also would have allowed for the Tower Scene/Miserere from *Il trovatore*, advertised as part of the evening's bill. The public paid $1.00 for general admission and $1.50 for reserved seats to hear the following cast sing with piano accompaniment: Pasquale — Sarti, Norina — Durand, Ernesto — Brignoli, Malatesta — Petrilli, Notary — Locatelli.

The *Journal* of 2 June 1869 carried accounts of Indian depredations in central Kansas, just two hundred miles to the west, along with a congratulatory review of the opera:

> Frank's Hall last night was crowded with the elite of Kansas City, and the rich dresses and brilliant colors that filled the room made a scene of beauty and fashion exceedingly attractive to look upon. . . .
>
> The opera passed off in a most acceptable manner, every one being in fine voice. M'lle Durand as "Norina," made a most charming widow. . . .
>
> Sig. Brignoli as "Ernesto" was exquisite. His voice has not that silver bell sweetness that it had ten years ago, but his wonderful tenor has still the power to charm the public into forgetting everything but his melody. . . .

Sig. Sarti . . . is a very excellent singer and actor. . . .

The entertainment was enthusiastically received throughout, and the curtain fell amid a storm of plaudits. So ended the first Italian opera in Kansas City. The ice has now been broken and we trust that other first class artistes will visit our city. We promise them all large and appreciative audiences.[26]

The driving of the Golden Spike in May 1869 made California accessible by rail, and the Brignoli Opera Company was one of the first to attempt the new route. Like so many others lured to the Pacific Coast by the promise of riches to be made, Brignoli paused in Kansas City for a two-night stand in November 1869, en route to San Francisco. Returning to Frank's Hall, Brignoli sported a reconstituted troupe of seven artists. For his soprano he had selected Isabella McCulloch, another South Carolinian (from Columbia), who at some point became his second wife. Antonietta Henne, another American, was the contralto. He had retained Petrilli and Locatelli, while adding veteran basso Augustino Susini. Paolo Giorza was the new music director and accompanist. C. A. Chizzola still managed the organization. On 5 November the troupe offered a three-part concert/scene recital: part 1, a short concert of operatic selections; part 2, act 1 of *Lucia di Lammermoor*, "in character"; and part 3, the Garden Scene from *Faust*, "in costume." The following evening the company introduced *The Barber of Seville*, in Italian, to Kansas City, before departing for Lawrence and Leavenworth, Kansas, St. Joseph, Missouri, and Omaha, Nebraska. Ever in a self-congratulatory frame of mind, the *Journal* exclaimed: "Kansas City can not only boast of a metropolitan trade, but metropolitan tastes and amusements."[27]

Despite such "metropolitan tastes," Kansas City still lacked the requisite first-class theater to attract "metropolitan amusements" on a regular, profitable basis. A new chapter in the town's cultural history began, however, on 6 October 1870, with the opening of the Coates Opera House, a fully equipped theater with ample seating capacity. Built at a cost of $105,000 by Kersey Coates, a prominent businessman, the theater itself stood on the second floor, above O. C. Day's Grocery and Feed Store (a common arrangement in the Midwest until the 1880s). Located at what became the intersection of Tenth Street and Broadway, the opera house was situated across the street from the city's finest hotel, also erected by Coates, on the edge of town. In an interview given thirty years after the opening, Coates's daughter, Laura Coates Reed, commented on the theater's rural surroundings and its social significance, as well as certain primitive aspects of daily life during her youth:

It was a great step forward in the social life of Kansas City, the night that the Coates Opera house was opened. It was an occasion when all the fashion of the town blossomed its brightest. . . . There were no pavements, and no street cars . . . in those days . . . and the sidewalks were all of wood. During dry weather the brown dust flew in clouds

Exterior of the Coates Opera House, Kansas City, Missouri.
(Courtesy of State Historical Society of Missouri, Columbia.)

down the roads of the town. When it rained the men wore rubber boots, and the women wore rubbers and tied them on. . . . The dust that covered the wooden sidewalks was changed by the rain to a slimy coating and when people walked along on the boards they held out their arms like a performer walking a slack wire. We had lamp posts, yes, but they were of the sputtering and uncertain variety.

The theater and the hotel, both built by my father, stood practically alone on what was called Coates hill. South of the theater was a deep pond. In front of it was a large area of vacant property and near it were some of the old forest trees that were here long before the white men came to Kansas City. Tenth Street was an earth dam to the pond.[28]

It should be pointed out that the opening of the Coates did not result in any "great step forward" in the social life of Kansas City's Afro-American population. Despite the Civil War, strict segregation prevailed in theaters all across the Midwest, with minorities being confined to the uppermost balcony. During the second season of operation at the Coates, an Afro-American courageous enough to buy a ticket in the parquet was ejected from the performance. In the aftermath of the incident, the manager of the Coates, John A. Stevens, wrote the following explanatory letter to the editor of the *Kansas City Times*:

> It has always been, and still is, customary in the United States for a
> particular portion of every theatre to be set apart for people of color;
> the Opera House in this city is no exception to the rule. . . . No colored
> person has been admitted to the parquette . . . until Thursday night
> last, and that was by accident. . . . During the performance a great
> commotion arose among the audience; I found it was owing to the
> presence of the colored man in the parquette, and I took measures to
> have him removed. . . . Colonel Coates, I presume, did not build his
> magnificent Opera House, nor do I manage it, for the purpose of
> settling the question of "Negro Equality." When the public are willing
> or desirous that colored people shall be admitted to the parquette and
> dress circle of my theatre, I shall admit them, but until then, I shall
> refuse to do so.[29]

Minorities would not gain equality in theaters until well into the twentieth century.

The Coates Opera House underwent remodeling in 1881, at a cost of forty-five thousand dollars. The theater was lowered to the first floor and the auditorium expanded to create a parquet, balcony, and gallery with a total capacity of eighteen hundred seats. The original leather upholstered benches, similar to church pews, were replaced with individual chairs. There were now four proscenium boxes and ten star dressing rooms. The stage measured thirty-six by seventy-two feet. Further remodeling occurred in 1891 and 1900, when Coates sold the theater after thirty years of ownership. It was destroyed by fire in 1901.[30]

The new place of amusement ensured its popularity by catering to female patrons. Aware that women had rarely attended theatrical events in Kansas City prior to 1870, the management of the Coates encouraged female attendance by introducing matinees for women and children. Soon the Coates Opera House became a gathering place for Kansas City society and remained the community's premiere theater until the end of the century.

The population of Kansas City exploded after the close of the Civil War and stood at 32,260 by 1870. It would grow to 55,785 by 1880, capping a decade of remarkable development.[31] Aside from the city's first opera house, the 1870s witnessed the establishment of the stockyards, a stock exchange, a city hall, a criminal court, a public library, an academy of science, a medical college, and a telephone exchange. The city attracted people from all walks of life, including such colorful figures as Wyatt Earp, Doc Holliday, Jesse James, and Wild Bill Hickok, all of whom could be seen on the streets in the 1870s. In the fall of 1870, the Academy of Music Piano House, located at 525 Main Street, opened for business, announcing "one of the finest stocks of pianofortes ever brought west. . . . All instruments fully warranted for five years."[32] The same store offered piano lessons: "We are determined to afford the best facilities for acquiring a thorough musical education. Terms — $15 per session of twenty lessons, payable one-half in advance."[33]

The construction of the Coates Opera House, combined with Kansas City's growing prosperity and increased accessibility by rail, did not immediately result in a surge of visits by opera troupes. In the first place, few such ensembles existed. Second, hardly any of these were willing to gamble on a far-flung trip to Kansas City. St. Louis (with a population of 310,864 in 1870, fourth highest in the nation behind New York City, Philadelphia, and Brooklyn, and ten times that of its sister city to the west) was still perceived as the extreme western edge of operatic profitability, San Francisco excepted. It should be remembered that opera impresarios at this time toured at their own financial risk. Kansas City therefore did not enjoy a steady parade of opera companies until the 1880s.

Following the 1869 visits of the Brignoli organization, five years elapsed before Kansas City heard a complete performance of an opera. In the meantime several concert companies came courting, not always with agreeable results. Not a square foot of space remained unoccupied when Ole Bull, making his first appearance in Kansas City, brought a small ensemble to Long's Hall on 8 April 1872. Soprano Gertrude Orme, tenor John ("Jack") H. Chatterton, and pianist Alfred Richter shared the program with the Norwegian violinist. Neither singer seems to have done much to advance the cause of opera, if the comments of the *Kansas City Times* may be taken at face value. According to the critic, it was not a good night for bel canto. Chatterton sang Donizetti's "Spirto gentil" in a throaty manner, while Orme rendered "Ah! non giunge" with a "metalic" [sic] voice, "almost barren of any heart" or feeling. Matters did not improve when Orme and Chatterton brought the concert to an end with an unnamed duet, "which was chiefly noticeable for wretched time."[34] Bull next ventured into Kansas City in February of the following year, accompanied by two new singers: soprano Graziella Ridgway and a baritone named Ferranti. This time, however, Bull and his troupe met with entirely favorable critiques.

On 2 September 1874 area newspapers reported that six surveyors from Lawrence, Kansas, had been killed by Indians near Ft. Dodge, Kansas, roughly 350 miles southwest of Kansas City.[35] Two days later, the Redpath English Opera Company gave Flotow's *Martha* at the Coates Opera House, the city's first complete opera since the Brignoli appearance five years earlier. The troupe came from St. Joseph, Missouri, where they had sung the same opera the night before. Little information about the company is available. James Redpath, who had come to Kansas years earlier and had been active as an abolitionist and newspaper publisher before returning to the East, was the manager of the troupe. Performers included Clara B. Nickols, soprano; Flora E. Barry, contralto; Charles H. Clark, tenor; Edward S. Payson, bass; and J. A. Howard, pianist; they were artists of little renown from Boston and New York. The opera was given with piano accompaniment and probably truncated (Payson portrayed both Plumkett and Tristan). In any event, a full house greeted the singers, as well as generally favorable reviews. While noting that the women's voices sounded somewhat tired and that the tenor was hopeless as an actor, the Kansas City *Times* trenchantly commented: "This way of presenting an opera without a chorus and orchestra is like playing *Hamlet* with Hamlet left out; and yet we cannot but admit that the people named above succeeded in giving a very creditable performance." The *Journal* praised all the voices and remarked that "the costumes were exquisitely rich."[36] Within the next four days, the Redpath troupe gave three additional performances of *Martha* in nearby Leavenworth, Atchison, and Topeka, Kansas.

A much more distinguished organization arrived a few weeks later, when the Adelaide Phillipps Opera Company appeared on 26 October at the Coates. Born in Stratford-upon-Avon, English contralto Adelaide Phillipps (1833–1882) performed extensively in the United States with both English and Italian opera companies. Her family moved to Boston while she was still a child, and she began singing professionally at an early age, undertaking roles with the Seguin English Opera Company during its 1846–47 and 1847–48 seasons. During her 1850 American tour, Jenny Lind heard Miss Phillipps and then initiated a fundraising drive to enable her to take lessons abroad. After studying with Manuel Garcia in London, the contralto debuted in Brescia as Arsace in *Semiramide* on 5 November 1853.

The following year she returned to the United States. In October John Sullivan Dwight heard her in concert and gave a ringing endorsement:

> Her singing did not in the least disappoint us. . . . She is . . . an admirable artist, one whose voice, execution, taste, expression, talent and evidence of reserved force afford rare satisfaction and still rarer hope.
> Her voice is a pure contralto of the most rich and musical quality . . . , powerful *enough*, refined and equalized by culture. . . . It is the voice of an expressive artist. The low tones are remarkably fine. . . . Her execution . . . is very smooth and even, and all is done in a good, honest, natural style, with nothing over-strained, and with the right expression always. . . .
> We found her one of the best Rossini singers we have ever heard. But what pleased us most was the simplicity, naturalness, and good sense that pervaded all her efforts. . . . We trust that she is destined to be . . . a true interpreter of the greatest masters of song.[37]

Phillipps made her debut at the New York Academy of Music, 17 March 1856, as Azucena in *Il trovatore*. On that occasion the *New York Tribune* stated: "Her voice is . . . a mezzo soprano of excellent quality, round and sympathetic. . . . Her appearance and bearing, too, are much in her favor."[38] In 1861 the contralto was back in Europe, appearing in France, Spain, Hungary, Belgium, and Holland. Phillipps sang in concert and opera in New York and other eastern cities in 1865–70 and made a second trip to Havana. In 1870, 1871, and 1872, she traveled across the United States with her own concert company, taking time out to appear with the Parepa-Rosa Opera Company in 1871 and 1872. During the 1874–75 season, she toured America at the helm of the Adelaide Phillipps Opera

Company. Joining the Boston Ideal Opera Company in 1879, Phillipps toured with that troupe for two seasons. Her final performance occurred in Cincinnati in December 1881. During her long and distinguished career in this country, her main low-voiced rivals were Annie Louise Cary, in Italian opera and concert, and Zelda Seguin, in English opera.

Although she had never sung in Kansas City, the adventuresome Miss Phillipps was no stranger to the West, having appeared in California in the late 1860s. In the summer of 1870, she must have embarked on another western tour, for on 22 July she headed a small troupe that gave a concert in Cheyenne, Wyoming. Later that same year she traveled west again. Ice on the Missouri River prevented her from reaching Nebraska City for a concert on 19 December, but she appeared in St. Joseph, Missouri, two nights later, despite below-zero temperatures. Phillipps came no further west than St. Louis in 1871 and 1872 and did not travel to the region in 1873.

With the price of reserved seats hiked to $1.50, the audience at the Coates Opera House heard a company consisting of Adelaide Phillipps, contralto; Tom Karl, tenor; Carlo Orlandini, baritone; R. Baccelli, buffo; Nicolo Barili, bass; and George Colby, music director.[39] Surprisingly, the troupe lacked a soprano, a most unusual circumstance. The program was supposed to feature excerpts from *Il barbiere di Siviglia*, *Don Pasquale*, *Nabucco*, *La traviata*, and *Il trovatore*. Unfortunately, the favorable review in the *Journal* provides no details of the performance and singles out only Mr. Karl for extended praise: "The tenor, Mr. Karl, deserves special mention for the unusual strength and volume of his voice, with which qualities are combined great sweetness and purity of tone."[40] A more extensive review appeared in the *Times*:

> The musical performance . . . by the Adelaide Phillipps opera combination was a rare treat, and was thoroughly enjoyed by all who were present. A well filled house complimented the appearance of the distinguished singer. . . .
> There was little to criticize, and much to admire. Instead of giving the program as announced . . . , the company essayed act 1st and 2d of . . . "Barber of Seville," and the 3d act of "Don Pasquale."[41]

The *Times* critic went on to note that Phillipps encored her *Barber* aria with an English ballad, which she sang "with such perfectness of expression and vocalization as to fairly carry away her hearers. . . . The other parts were well sustained, and Mr. Locke [Charles Locke, then manager of the Coates] has the thanks of everyone who attended for such a creditable entertainment."[42]

After the 1874 engagement in Kansas City, Phillipps remained in the Missouri River valley for nine more days, appearing in Leavenworth, Atchison, and St. Joseph, as well as Lincoln and Omaha, Nebraska. Aside from an 1875 engagement in Hannibal, Missouri, she did not return to this part of the Midwest after her 1874 tour.

A three-year operatic drought followed the Phillipps engagement. Relief finally came in the form of the Richings-Bernard Grand English Opera Company, which arrived in early June 1877.[43] Soprano Caroline Richings-Bernard had sung in Kansas City on three earlier occasions at the head of her own concert company (27 April 1874; 19 and 30 March 1875), but this was her first appearance in opera. Purportedly comprising forty people, her troupe opened its Missouri River valley tour in Omaha on 31 May, before moving on to St. Joseph, Missouri, on 5–6 June, and Leavenworth, Kansas, on 7 June. The company included a small chorus and orchestra — the first such operatic ensembles ever heard in Kansas City. The orchestra was probably augmented with a few local instrumentalists, as had been the case in Omaha. Aside from Miss Richings, the principal artists were Mrs. Henri Drayton, contralto; Harry Gates, tenor; and Pierre Bernard, tenor/baritone/conductor (as the occasion demanded!). The troupe opened on 8 June with the Kansas City premiere of *Trovatore*, with Richings, Drayton, Gates, and Bernard in the four leading roles. Matinee and evening performances of Wallace's *Maritana* and Balfe's *Bohemian Girl*, respectively, followed the next day. These three operas constituted Kansas City's first full-scale productions of grand opera in English.[44] Unfortunately, the newspapers failed to announce the casts for the latter two offerings.

Although inclement weather and the inevitable muddy streets curtailed the size of the audience, favorable notices greeted *Trovatore*. The lack of a full house prompted the *Times* to defend the city's cultural reputation, while urging greater attendance in the future:

> The English opera is something quite new to Kansas City; but its favorable reception last evening and its introduction under such noted auspices ensures its permanent popularity in Kansas City hereafter. The people of this city have been accused sometimes of possessing a taste for the lower and more vulgar class of amusements; but the hearty . . . reception given the . . . Opera Company last night . . . refutes this idea. We . . . express the hope that the legitimate drama and the opera will receive a better reception in Kansas City in the future than burnt cork minstrelsy, circus nonsense and the blood-and-thunder melodrama. . . . Had the weather been favorable last night the Opera House would have been crowded.[45]

The Richings troupe left Kansas City on 9 or 10 June but did not go far afield. After appearances in St. Louis (11–16 June), Hannibal (25 June), Boonville (27 June), and Sedalia (28 June), the organization returned to Kansas City for a performance of *Martha* on 2 July. During its absence the size of the troupe may have been curtailed to reduce expenses, for the advertisement of *Martha* in the *Kansas City Journal* proclaimed thirty artists, down from the forty advertised in June. In any event, both the *Times* and the *Journal* gave favorable accounts of Flotow's opera. The company next appeared in nearby Atchison (3 July), St. Joseph (4 July), Topeka (5 July), and Wichita (9 and 10 July) before heading west toward Colorado, where they opened a season in Denver on 16

July. Richings would never sing in Kansas City again. After she returned from a tour of the Far West the following winter, her troupe disbanded in Denver before reaching the Kansas City area. Thereafter she retired from the operatic stage.

At the beginning of 1878, the C. D. Hess Grand English Opera Company had two short engagements at the Coates, 14–16 and 21–22 January. Hess's roster contained the names of three well-known artists: mezzo-soprano Zelda Seguin; her husband, bass Edward Seguin; and tenor William Castle. Zelda Seguin and William Castle were, at this time, perhaps the best singers in English opera in their respective voice categories, while Edward Seguin was known for his skillful interpretation of comic and character roles. Despite its name, the troupe restricted its offerings to lighter fare, including one performance each of *The Bohemian Girl* and *Fra Diavolo*.

Although the Hess company drew an enthusiastic response from the press and public, the most exciting event surrounding the troupe's engagement was, without a doubt, an attempted robbery. In broad daylight on the morning of 22 January, a young man grabbed the purse of soprano Emilie Melville as she walked the short distance from the Coates Opera House to the Coates Hotel. A number of men and boys gave chase and cornered the thief until a policeman arrived. The purse, containing the considerable sum of thirty dollars, was returned to its owner.[46]

No other opera company visited Kansas City in 1878. But in March the public was treated to two concerts by the famous Croatian soprano Ilma di Murska, who had split off from the Richings-Bernard Opera Company when it began to unravel in Denver. Now she was withdrawing eastward, giving hastily arranged concerts to finance her retreat.[47] Traveling with her were Cornelius W. Makin, bass, and John T. Hill, violinist and pianist.

Di Murska received a cool reception in Kansas City. Small houses greeted the soprano, with less than 150 attending the second performance. The *Journal*, which praised her "wonderful flexibility" and "purity and richness of tone" after the first concert, reversed course in its assessment of the second, calling her "an ill-tempered, sour-visaged, vixenish sort of a person," and advising her "to cultivate a pleasing manner and train the corners of her mouth upward instead of downward."[48] What prompted the *Journal*'s abrupt change of mood cannot be determined. Some of the ill feeling could have been caused by di Murska's refusal to respond to every encore request (the press made no mention of what was on the regular program for either concert). Needless to say, the soprano never revisited Kansas City.

C. D. Hess returned with an English opera company the following year. For this 1879 troupe, he retained Zelda Seguin and William Castle, while strengthening his forces with the addition of soprano Emma Abbott, destined to become America's most popular diva in the 1880s. Hess also hired for principal roles soprano Annis Montague, C. H. Turner, who alternated between tenor and baritone parts, and basses Gus Hall and James Peakes. The company traveled with a chorus of modest size, as well as a small core of instrumentalists, which was augmented with Kansas City players.[49]

With prices of admission ranging from 50 cents to $1.25 at the Coates, Hess opened on 26 February 1879 with the Kansas City premiere of Gounod's *Faust*, starring Emma Abbott and William Castle (Hall sang Valentine; Peakes was Mephisto). This was followed by Planquette's *Chimes of Normandy* on 27 February, with Montague, Seguin, Castle, and Turner; Balfe's *Bohemian Girl* on 28 February, with Abbott, Seguin, Turner, and Hall; and two performances on 1 March: a matinee of *Martha*, starring Montague, Seguin, Turner (as Lionel), and Peakes; and, in the evening, the first Kansas City performance of Thomas's *Mignon*, with Abbott, Montague, and Castle in the leading roles.

The *Journal* liked *Faust*, and had nothing but praise for the two leads:

> Those who had seen Miss Abbott in concert were not prepared for the dramatic force which she displayed throughout the piece. Thoroughly conscientious at all times, she sings in good taste. . . . In the stronger dramatic passages she showed a power far beyond that which is usually seen in opera. . . .
> Mr. Castle sang with the same spirit and effect as ever.[50]

As is well known, the lyric art has not always brought out the best in human nature. Squabbles have often arisen, and not always among the performers. Not surprisingly, this phenomenon attended the Hess season. Although the *Journal* had welcomed Hess's company with open arms, elsewhere the greeting had been less friendly, prompting the *Journal* to issue a reprimand on its editorial page:

> Criticism is the element of people out of sorts with themselves and everybody else. . . .
> The statement made in a very pretentious critique yesterday morning, that Miss Abbott failed in the "long note" in the spinning song on Wednesday night was so manifestly unjust as to deserve a correction. If a writer has to go so far as to misrepresent in order to find something to condemn, it is no more than right that correction be made. In the effort commented upon so unjustly, Miss Abbott was so successful that the most hearty applause was awarded her.[51]

As the short opera season progressed, the *Journal* remained steadfast in its support of the Hess troupe and, in particular, Emma Abbott. The paper praised her naturalness and spontaneity on stage, her lack of self-consciousness and affectation. And when it remarked, "She never forgets that she is an American girl," one could sense not only a hint of impatience with foreign-born divas but also an emerging national pride in home-grown artists.[52] The *Journal*'s assessment of the season left no doubt that Abbott had taken the town by storm. The little prima donna from Bloomington, Illinois, who had been busy during the week signing autographs on ladies' programs, had convincingly exhibited her drawing power among all classes of society:

> Our brief opera season is over, and what a treat it was for the major-
> ity of our people. . . . People in society and those out of society, who
> rarely ever go to the opera house, were there. And who that saw her
> will ever forget Emma Abbott; forget her as a lovely, true and noble
> woman, or as an actress of magnetic power, or her exquisite voice?[53]

In closing, the *Journal* noted with approval that many ladies had not worn bonnets to the opera.

A contingent from the Kansas legislature attended the final performance. Five coaches, loaded with a number of legislators and their wives, made up a special train organized by the manager of the Atchison, Topeka, and Santa Fe Railroad. According to the *Journal*, the journey from Topeka to Kansas City was enlivened by several enterprising politicians, who, "wishing to lead the company up gradually to the divine melody of last night, organized themselves into an opera troupe on their own account, and gave their listeners such music as whetted their ears for Emma Abbott."[54] For the convenience of all passengers, the special train returned to Topeka immediately after the final curtain.

The war of words that had commenced a few days earlier had not yet run its course. Immediately after the troupe's departure, one more salvo was fired by the critic at the *Mail*, who took exception to the views expressed by the *Times*:

> Kansas City is told that she has a critic who will not only teach the
> town, but all other critics, how to comport themselves. . . . A morning
> paper, in order to cover the blunders of this critic *par excellence*, pub-
> lished over three columns of brilliant gloss work yesterday morning
> [Sunday, 2 March], to show the public that it really appreciated the
> opera after all, and did not mean to be insipidly stupid or maliciously
> fault-finding. . . . The fact is that the criticisms were no criticisms at all.
> They did not rise to that dignity. They never got above fault-finding.
> Any scold could have done just as much. To do justice to criticism, the
> critic must know as much about the subject criticized, or even more, as
> the artist. . . . The verdict of the public is that there was little to find
> fault with in the season of opera just closed. In this opinion the public
> is the best critic.[55]

The *Journal* noted the feud between its sister papers, but did not join in the fray. And with the departure of the troupe, the matter seems to have been quickly forgotten.

Aside from a November concert by Carlotta Patti, Kansas City heard no more grand opera in 1879. However, at the close of the decade, the city stood on the verge of an operatic golden age. Whereas only four companies had actually presented complete, staged grand opera between 1860 and 1879, the number of such companies jumped to twenty in the 1880s. During the latter decade Emma Abbott herself would bring a company on thirteen different occasions. And the public would often enjoy two or more opera seasons annually.

Nevertheless, the two decades from 1860 to 1879, especially the last ten years of that period, reveal impressive (and perhaps surprising) statistics. There were no fewer than ten operatic premieres in Kansas City. Two of these, *Don Pasquale* and *Barber*, were sung in Italian; the remainder, including *Trovatore* and *Faust*, in English. Fourteen performances of ten different operas took place. In addition, the public of this frontier community had the privilege of hearing such world-class singers as Anna Bishop, Pasquale Brignoli, and Adelaide Phillipps, as well as half a dozen other singers of distinction. These names and numbers look impressive, even today. And they suggest that the Midwest was not quite the cultural wasteland depicted in the history books.

NOTES

1. The name was changed to Kansas City (Missouri) in 1889.

2. *Kansas City Journal of Commerce*, 7 May 1859, p. 3.

3. Ibid., 7 July 1859, p. 2. The Court House was located on Main Street, between Fourth and Fifth.

4. Ibid., 22 July 1859, p. 3.

5. United States Census, 1860, *Population of the United States in 1860: Compiled from the Original Returns of the Eighth Census* (Washington, D.C.: Government Printing Office, 1864), p. 292.

6. *Kansas City Journal of Commerce*, 17 April 1860, p. 3.

7. According to Nicholas Temperley, Anna Bishop "was one of the most popular English singers of her generation. Her voice was brilliant, her technique masterly; but she lacked the expressive power of Jenny Lind or Clara Novello." See *The New Grove Dictionary of Music and Musicians*, ed. Stanley Sadie (London: Macmillan, 1980), vol. 2, p. 741. On her return from the Continent in 1846, the London *Morning Post* had this to say about her performance as Isoline in Balfe's *Maid of Artois*: "This lady has rare qualifications for the stage, a soprano voice of excellent quality, unerring intonation, facile execution, artistic feeling, and . . . perfect musical accent. Her register extends from E flat on the first line to D flat in alt. She is of middle size and symmetrically

formed — her eyes are large, lustrous, and full of fire — her actions free, graceful and dramatic" (*The New Grove Dictionary*, vol. 2, p. 741).

8. C. D. Odell, *Annals of the New York Stage*, vol. 5, p. 321 (Bishop's debut occurred in August 1847). Richard Grant White had a less favorable impression of Bishop's first New York appearance. While noting that she had "retained the remarkable beauty both of her face and her figure," and admitting that she sang "in very good style and with clever execution," White complained that "her voice, never of first-rate quality, was worn and somewhat husky." See Richard Grant White, "Opera in New York," *Century Magazine*, vol. 23 (April 1882), p. 879.

9. Odell, *Annals of the New York Stage*, vol. 5, p. 321. Late in 1859, John Sullivan Dwight heard her in oratorio and wrote the following assessment in his journal: "To be sure, she avoided low notes, and there was the same old tendency in her high voice to the upper edge of pitch. . . . Some of her notes have still a splendid resonance, which fades away in others. But there was the sure, artistic, eloquent and telling execution throughout; the finest English singing (at least of elaborate and florid music) that we have heard. Miss [Louisa] Pyne may execute as fluently and finely, but with far less vitality." See *Dwight's Journal of Music*, vol. 16, no. 10 (3 December 1859), p. 286.

10. *Lexington Weekly Express*, 7 July 1860, p. 2, and 14 July 1860, p. 3. The issue of 7 July states that Bishop was to give a concert in Lexington on 9 July, but the 14 July issue mentions only the 13 July performance.

11. *Kansas City Journal of Commerce*, 15 July 1860, p. 3.

12. Ibid., 17 July 1860, p. 3.

13. Ibid., 18 July 1860, p. 3.

14. Hannibal *Daily Messenger*, 31 July 1860, p. 3. A rail line connecting Hannibal with St. Joseph had been completed in 1859.

15. *Kansas City Journal of Commerce*, 29 July 1860, p. 3.

16. Ibid., 15 December 1865, p. 3.

17. Ibid., 11 July 1865, p. 3.

18. Frank's Hall opened on 8 February 1867 and was destroyed in December 1878, when the roof collapsed. In addition to the above-mentioned Lockridge Hall, two other public halls were in operation in the 1860s. Long's Hall, situated on Main Street between Fifth and Sixth Streets, was first advertised in the fall of 1860. Of lesser importance was Turner's Hall, owned by the German Turner Society. Originally near Fifth and Main Streets, it was reestablished near Tenth and Main Streets in 1864, and relocated again at Twelfth and Oak Streets in 1872. See Louise Jean Rietz, "History of the Theatre in Kansas City, Missouri, from the Beginnings until 1900" (Ph.D. diss., State University of Iowa, 1939), pp. 24–25, 29–30, 33, 34; Janet Loring, "Coates' Tales," *Missouri Historical Review*, vol. 56 (July 1962), p. 320; and an interview with Laura Coates Reed in the *Kansas City Star*, 1 February 1901, p. 1.

19. John L. DiGaetani and Josef P. Sirefman, eds., *Opera and the Golden West* (London: Associated University Presses, 1994), p. 106. William C. Quantrill was the leader of a Confederate guerrilla force that sacked and burned Lawrence, Kansas, on 21 August 1863. Most of the town was destroyed and 150 people were killed.

20. Odell, *Annals of the New York Stage*, vol. 6, p. 393.

21. *Dwight's Journal of Music*, vol. 7, no. 9, 2 June 1855, pp. 69–70. Calling Brignoli "a master of tone-production," the impresario George Upton had nothing but praise for the singer: "His tones had a silvery quality and were exquisitely pure. He never forced his voice beyond the limit of a sweet musical tone, and rarely expended much effort except in reaching a climax. . . . He never sang the high C . . . , though he could reach it with ease, for he had great range and power of voice. He used to say that 'screaming is not singing.' . . . His highest ambition was tonal loveliness. . . . To hear him sing . . . was to listen to vocalization of absolute beauty, to an exposition of *bel canto* of the Italian romantic school as perfect for a tenor as was Adelina Patti's for a soprano." See George P. Upton, *Musical Memories: My Recollections of Celebrities of the Half Century, 1850–1900* (Chicago: A. C. McClurg, 1908), p. 122.

22. *Dwight's Journal of Music*, vol. 14, no. 14 (1 January 1859), p. 318.

23. In 1876, when the singer had reached the age of fifty-two, Dwight heard him as Ottavio in *Don Giovanni* and gushed that he sang "Il mio tesoro" "like a young man of twenty-five, with such fervor and such beauty, and such wealth of tone, that he was . . . obliged to repeat it" (*Dwight's Journal of Music*, vol. 35, no. 25 (18 March 1876), p. 199.

24. Sculley Bradley, Harold W. Blodgett, Arthur Golden, and William White, eds., *Walt Whitman, Leaves of Grass: A Textual Variorum of the Printed Poems*, vol. 3: *Poems, 1870–1891* (New York: New York University Press, 1980), p. 715.

25. DiGaetani and Sirefman, *Opera and the Golden West*, p. 106.

26. *Kansas City Journal of Commerce*, 2 June 1869, p. 4.

27. Ibid., 6 November 1869, p. 4. The decade closed with the first Kansas City appearance of the Mendelssohn Quintette Club of Boston at Frank's Hall, 22 December. With them was soprano Jennie Busk, who introduced the young community to the aria "Bel raggio," from *Semiramide*.

28. *Kansas City Star*, 1 February 1901, p. 1; Rietz, "History of the Theatre in Kansas City," pp. 44–45; and Janet Loring, "Coates' Tales," pp. 319–20. Kersey Coates hired and maintained a resident stock company during the theater's first season. When the initial season ended in the red, Coates made up the deficit himself. Smaller stock companies were hired for the second and third seasons.

29. *Kansas City Times*, 3 January 1872, p. 1.

30. Rietz, "History of the Theatre in Kansas City," pp. 46–48, and Loring, "Coates' Tales," p. 320.

31. United States Census, 1870 and 1880, *Compendium of the Tenth Census* (1 June 1880), part 1 (Washington, D.C.: Government Printing Office, 1883), pp. 392, 393.

32. *Kansas City Journal of Commerce*, 15 September 1870, p. 1.

33. Ibid.

34. *Kansas City Times*, 9 April 1872, p. 4.

35. *St. Joseph Morning Herald*, 2 September 1874, p. 1.

36. *Kansas City Times*, 5 September 1874, p. 4; *Kansas City Journal of Commerce*, 5 September 1874, p. 4.

37. *Dwight's Journal of Music*, vol. 8, no. 2 (13 October 1855), p. 14.

38. Ibid., vol. 8, no. 25 (22 March 1856), p. 199. On another occasion, Dwight referred to her Azucena as "a sort of walking, singing *auto da fe*" (ibid., vol. 10, no. 6 [8 November 1856], p. 46).

39. Irish tenor Tom Karl (1846–1916) sang for a number of years in Italy before coming to the United States, where he became one of the most prominent tenors in English opera in the 1870s and 1880s. He joined the Boston Ideal Opera Company in 1879 as its leading tenor and later toured as a mainstay of the Emma Abbott Grand English Opera Company and the Bostonians. His main rival in English opera was tenor William Castle. See Nicolas Slonimsky, ed., *Baker's Biographical Dictionary of Musicians*, 5th ed. (New York: G. Schirmer, 1958), p. 808; and Oscar Thompson, *The American Singer* (New York: Dial Press, 1937), pp. 51, 52, 88, and 129.

40. *Kansas City Journal of Commerce*, 28 October 1874, p. 4.

41. *Kansas City Times*, 27 October 1874, p. 4.

42. Ibid.

43. Caroline Richings (1827–1882), born Mary Caroline Reynoldson in England, was adopted by the actor Peter Richings and brought to the United States while still a child. She debuted in English opera in *The Child of the Regiment* at Philadelphia's Walnut Street Theatre in 1852. Her debut in Italian opera, in the role of Adalgisa, took place at the Philadelphia Academy of Music in 1857, under the auspices of Max Maretzek. In January 1859 she took to the road at the head of her own English opera company, managed by her adoptive father. When Peter Richings retired in the fall of 1867, she became sole manager. A few months later she married tenor Pierre Bernard. The Richings-Bernard company was the first important English opera troupe to tour the United States, and Richings remained a constant promoter of opera in the vernacular. According to John Dizikes's *Opera in America*, "She was an excellent actress with a serviceable voice. . . . She often translated the librettos herself, not hesitating to edit and adapt the operas to her company's needs." At the time of her death, of smallpox, she directed the Richmond (Virginia) Conservatory of Music. For an obituary, see the *Musical Courier*, 21 January 1882, p. 28.

Richings's troupe included Mrs. Henri Drayton, Hattie Moore, Amy Phillips, Pierre Bernard, Harry Gates, Frank Howard, and W. H. Kinross. Although newspaper accounts are sketchy regarding casting, it appears that Richings and Drayton assumed all the leading soprano and mezzo roles, respectively. Harry Gates was responsible for the leading tenor roles. Pierre Bernard, a tenor of less accomplishment, conducted some of the performances but sang in others, taking the baritone role of Count di Luna in *Trovatore*! Frank Howard and W. H. Kinross essayed the baritone/bass roles. Prices of admission ranged from 50 cents to $1.00 in Missouri, Kansas, and Nebraska, but the troupe hiked the most expensive tickets to $1.50 when they appeared in Denver later in the summer.

44. Although the Redpath Opera Company had given *Martha* in English at the Coates Opera House on 4 September 1874, that troupe contained only four singers and lacked an orchestra and chorus.

45. *Kansas City Times*, 9 June 1877, p. 4. No reviews of the 9 June performances of *Maritana* and *Bohemian Girl* appeared in the newspapers.

46. *Kansas City Journal of Commerce*, 23 January 1878, p. 5.

47. Ilma di Murska (1836–89) debuted in *Martha* at Florence, Italy, in 1862. After appearances in Budapest, Berlin, Hamburg, and Vienna, she debuted as Lucia at Her Majesty's Theatre, London, in 1865. For the next eight years, she was a mainstay of Mapleson's London troupe. Her American debut took place in 1873. She rejoined Mapleson for a season in London in 1879, by which time her voice was in decline. Her interpretation of the Queen of the Night was held in particularly high esteem by her contemporaries.

48. *Kansas City Journal of Commerce*, 10 March 1878, p. 4, and 12 March 1878, p. 8.

49. According to the *New York Dramatic Mirror*, C. D. Hess had traced the following itinerary prior to his 1879 appearance in Kansas City: Cincinnati, 16–21 December 1878; Louisville, 23–28 December 1878; Peoria, 1–2 January 1879; Terre Haute, two

nights, probably 3–4 January, though the *Mirror* provides no specific dates; Chicago, 6–11 January; New Orleans, 20 January–8 February; Austin, 20 February; Dallas, 21 February; Sherman, Texas, 22 February; and St. Joseph, Missouri, 24–25 February. After his departure from Kansas City, Hess took his troupe to St. Louis, 3–8 March; Quincy, Illinois, dates unknown, probably 10–11 March; Jacksonville, Illinois, 12–13 March; Sterling, Illinois, 14–15 March; St. Paul, 20–22 March; and Minneapolis, 24–26 March.

50. *Kansas City Journal of Commerce*, 27 February 1879, p. 8.

51. Ibid., 28 February 1879, p. 5.

52. Ibid., 1 March 1879, p. 4.

53. Ibid., 2 March 1879, p. 2.

54. Ibid.

55. *Kansas City Mail*, 3 March 1879, p. 3.

Beniamino Gigli
An Appreciation

JACQUES CHUILON

IT IS widely acknowledged that the Italian tenor Beniamino Gigli (1890–1957) possessed one of the most beautiful voices of all time. Yet sometimes the stock phrase seems to turn, paradoxically, to Gigli's disadvantage, as when beauty is associated with a lack of intelligence (implying that intelligence is always more desirable than beauty). In such cases, the cliché inevitably injects a note of reserve to the compliment, diminishing its effect and causing one to pair vocal beauty with interpretive shortcomings. Gigli, claim the so-called guardians of good taste, may have had a beautiful voice overall but, because of certain defects, cannot be called a truly great artist. Whether this opinion reflects genuine high standards or a lack of open-mindedness, and whether such criticism is justified, shall be the main focus of this article.

First of all, to stress my opening point—and contrary to popular opinion— a beautiful voice is not a gift from heaven over which an artist has no control. During a career as long as Gigli's, the voice inevitably becomes the result of renewed demands, practice, and artistic taste. What starts out as luck turns into the creativity of an artist who, on recognizing the capabilities of his voice, preserves and develops them (is not the highest quality of a creative artist the ability to distinguish between what is right and wrong for his voice?); it is therefore unfair not to credit Gigli for this entirely independent facet of his artistry. There are so many young singers who sacrifice freshness of voice for an imagined maturity, who ruin their voices in an effort to make themselves sound older! One might well question the purpose of such an approach. Should not singing be primarily a matter of trying to embellish one's instrument, in the sense of enhancing its possibilities? Is not beauty an important aspect of one's art? If God granted Gigli a prodigious vocal talent, his recordings prove that he deserved the favor. In fact, he is not among those tenors whose earliest records are the best and whose first performances reduce fans to tears. His voice was beautiful, certainly, but how he enriched it, how he worked and reworked the music, perfecting an aria and giving free rein to interpretation!

Oddly enough, those who consider themselves upholders of modernity (a word that usually evokes a sort of fickle eclecticism, individualism, or even the

Beniamino Gigli (this and all subsequent photos courtesy of Jacques Chuilon).

death knell of traditional art) have been known to claim that Gigli was devoid of artistic taste. Of course, what these detractors really mean is that Gigli was an old-fashioned artist, out of sync with the style of today. Sometimes it is well to distinguish between artistic expression that seems to emanate naturally from within and that which often merely reflects passing trends; yet it must also be admitted that any artist necessarily performs in his own era. There will always be one part of performance that sounds original, personal, and timeless, and another that reflects the idiosyncrasies of time and historical context. Just as we recognize a Louis Quinze chair, a nineteenth-century painting, or a piece of Baroque music, so can we identify a singer of the 1920s, 1930s, or 1950s. Listeners must learn to familiarize themselves with the taste of earlier times instead of judging artists of the past by today's standards. Indeed, that temporal distance enriches us and opens up new horizons. It is naive to expect an artist of the past to resemble those of today and to think that performances recorded now will sound just as fresh fifty years from now. Such a misconception is the source of those "reinterpretations" that supposedly purge the classics of centuries of performance traditions and of the illusion that the score contains everything one needs to realize a composer's intentions.

It should also be pointed out that the way we perceive historical time tends not to be linear and chronological; instead, the effect is like that of a camera shifting between close-ups (the here-and-now) and long shots (the past, where artists who lived in different centuries intermingle, washed in the flood of memory and eventually drowned by progress). For a while Maria Callas was considered not only modern but also the model to which all female singers should aspire, an artist on whose high accomplishments one could draw in creating a new interpretation; everyone who preceded her was cast in the shadow of her greatness. Today (despite all the latest marketing efforts to capitalize on her fame), Callas is no longer emulated by young sopranos, and it is all too clear that yesterday's diva is fast becoming the stereotype of the old-fashioned opera singer. After she escapes this purgatory, Callas (or our memory of her) will attain that borderless plateau where all great artists merge together.

For today's public, and for those used to the generation of postwar singers who stood for "stylistic renovation," Gigli still (though not for much longer) represents the outmoded singing style of a bygone era. But soon our paragons of modernity—like Domingo and Carreras—will themselves have become singers of the past. Those for whom the style of the 1950s and 1960s represents merely one artistic metamorphosis among many will no longer view Gigli as the epitome of a fashion that needs to be put down but simply as one example—like any other artist—of a particular aesthetic, and he will then attain immortality. The time is so near, in fact, that it is silly to continue to claim that Gigli is outmoded, especially when the tenors who are supposed to have eclipsed him once and for all are already well past their prime. We are clearly approaching the day when Gigli shall recover his past glory and when those who spoke ill of him will be regarded as fools.

One of the aspects of Gigli's voice that has inspired the most commentary is not his splendidly radiant *forte* but rather his "angel voice," infinitely poignant in certain nuances. It is disquieting for some listeners, who react to it with a certain embarrassment, as though they had just caught a glimpse of the singer naked. There are those who avert their glance and ignore the effect of this immodesty, misinterpreting it as a sign of emasculation or even homosexuality. Because, in listening, the hearer essentially inhabits the singer's own space for a moment in time, such reluctant participants are merely denying that such feelings exist within themselves! Instead of reacting to the performance itself, they project their own prejudices and hang-ups onto the singer. Of course, the emotion involved here is not a genuinely artistic one. It is not the music, the voice, or the interpretation that is in question, but what the listener brings to it.

A more genteel version of the same complaint is the claim that when Gigli's tone softens, the voice loses its virility and becomes too sweet. No one, such critics declare, could ever sing like that today and get away with it. But it makes just as much sense to say that no composer of our time could write in the style of the very music Gigli sang. Hence it logically follows that it would be a mis-

Gigli as the Duke in Rigoletto.

take to sing old music in the style of our time. Thus the criticism flies back in the face of the critic. In fact, it is our responsibility to try to understand the artist's performance, just as we are obliged to do when contemplating a Greek sculpture or a Renaissance painting that has not been retouched or repaired for the modern viewer. The question of virility (about which, need it be said, Gigli's private life never occasioned the tiniest false rumor) arises from the fact that Gigli's timbre gives way to *piano* nuancing without the slightest residual roughness. Of course, some listeners prefer to hear the effort and its less than perfect outcome. They don't want the angular, muscular — hence "masculine" — character of the voice to be smothered, and they like to sense the difficulty involved in scaling it down without losing the ability to return to full volume at any given point. Clearly, such imperfection can be capitalized on and turned into a sign of strong temperament or prowess, to the extent that the technical deficiency becomes, paradoxically, worthy of admiration! A sweet, caressing timbre is felt by some to be a sort of dangerous softness, even an irresistible temptation, a kind of terrible narcotic. "Real men" are hard, not soft!(It should be noted that men who are preoccupied with their ability to maintain an erection — the larynx being to the production of timbre what the penis is to sexual performance — show less proof of their manhood than fear of losing it. But, rest assured, the situation is far from hopeless: as with any phobia, a treatment of gradual habituation produces excellent results).

If readers feel I am wandering from the main topic, they may recall a time not so long ago when nothing was more desirable than for tenors to possess the timbre of a baritone, for baritones to sound like a bass, and for sopranos to sound like a mezzo! Lightness was so widely regarded as a lack of profundity that entire audiences, I wager, would sooner have applauded tenors with the timbre of a *basso profundo*. In those days to be a coloratura soprano was to risk being labeled a mechanical birdcaller. In retrospect, one can just imagine how many voices went unnoticed due to such foolishness! An entire repertoire became inaccessible, because it required vocal qualities that lay beyond the capability of those "descending organs." Such music, it was reasoned, was of no interest to "real" singers and only the concern of the "easy voices" [*voix légères*] —implying "easy virtue" (in light of my previous comments, readers will no doubt discern the implicit sexual connotation).

From these bad habits a new criterion for masculinity gradually emerges, an apparently more subtle one that women can also appreciate: that criterion is "effort." The listener who cares little for artistic niceties is content to judge singers on the basis of the challenges they must conquer in order to please. Any audible tension, where the timbre sounds on the verge of breaking, is only to be admired. Obviously, Gigli's celestial voice does not fulfill its duty, since it seems to float with ease in a state of weightlessness. Hedonists appreciate the pleasure it gives to them, because it is free of base labor and borders on the sublime; others reject this blasphemous defiance of the earthly law of gravity and thereby contest its technical legitimacy. Their criticism assumes the form of a question: "Isn't this ineffably sweet voice in its essence merely a falsetto?" (Translation, according to the principle of effort defined above: "Inasmuch as it is acknowledged that a falsetto is easy to achieve, such being the case, this voice must have no merit.")

To answer this question one has to reexamine some basic principles of singing. The technical name for the sweet vocal emission we have been discussing is *voix mixte*. The velvety quality of its timbre is particularly noticeable when a tenor sings softly in the upper middle and high registers. It can be employed by other singers, especially baritones and basses, although, like the "chest" high C, it elicits the most heated controversy in connection with tenors. The "full voice" as it is generally applied to opera is actually a blending of two registers, those of the chest and head (or falsetto). The *voix mixte* (also referred to as *falsettone*, although the term often leads to confusion) occurs in soft singing, when the falsetto takes over without dissociating itself from the mix. The untrained ear could easily misinterpret it as a pure falsetto, but the characteristics of the latter differ from those of *voix mixte*. Indeed, falsetto is a completely separate register that encompasses less than two octaves; it has a tendency to fade in the lower notes, in the very spot where the chest register reaches its highest point of tension. This critical zone is called the *passaggio*. Singing a few notes in falsetto and then in full voice tends to cause an audible shift of timbre, like a hiccup.

No such awkwardness emerges in Gigli's voice, precisely because he uses the *voix mixte*. Even when the proportions of the mix vary, both registers always remain solidly fused, allowing him to make a crescendo toward full voice or to descend to the low register—which could not be done in pure falsetto. For example, it is impossible to sing "Dalla sua pace" in falsetto, because the vocal line descends too low. Not surprisingly, it is Gigli's use of his sweet timbre here that makes his recording of that aria stand out from all the others. Furthermore, the falsetto range extends higher than the *voix mixte*, whose usage obviously remains centered on the area of the full voice. A singer who uses falsetto would hardly deny himself the chance to exploit the high notes facilitated by such an approach. That Gigli never does merely gives further credence to the *voix mixte* school of thought.

Therefore, the advantage of a singer's choice of *voix mixte* over falsetto stems not from the difficulty of achieving it but from the fact that it helps to unify the voice and permit it to go everywhere, from *forte* to *piano* and vice versa, from low to high and from high to low, smoothly, without a break. But to achieve *voix mixte* one must avoid any excess pressure on the chest voice, which some tenors rely on for more power and masculinity. The attractive sensuality of *voix mixte* is due to the lower concentration of chest voice in falsetto, which keeps the timbre warm. A pure falsetto would sound colder, harder. Ironically, today's audiences prefer the detached purity of falsetto as opposed to the emotion of *voix mixte*; hence if they believe (in this instance, wrongly) that Gigli uses falsetto, they ought not to criticize him for it—but there is more to the issue than that. For falsetto has never been more widespread than it is today, even in repertoire where it should not be used. Incredibly, opera audiences have ended up believing that castratos used to sing in falsetto, despite the fact that the principal reason for castration was to give male singers the ability not to have to resort to it! Gigli, who of course also could sing in falsetto, gives an amusing demonstration of it in his 1938 film *Solo per te* by singing a few of Zerlina's phrases from "Là ci darem la mano." (It goes without saying that his falsetto differs from the extraordinarily pure timbre of his *voix mixte*.)

After Gigli retired from the stage in the mid-1950s, the most popular tenor sound was that of the *spinto*, which literally means "pushed." Those who defend this technique as the only acceptable one (despite its serious disadvantages) inevitably find themselves in opposition to the use of *voix mixte*, which *spinto* tenors avoid. Indeed, due to their laryngeal rigidity, *spinto*s can only "deresonate" certain phrases. The reason for this is that their entire technique is based on the management of tension, which can never be totally eliminated, whereas the bel canto technique of Gigli, on the other hand, consists of harnessing the muscle's relaxation. Even though today there is a tendency to describe the great *spinto* tenors as "bawlers," it is difficult not to feel ambivalent toward them: one can deplore their lack of refinement as well as be seduced by their animal magnetism. We become the victims of our conception of Art-as-Progress, which leads us to believe that our modern singers necessarily surpass those of yesteryear. But apart from the marvelous Mario Del Monaco (who, by the way, was not just a *spinto*, and whose art is underestimated today, if only because a group of pseudo-intellectuals deaf to his incisive and expansive phrasing have proclaimed his lack of subtlety), what a quantity of nonentities, of small, piercing voices have been produced under this system![1] Today's ears have grown so accustomed to hearing a dull timbre when a *spinto* sings softly that opera audiences now think that tenors ought to cultivate the sound and avoid the roundness and resonance of the *voix mixte*!

Since for every action there is a reaction, an entire new breed of listener, tired of the big postwar voices, soon championed the little voices, worshiped falsettos, and found them being applied to a repertoire that had long been neglected, though without the tiniest evidence that the music should be performed in such a manner. But these two new developments had the same result: the disappearance of the *voix mixte* and of the knowledge that *piano* singing demands more often a softening of texture than a lowering of volume. That concept is what allowed the voices of the past to carry to the last row of the balcony.[2]

As stated earlier, when the voice ascends to the high register, it has to traverse the *passaggio*. Even if the mid-register is able to support an approximate adjustment of the mix, this middle-to-high area will expose any defects in one's vocal technique even before the voice reaches what might seem the most difficult spot: the highest notes. There is general agreement that this crucial area of top-of-staff E-F-G is particularly well calibrated in Gigli, that is to say, the timbre and the volume of these notes retain their clarity and fullness on the way up.[3]

It is sometimes said (and meant as a compliment) that Gigli's voice was naturally placed "in the mask," but, in reality, nothing about his voice gives any indication that this was so. Indeed, singing "in the mask" is characterized by a marked "forward" projection. It will be recalled that the great tenor Angelo Masini (1844–1926) and the Accademia di Santa Cecilia where Gigli studied taught just the opposite, namely, the famous old maxim "If you want to shoot the arrow far, you have to pull the bow way back." The "voice in the mask" produces a pointed timbre that sounds a bit like a shout from behind a closed door, whereas Gigli's voice is as round and full as can be. His tones are emitted from the pharynx, not in the mask.[4] Reliance on the larynx involves emphasizing the rugged aspect of the timbre, going down as far as the chest voice, with nuancing proceeding from there. Cultivation of the pharyngeal area, on the other hand, enhances the voice's resonance, range, and flexibility and "lifts" it above any laryngeal roughness. The pharynx is in fact the primary resonator that envelops and enlarges the voice, provided one knows how to use it, by mastering a technique of breath support different from diaphragmatic (or abdominal) breathing. The latter involves, in place of a thoracic lift, a pushing forward of the diaphragm, thereby gradually causing the thorax, which remains stationary, to rigidify during singing. This system generates subglottal tension and precludes pharyngeal expansion. It goes without saying that the "support" system used by Gigli is the one that makes proper use of the diaphragm, whereas the concept of "diaphragm breathing" is typically preached from the wrong pulpit nowadays.

With regard to interpretation, it has become commonplace to point out the presence of certain old-fashioned mannerisms that supposedly detract from one's appreciation of Gigli's recordings — especially the sentimental sobs. But anyone who counts the sobs in the recordings of Gigli and then compares them with those of, say, Franco Corelli will discover that the greater offender is not Gigli. Moreover, one will notice how reserved Gigli's elegantly musical phrasing sounds, and how exaggerated, grandiloquent, and sentimental Corelli's seems by comparison.[5]

The debate does not end there, however. The sob is not a shameful liberty that a great artist should avoid at all costs but an interpretive effect that has been cultivated since the eighteenth century and that the verismo era brought to perfection. Essentially, the sob is produced by an excess of vocal tension, expressing an irrepressible burst of emotion. Under this excessive pressure the voice reacts with a sort of clutch, or wrong note. The singer who wishes to use this effect must learn how to harness it without endangering the condition of his instrument. Therein lies the key: for some singers, the sob is the result of a faulty vocal adjustment; for others, it is an expressive ornament. Gigli uses the sob with refinement, and at no time does it seem to pose any threat to his voice.

Generally, I see no reason why one should actively avoid using the sob altogether, simply for the sake of repudiating an element of musical style. What is the point in reviving music of the past if it is to be thus distorted? If we strip the front of a Renaissance building of its decorative relief sculptures we are left with a modern facade, but why do that? The sob is not all that sinful (as with many things, it must only be used in moderation), and if Puritan listeners find it distasteful today, they should still be willing to tolerate it in certain styles of music, realizing that the future might witness its resurgence. Admittedly, among the recordings of Gigli, one might point to a few arias where today one would not feel the need for as many sobs. But surely we ought not to let that minor issue blind us to the overall greatness of Gigli's recorded legacy.

Another interpretive device used by Gigli is portamento — nowadays taboo but at one time highly valued. Most modern-day singers shun "scooping," and until quite recently there was a concerted effort to rid the entire repertoire of this species of "bad tradition." Of course, the modern aesthetic that preaches "less is more" is very gradually losing strength, as the art of singing begins to adopt other criteria. It should be understood that in the 1950s and 1960s, musical taste and the repertoire then in vogue had an effect on the standards of vocal technique. To say that the situation was no better or worse than the one that preceded it would not be completely true, for there are certain artistic standards that are more or less advantageous to the development of a singer's vocal potential, and others that lead to premature damage of the voice. Dramatism kills the voice, and beautiful tone nurtures it. In general, because of the decline in technical standards since the 1950s and 1960s, portamento can no longer be executed without placing a terrible strain on the timbre in voices whose center of gravity has descended into the throat, the better to express visceral emotions. That deep, dark resonance (wrongly associated with vocal strength and energy) hardly lends itself to the smooth connecting of notes; only sopranos can still get away with it. Portamento was therefore written off by the public as ridiculous, unacceptable, although no one could say why. But when it is done with limpid tone in a delicate and flowing manner, as Gigli does in countless recordings, it is quite simply divine. The theoretical treatises are unequivocal about it: until the dawn of the twentieth century, the use of portamento was expected of all singers. To avoid it is no indication of progress, but a sign of vocal unrefinement. Since nothing is permanent in the world of music, it would not be surprising for the use of portamento to become fashionable again in the future.

Another important element of style worth mentioning is rubato, which Gigli uses in moderation. A flexibility with tempo brings the music of the past down from its pedestal and rescues it from the conventional dullness of a steady beat. As for interpolated high notes — those not written in the score but traditionally performed, often with the composer's blessing — Gigli does not shy away from them (i. e., the high C in "Di quella pira" or the high B at the end of *Arlesiana*'s Lamento di Federico), but one would have to be a real curmudgeon to criticize him for it.

Gigli's beautiful lyric voice adapted extraordinarily well to both the lighter and the heavier tenor repertoire. What singer of today would be able to tackle such a variety of roles with the success that Gigli achieved in them? He has been compared to a number of other greats, above all Caruso, who died at about the same time Gigli's career was starting. It could be said that Caruso's premature end hastened the young Beniamino's inevitable rise to fame, though the push in the right direction could have been disastrous to him if he had not been well prepared. It is sometimes alleged that Gigli tried to imitate Caruso, but to leave the comment at that implies something pejorative. That he was impressed by Caruso is a certainty — what tenor in the 1920s would not have been? Great artists often owe their early success to the influence of a famous predecessor, the proof of their talent lying in their choice of a mentor of quality. And, to a certain extent, in some of his expressive shades and other vocal effects, the young Gigli projected — perhaps instinctively — the kind of charisma that Caruso did toward his public. Yet it did not prevent his own individuality from emerging the instant he opened his mouth. In fact, the two voices have very little in common, as a comparison of their recordings of the arias from *L'elisir d'amore* and *Les pêcheurs de perles* illustrates, for example. To recognize that Gigli's recordings of "Una furtiva lagrima" and "Mi par d'udir ancor" [Je crois entendre encore] are markedly superior is not to cast aspersions on the artistry of the great Caruso. Caruso's singing is too human, too flesh-and-blood, to convey the quasi-mystical ecstasy and the sheer poetry in which Gigli excels. Many gifted young talents are compared to their glorious forebears when they make their debuts, but when they prove themselves and are recognized for what they bring of themselves to the music, descriptions like "the new X" or "the new Y" seem ridiculous. Thus it is with Gigli and Caruso, yet in comparing these two legendary tenors, it must be taken into account that Gigli's career was longer, his repertoire more varied, and his fame even greater than that of his predecessor.

Comparisons are also commonly made between Gigli and Schipa, usually praising the refined musicality of the latter and criticizing the popular appeal of the former. Arguments of this sort could be advanced only by those who pass themselves off as serious, cultivated musicians. But because it is easy to identify Schipa's vocal defects (the absence of *voix mixte* and, as a result, breathiness at the half-tone level; short, lackluster high notes and no high C; an acerbic, almost hoarse timbre), such judgments do not appear to me to be based on solid ground. That one might love Schipa while accepting his limitations is certainly understandable, but to turn around and proclaim him superior seems nonsensical.

The name of one other singer is often evoked to make the Gigli worshiper bite the dust: Jussi Björling. The Swedish tenor is felt to be the epitome of good taste, free of the Italian's unbearable sobbing. Granted, one hears nary a sob from Björling, but does that make him the greater artist and better singer? Some would say unhesitatingly, "Yes!" However, although Björling's top is radiant, his mid-range is not as round, colorful, or sensual as Gigli's. It often sounds constricted, which is perhaps why it gives some the impression of a chaste reserve, a sort of ardent purity. Björling's mid-range is even nasal on occasion and the voice often shaky on high notes. But, despite the brilliance — and the sweetness — of his voice, never do Björling's timbre and expression match the variety of Gigli's. Björling was, I hasten to emphasize, a great tenor — who, from what I understand, admired Gigli — but I do not believe one should cite him as an example of how his Italian colleague ought to have sung.

But what purpose is there in discrediting Pavarotti, Corelli, Caruso, Schipa, and Björling while praising Gigli? None, I admit — although I haven't discredited them, I have merely weighed their singing objectively in the light of similar reservations that their admirers direct toward Gigli. In order to respond to recent complaints leveled against Gigli, it is only logical to see if other tenors are exempt from the same (or similar) criticism.

Consider, for example, the oft-repeated remark that Gigli was not a good actor, that it was better to listen to him sing than to watch him perform. Forging ahead as before and putting our other tenors to the test: Caruso was certainly a great tragicomic actor; his films prove it. I recommend viewing certain sequences in his silent film *My Cousin*, in which he plays two contrasting roles — for example, the scene in which the poor cousin experiences opera for the first time, or the one in which the unhappy sculptor is forced to audition in front of the great singer, which gives Caruso the chance to show in a silent film that

Gigli, ca. 1936.

the ear is not the only factor involved in detecting an inferior voice. Schipa was a good actor, but Björling was not. Del Monaco's acting was vibrant, inspired. Corelli's physical appearance was captivating (I admit, his legs were sexier than Gigli's), but most of the time he gazed vacantly at his colleagues with a seeming indifference to everyone but himself. Pavarotti's admirers are content to see the tenor as himself in every role; what he does is not so much act as move from one spot to the next.

In light of this cursory bird's-eye view, the complaint that Gigli couldn't act begs serious reconsideration, even reevaluation. Indeed, in the films that he made Gigli proves himself an excellent actor, in both the intimist and the humoristic veins. He would not have made so many films if such had not been the case. The characters he plays in them reflect his own physique and personality: no handsome romantic leads for him. On the opera stage, however, he had to play larger-than-life personages that he could not have identified with — for he modestly considered himself an ordinary man with a great talent. Such a confession exposes Gigli's honest, down-to-earth self-image as well as his levelheadedness and inner peace, which come across naturally in his singing (perhaps it is this baring of the soul that disturbs some listeners). It was not only Gigli's voice but his mental attitude that accomplished the miracle, and with greater success than that of some of the more physically attractive singers. He could communicate youthful ardor or amorous melancholy, but his lack of false illusions about his looks kept his ego uninflated and his acting more restrained than that of many of his colleagues. But because today his sort of restraint has come back into fashion, it seems unfair to keep rehashing the same petty criticism about Gigli now. All that is ever said about his physical appearance is that he was ugly, which is far from the truth; there are many tenors homelier than Gigli who have escaped such a derogatory remark. As for his waistline—well, I'm afraid he outdoes the Pavarotti era in that respect, too!

A Sampling of Gigli on Record

The following commentary by Jacques Chuilon began as a review of Romophone's recent multivolume CD reissues of Gigli's Victor and HMV recordings; thus the division of the material under opera-title headings reflects the repertoire covered on the Romophone sets and not necessarily the author's order of preference. Most of the Romophone items, as well as additional studio recordings and live concert material mentioned here, can be found in one or more of the other CD compilations listed in the discography at the end. Catalog information for complete opera recordings and video materials is given in parentheses in the text.—Ed.

Mefistofele: "Dai campi, dai prati" is the aria that served as the vehicle for Gigli's first recordings for HMV (in 1918) and Victor (1921). The 1921 version surpasses even the very beautiful earlier one, the timbre sounding richer, the final high B-flat more brilliant. The 1927 Victor version has such a different vocal color that the aria sounds transposed down a half-tone, but it isn't. As for "Giunto sul passo estremo," the unsurpassed 1921 Victor again shows how much Gigli's voice had gained in maturity and expression since the 1918 HMV effort.

Tosca: Gigli sounds radiantly inspired in his third (1926) "Recondita armonia" (there is a fourth, equally splendid performance in his 1938 complete *Tosca* [Grammofono 2000 GRM 78591]). The 1921 Victor "E lucevan le stelle" naturally surpasses the 1918 HMV version, though the 1938 performance achieves the unsurpassable. In his later recitals Gigli displays many different approaches to Cavaradossi's last-act aria, for example, in the 1951 recital at the Grand Rex Theater in Buenos Aires (issued on Atrium ATR 003 CD). Gigli offers an impressive singing lesson with this aria in his 1939 film *Du bist mein Glück* (Bel Canto Society videocassette 500). Gigli recorded "O dolci mani" as a single extract only once, in 1921, and he sings it with all the tenderness one could ever wish for.

La Gioconda: One cannot listen to Gigli's "Cielo e mar" without thinking of the anecdote about his 1914 debut in Rovigo, when at the first performance he backed out of singing the traditional high B-flat at the end. When he heard people say that his range was limited and that he did not have a high B-flat (even though the same note is written to be sung obligatorily elsewhere in the aria), Gigli decided to take on the challenge. At the second performance he sang the note in question, causing a sensation—his first real triumph. Worth seeking out is the 1927 Vitaphone sound film in which Gigli sings the aria in costume and then bows to some off-camera applause. There is a 1918 HMV "Cielo e mar," but it is the superb 1929 second Victor version (with better sound than the 1921 issue) that is most recommended.

La favorita: The 1921 Victor "Spirto gentil," an aria Gigli first recorded for HMV in 1918, is superb, although transposed down a half-tone, thus ending on a splendid B natural. There are two other magnificent versions in the original key, with the high C: one taped live in 1949 during a BBC recital (issued on Eklipse EKR CD 21) and the other from 1950, recorded for the film *Taxi di notte* (available on CLAMA CD5). The 1950 version is especially sumptuous; the sixty-year-old tenor had not lost his high notes.

Faust: The 1921 Victor recording of "Salve, dimora" is superior to the 1918 HMV, although both are sung in G instead of A-flat. Curiously, however, the brighter timbre of the twenty-eight-year-old tenor adapts itself better to the downward transposition than does the deeper resonance of the voice three years later. No doubt unsatisfied with the results, Gigli made another recording of the aria in 1931, this time in the original key and crowned at last by a magnificent high C. The extrovert tone might surprise the listener, but the beautiful sound is irresistible.

Iris: The 1918 HMV "Apri la tua finestra" displays the tender charm of adolescence, the 1921 Victor all the conviction of budding manhood.

Le roi d'Ys: In 1922 Gigli sang the role of Mylio in the Metropolitan Opera premiere of Lalo's opera. The same year, he made a recording of the aria "Vainement, ma bien aimée" for Victor. He would repeat this miracle of freshness in a live performance captured in 1949 (on the above-cited Eklipse CD)—proof that the studio was not a place where Gigli would have tried out things that he couldn't achieve in public. The 1946 HMV studio recording should not be overlooked, either.

Pagliacci: Canio was not written for a voice like Gigli's, and yet he made it so uniquely his own, stamped with genuine emotion in a sunny timbre, that he will always be associated with the role. His first recording of "Vesti la giubba" was made for Victor in 1922. It is intense, poignant, but also dignified and under control (in the 1934 complete recording for HMV he pulls out all the stops). The aria turned up so frequently in Gigli's recitals throughout his career that numerous live performances exist of it—all displaying an artistic freshness that captivates every time.

Andrea Chénier: Gigli himself considered Andrea Chénier one of his favorite roles. In 1922 he recorded "Un dì all'azzurro spazio" and "Come un bel dì di maggio" for Victor. The performance of the former is so beautiful, so glorious, that it defies description. One can only marvel at the fortissimo high B-flat on "T'amo!"—declared with passion enough to melt the heart of any listener. Gigli

Gigli as Andrea Chénier.

would record two more versions in 1941, separately and in the context of the complete opera. Of the two I prefer the one conducted by Umberto Barrettoni, freer and more expressive than that of the complete recording under Oliviero De Fabritiis. There are some live documents of the aria worth sampling, despite variable sound quality: one from 1938 (on *Beniamino Gigli in Opera [1934–1940]*, Eklipse EKR CD 30) and another captured on 21 December 1953 under the baton of Nino Sanzogno (Arkadia GI 801. 2) and paired with Gigli's superb rendition of "Come un bel dì."

L'Africaine: Gigli recorded "O paradiso" twice for Victor — in 1923, when he first sang the role of Vasco da Gama at the Metropolitan, and in 1928. The second is a monumental performance, every element of which works to produce an unparalleled example: the sweet, velvety voice in the beginning; the ascent to high B-flat on "tu m'appartieni" (without the 1923 version's glottal attack à la Caruso); the subsequent tone of authority; the rightness of the tempo; the relish with which he projects the words "a me"; and the final high B-flat. A number of live recordings show the extent to which this aria suited Gigli, who still sounds electrifying in it in a 1955 Vienna concert at age sixty-five (issued on Bongiovanni GB 1055/56-2).

Roméo et Juliette: The 1923 "Ange adorable" and "Ah, ne fuis pas encore" with Lucrezia Bori are wonderful souvenirs from the Gounod opera, which the pair had just sung a few months earlier in Philadelphia and would sing together again in Atlanta soon thereafter. The tenor's French is quite good, his expression representative of the youthful ardor he could project so well. It is curious that an "Ah! lève-toi, soleil" that he presumably recorded in the same year is not issued in the Romophone collection.[6] As consolation, we can only turn to the sonically inferior 1934 live recording on the Eklipse compilation (EKD CD 30); it also includes the duets, this time with Mafalda Favero as Juliette. Gigli sounds even more irresistible here, perhaps the most breathtaking moment occurring, in the quiet coda of the act 2 duet, with Gigli's utterly sublime intoning of "Va, repose en paix."

Martha: We know that Gigli used to warm up his voice with "M'appari," the opening phrases of which traverse that perilous zone referred to as the *passaggio*. He sang it in recital throughout his career, which is to say he made it his own. The 1923 Victor recording is passionate, the 1929 more sensual. It is difficult to choose among the many live Gigli versions of this aria, though one might try a 1951 (on Atrium) or a 1955 (on Bongiovanni).

L'elisir d'amore: The 1925 Victor "Quanto è bella" is bound to delight the listener as much as will the 1949 HMV version with the Philharmonia Orchestra under Stanford Robinson. "Una furtiva lagrima" figures among the greatest of Gigli's recorded performances—twice. The Victor recording of 1929 (the year after his Nemorino debut) is glorious, but the singer sounds even more inspired on the 1933 HMV recording under John Barbirolli. There is also a magnificent live performance from the 1953 concert under Sanzogno (Arkadia GI 801.2).

Lucia di Lammermoor: The two 1925 takes of the first half of the Tomb Scene (one of them unpublished) contain some extraordinary interpretive touches, even if it sounds as though the tenor is trying to deliver more than his voice is capable of doing. Two years later the goal is achieved in a remake of the same scene, marking the difference between youthful exuberance and artistic maturity: the ascent to the high B-flat blossoms more fully, and the expressive contrasts in timbre are more distinct. (There is another unpublished take from the 1927 session; the performance is noticeably different but no less polished; it has the atmosphere of an encore an imaginary audience might have demanded, sung in the heat of excitement in a way that would never be duplicated.)

There are also two recordings of "Giusto cielo, rispondete" (the *tempo di mezzo*, with chorus and bass soloist), both from the same session of 12 December 1927 and difficult to choose between. The first recording seems to flatter Gigli's voice more, though the tenor sounds more committed and intense in the second. Ezio Pinza sounds better in the second, but, on the whole, balances are better perhaps in the first version. Of the two recordings of "Tu che a Dio," the later (1927) version surpasses the 1925 effort.

Topping the *Lucia* selections is the historic and unsurpassable 1927 recording of the Sextet with Amelita Galli-Curci, Louise Homer, Angelo Bada, Giuseppe De Luca, and Ezio Pinza. This substantial body of extracts constitutes a magical assemblage, indispensable for comprehending the performance style of Donizetti's opera.

Gigli as Edgardo in Lucia di Lammermoor.

Rigoletto: The famous *Rigoletto* Quartet sung by Gigli, Galli-Curci, Homer, and De Luca was recorded the same day—16 December 1927—as the afore-mentioned *Lucia* Sextet. A masterpiece, the two takes that exist of this selection demonstrate that a successful performance by great artists is never an unre-peatable act of chance; certain differences may be detectable, mainly involving balances, but it is clear in both takes that these singers are masters of their inten-tions.

Manon Lescaut: On 27 October 1926 Gigli recorded a "Donna non vidi mai" to die for. Indeed, how could he disappoint in an aria that seems as though it were written specifically for his sun-filled voice? In the 1940 film *Du bist mein Glück*, Gigli recaptures this blaze of glory (the soundtrack of the aria is included on the now out-of-print Legato Classics compilation LCD 106-1).

Tenor-Baritone Duets: "Solenne in quest'ora" is the first of three duets that Gigli recorded in 1926 with Titta Ruffo, whom many opera buffs consider one of the greatest opera baritones of all time. At the height of his career, Ruffo impressed audiences with the power of his voice, which might explain his popularity; but how can the serious musician tolerate Ruffo's limited musicality or his unreliable phrasing and rhythm just for the thrill of a few extra decibels? (On a record, the loudness of a voice can be regulated mechanically, hence it is the musical and vocal quality of a singer that counts the most.) It is one of those frequent paradoxes in the world of art that Ruffo's defenders imagine themselves part of an avant-garde, when in fact the qualities they attribute to their idol are no more than run-of-the-mill. When the same people then criticize Gigli for being vulgar or deny his artistry, it's the world turned topsy-turvy! What is certain is that the Apollonian clarity of Gigli contrasts singularly with the gravelly timbre of his colleague Ruffo.[7]

With Gigli as the common denominator in a double series of duets from *Forza*, *Bohème*, and *Gioconda*, the listener can compare Ruffo and De Luca in a context more revealing than that of the bravura aria. On these recordings De Luca is a year older than Ruffo is on his, but his voice is in much better condition and his musicality completely eclipses that of his baritone counterpart.

In "Solenne in quest'ora" with Ruffo, Gigli shines as usual, but with De Luca he attains the sublime at his very first phrase — the purity of expression breathtaking, the "Addio"s infused with genuine emotion. The *Bohème* duets are also excellent, with the artistry of De Luca inspiring Gigli to greater warmth of feeling. There are two takes of the *Gioconda* duet with De Luca from the same session in 1927, both similar and both published, though the second recording flatters the voices more than the first. The 1926 version with Ruffo hardly merits attention, in my opinion.

Gigli and De Luca achieve what is perhaps their most accomplished work on disc in their 1927 *Pearl Fishers* duet. It is an unforgettable performance, the voices blending exquisitely in the final cadenza. With the possible exception of Edmond Clément and Marcel Journet's 1912 Victor version, no other recording of this piece attains quite the level of sensuality and poetry heard here.

La traviata: The 1928 Victor "De'miei bollenti spiriti" is another high point in Gigli's recorded legacy; the voice's loving caress and charming, youthful *slancio* go so far beyond the ordinary interpretation of this aria that listeners feel they are hearing it for the first time, or as though Verdi wrote it for Gigli to sing. One hears the same qualities in Gigli's performance of the entire role of Alfredo, in a 1939 live performance at Covent Garden with Maria Caniglia, conducted by Vittorio Gui (Minerva MN A28/29) and even in the later recitals (for example, in the aforementioned 1951 Buenos Aires concert).

Mignon: Gigli's first Metropolitan Opera appearance in the role of Wilhelm Meister was in 1927. The following year he made recordings of the tenor's two principal solos: "Ah, non credevi tu" and "Addio Mignon fa core" are a ravishing blend of tuneful simplicity and refined sentimentality.

Les pêcheurs de perles: Two years after the sublime *Pearl Fishers* duet on Victor with De Luca, Gigli duly recorded the tenor aria "Mi par d'udir ancora" (Je crois entendre encore). (Romophone's second volume of the Victors also includes an unpublished take of the piece from the same December 1929 ses-

sion.) His 1931 HMV recording of the piece, transposed up a semitone, is beautifully melancholic; it documents for eternity the epitome of Gigli's style, with
rounded *i*'s and the added flourish on "divin sovvenir," this time ascending to
high B.

Sadko: In a 1932 Victor recording of the Song of India Gigli demonstrates
his ability to evoke the magical, exotic atmosphere of "the inscrutable, age-old
mystery of the orient." His miraculous legato makes the French text he uses
sound all the more seductive.

Conclusion: The above commentary does little more than scratch the surface
of Gigli's vast recorded legacy. For example, any basic library of Gigli on disc
should not be without his "O dolce incanto," "Che gelida manina," "Ombra mai
fu," "No! Pagliaccio non son," Lamento di Federico, "Celeste Aida," "Dalla sua
pace," "Amor ti vieta," "Di quella pira," "Rachel, quand du Seigneur," "Ah! dispar, vision," and "Ah non mi ridestar," not to mention other remakes of titles
already discussed. Nor have I touched on the song repertoire that turns up here
and there in the Romophone sets. As for the technical realization of the transfers on Romophone's Gigli sets, not all the selections sound as good as they
could, and a few of the arias have been transferred more successfully elsewhere.
Nevertheless, I heartily recommend the Romophone compilations for their
cumulative impact, for the unpublished titles they make available to us, and for
the overall quality of the presentation.

Today, unfortunately, singers in Italy and around the globe are all too unin-
formed about singers of the past. If pressed to name a great tenor of yesteryear,
the majority would probably point no farther back than the young Di Stefano
(emphasizing "the young" in the same way they would refer to a great wine, to
prove their exquisite taste). I can understand why so many like the voice of the
young Di Stefano. His ardor and occasional attempts to reach beyond his grasp
endeared him to audiences. The voice was certainly attractive, and he was a very
good singer, but his limitations stand out as soon as one compares him to Gigli.

No doubt one must accept the fact that there will always be artists who do not
rise to the level of the greater ones who preceded them. The improbability that
the work of a Mozart or a Veronese will ever be surpassed doesn't prevent composers and painters from recognizing and benefiting from such geniuses, while
the door remains open to those who want to try to rival them. Yet blind arro-
gance pushes some to proclaim that it is better to ignore those who might
influence you in order to avoid corrupting your own personality—that is, art
being lawless, perfecting oneself is not an issue. What senseless vanity!

The Italians' lack of interest in one of their most famous compatriots does
not justify the apathy that has tended to creep into Anglo-Saxon perceptions
of Gigli. More than a question of taste, it would seem to stem from cultural
and religious differences. Gigli is in fact the epitome of the Catholic and all its
implied blending of the corporeal and spiritual, the heritage of Greco-Roman
civilization. The spirit does not deny the body and the senses, but, on the contrary, brings them to the fore. There is nothing of the Protestant or Puritan phi-

Gigli as Des Grieux in Manon.

losophy in this fusion of the sensual. One suspects that a more austere education than that of the Mediterranean culture repudiates anything that might be regarded as pagan. There is nothing rustic or homespun about Gigli, and no singer conveys transcendence better than he, as, for example, in the "Ingemisco" of the Verdi *Requiem* (in either the studio recording under Serafin or the live performance under De Sabata). Does anyone give a more moving performance of the Gounod "Ave Maria"? To deny Gigli's greatness is surely to betray one's ignorance of an entire culture that engendered the glorious flowering of Baroque art. Beniamino Gigli, one of the geniuses of vocal art, belongs to the operatic Parnassus. Rare is the singer who does not pale by comparison when heard alongside him — why deny it? The best thing one can do is to listen again and again to his records. Many a young tenor of today (nay, all singers) would do well to make a regular practice of listening to Gigli for at least an hour every day, for study or as a remedy for their vocal bad habits. We know that Del Monaco did not hesitate to affirm his admiration for Gigli (as well as for Caruso), and it did not prevent him from achieving his own vocal personality. Far from imposing a model to copy slavishly, a master like Gigli provides an example that inspires all singers to find in themselves the keys to understanding how the voice functions, to let the art of singing flow in their veins.

SELECTED GIGLI DISCOGRAPHY

Beniamino Gigli: Collezione completa delle incisioni operistiche. Volume 1: Tutte le incisioni acustiche effettuate dalla HMV e dalla Victor (1918–1923). Istituto Discografica Italiano (distributed by Qualiton Imports) IDIS 274/75

Beniamino Gigli: The Complete HMV Recordings Volume 1 (1918–32); Volume 2 (1933–35); Volume 3. Romophone (distributed by Harmonia Mundi) 82011–2, 82017–2, 82020-2.

Beniamino Gigli: The Complete Victor Recordings. Volume 1 (1921–25); Volume 2: (1926–28); Volume 3 (1929–32). Romophone 82003-2, 82004-2, 82005-2.

Beniamino Gigli: Heroes. EMI Classics (distributed by EMD) 5 66809 2

Beniamino Gigli in Concert. Eklipse (distributed by VAI) EKR CD 21 (out of print)

Beniamino Gigli in Opera (1934–1940). Eklipse (distributed by VAI) EKR CD 30

Beniamino Gigli: Volume 1 (1918–1924). Nimbus Prima Voce (distributed by Allegro Corporation) NI 7807

Beniamino Gigli: Volume 2 (1925–1940). Nimbus Prima Voce NI 7817

NOTES

1. Forcing the tone does not automatically enlarge the voice; it may make the voice ring out more, but it requires the singer to keep the pressure close to its maximum level, which creates a false impression of size.

2. Whether one realizes it or not, many of today's conductors, coaches, and directors collectively insist on this "low-volume singing," now that the "big voices" (over whose disappearance they shed crocodile tears) are no longer performing. The "low volume" demanded by these powerful individuals, whom singers are expected to obey, is not the *piano* of a Gigli, whose soft singing they would find too loud, too resonant. What they want resembles a stifling or a holding back of the tone, in the manner of a whisper. Instead of hearing an operatic voice make a nuance, they would rather feel it shift its center of gravity, leave its proper singing position, and adopt a quality more suited to speech. Their inspiration for this comes not from the theater but from the cinema. For them, the drama prevails over the music, which is only there to underline, to illustrate. These pseudo-intellectuals want the singer to act and care little about vocal splendor, while the conductor rubs his hands gleefully at the chance to make his orchestra thunder. Is it

any wonder that today's critics pay so little attention to the singing and that a large segment of the public takes refuge in recordings, which many claim sound clearer than anything one hears in the opera house (as though the technique of singing were adjusted to the studio microphones). There is so much misinformation on this matter that I have actually had "modern school" singers thoughtlessly say to me, after listening to one of Gigli's records, that his pianissimo would never carry beyond the footlights. Yet it is precisely that kind of emission that projects, whereas the "*dis*resonance" so common nowadays sounds inaudible from a distance.

3. For the sake of comparison, in Pavarotti's traversal of these same notes one detects an increase in tension, a sort of stiffness or tightening. It amounts to a kind of precision stoppage of what might otherwise lead to a wrong note.

4. One should not confuse the pharynx (the back of the throat, between the mouth cavity and esophagus) with the larynx (the upper part of the trachea that contains the vocal cords). Pharyngeal vocalism is often described as "singing on the breath," whereas laryngeal vocalism (or singing "in the mask"

or even from the chest) determines the notion of "singing on the timbre." The difference between them is not a question of taste but one of efficiency.

5. I recommend, for comparison, the arias from *Andrea Chénier*, *Tosca*, and *La Gioconda* recorded by Corelli on an EMI recital disc (CDM 7692362; out of kindness to Corelli, we'll pass over the *Favorita* aria); the same selections can be found on the first disc of volume 1 of Romophone's Gigli series (*The Complete Victor Recordings [1921–25]*; 82003-2).

6. An unpublished "Ah! lève-toi, soleil" recorded in February 1923, a month before the duet sessions with Bori, is listed in the discography in *The Memoirs of Beniamino Gigli*, trans. Darina Silone (London: Cassell, 1957), p. 239.

7. With another technique Ruffo could have refined his timbre and scraped the barnacles off his phrasing to soar into the heights and communicate a totally different impression. I admit that Ruffo was a good actor and that it must have been exciting to watch him on stage as he kneaded melodies to increase their dramatic impact, but his records do little more than document his tendency to deconstruct the music, a bit like Chaliapin.

Ruffo reportedly wanted to study under Persichini, the teacher of Battistini (whom he always considered a rival, even though a generation separated the two), but Persichini rejected Ruffo in favor of Giuseppe De Luca. Many regard this as proof of bad judgment: to prefer the lightweight De Luca to the great Ruffo, the father of the modern baritone! But in the final analysis, if we compare the recordings these two baritones made later in their careers, Persichini's early opinion of them makes perfect sense.

Books

Richard Wagner, Fritz Lang, and the Nibelungen: The Dramaturgy of Disavowal

David J. Levin

Princeton, New Jersey: Princeton University Press, 1998
207 pages, $29.95

In "The Greatest of the Monsters," W. H. Auden observes that "Wagner, like Milton, another monster, whom he resembles in more ways than one, is a striking example of an artist whose actual achievement is quite other than his conscious intention."[1] Yet a pronounced trend in recent Wagner criticism has been its fascination less with the character of that "actual achievement" than with attempting to unravel how the composer's putative intentions — above all in their most toxic, unsavory aspects — are inflected in his works.

Clearly David J. Levin's book belongs to the latter category, although its focus extends beyond Wagner's *Der Ring des Nibelungen* to the first part of Fritz Lang's film treatment of the medieval *Nibelungenlied*. Both works not only share the same source material but provide an "elaboration of what we might term an aesthetics of national identity" (p. 5). The operative term here is "aesthetics," as Levin, a Germanist at Columbia University, explains at the outset: "What these works endorse as good (an ethical judgment) will be presented as good art (an aesthetic judgment); and conversely, what is ethically bad is marked as aesthetically bad. Thus, a good character in these works is marked by aesthetic qualities that the work endorses, while a bad character is marked by aesthetic qualities that the work loathes" (p. 5).

To bolster this rather Manichean formulation of his thesis, Levin draws on psychoanalytic models such as Melanie Klein's notion of the splitting off of the bad object and, most importantly, Freud's concept of disavowal, whereby a perceived lack or flaw (an aesthetic one in the case of Wagner and Lang) is compensated not by denial but by a symbolic embodiment or refiguration of that flaw. In other words, "these works figure their own aesthetic shortcomings, but fob them off onto a character within the work who is eventually unmasked and killed off as an aesthetic bad object" (p. 11).

An introductory chapter sets the stage for the particular focus of Levin's argument, with excursions into Freud's technique of educing disclosure through the analysand's narrative reiteration in *The Interpretation of Dreams*. Levin also expounds on how Siegfried and Hagen figure in the medieval *Nibelungenlied* in terms of their respective relationships to representational control. He devotes the greater part of his analysis to specific manifestations of the process of disavowal in Wagner's *Ring*, which reveals the composer's desire for "a totalizing representation, one that will allow the tale to be rendered from start to finish, in all of its complexity" (p. 13). This leads to a discussion of the period of the *Ring*'s genesis as well as Wagner's theoretical tracts from that time — especially *Opera and Drama* — to establish the crux of Levin's argument. Essentially, that argument centers on two distinct modes of telling the tale: *Erzählung* (narration or description of what has occurred) and *Darstellung* (direct, present-tense presentation through dramatic enactment). Wagner considered *Darstellung* the superior mode, according to Levin, because of its immediate appeal to the senses. "Narration, on the other hand, took a different and artistically less viable route . . . which produced rumination and inhibited immediate sensory comprehension" (p. 32). Most important for Levin's purposes is his assertion that, in Wagnerian aesthetics, narration is problematic because "it produces reflection by addressing itself to the mind, while he aims for a stronger — we might say, more abject — identification on the part of his audience" (p. 40).[2]

It's certainly odd that Levin, who himself has experience as a dramaturg, should fail to note the preference for *Darstellung* as an obvious matter of practical effectiveness for the stage. After all, Wagner wasn't setting out to write an oratorio; far from being an "idiosyncratic" gesture, Wagner's impulse to expand the original, narrative-laden drama *Siegfrieds Tod* into a cycle enacting its chief antecedent events, accompanied with compelling stage visuals, is in keeping with a view of theatrical praxis going back to Aristotle's *Poetics*.[3]

So how do we account for the paradoxical abundance of lengthy narrative passages that ended up in the *Ring*? Levin posits that "the recurring instances of monologue create an audience as community, an audience that is bound into an impromptu — but politically and aesthetically significant — union by the mechanics of address and identification" (p. 83). But Wagner's "dramaturgical dilemma" over the use of narration[4] leads him to emphasize its potential for manipulation in the hands of Mime and Hagen. To this distinction between good and bad narration, Levin educes a constellation of antinomies drawn mostly from Wagner's extravagantly metaphoric theory of language in *Opera and Drama*: authentic/inauthentic language, nature/culture, innocence/corruption, and (from *Das Judentum in der Musik*) the community/the foreigner and the indigenous German/the rootless Jew.

The negative side of these polarities, in Levin's view, becomes embodied in the *Ring*'s villainous characters, who thus serve as a sort of "overdetermined" scapegoat "to guarantee the bond binding the rest of the characters, many of whom, not so coincidentally, end up being naturally related" (p. 94). Levin arrives at this astonishingly reductive conclusion through a close, "micrological" reading (to borrow T. W. Adorno's term from *Versuch über Wagner*) of the scenes between Siegfried and Mime in *Siegfried* and of Hagen's murder of the hero in *Götterdämmerung*. Thus Mime's reiterated lies and dissembling in the "rearing-song" make him an emblem of the bad-faith narrator, one who is "all talk and no action." Siegfried's success at forging his father's broken sword by contrast dramatically marks him as the "agent of *Darstellung*" par excellence, who later kills Mime when the "language of nature" opens his ears to the narrative treachery of his scheming foster parent. Mime's relation to language, moreover, reinforces for Levin the well-worn interpretation of the dwarf as an anti-Semitic caricature.

Likewise with Hagen, although his savvier ability to manipulate narration will have more ominous consequences within the *Ring*. Levin applies close scrutiny to the mechanics of Siegfried's murder, by which Siegfried is duped into a mode of narration stage-managed by Hagen. The latter is thus, for Levin, a master of the "linguistically alienated" state of the Gibichung society who "manipulates language with no apparent heed to its natural reference and with every attention to his personal gain" (p. 82). Levin interprets the climactic scene of Siegfried's slaying through his vulnerability to "culture's manipulations" as the metaphoric equivalent of the linden-leaf spot that left Siegfried vulnerable after bathing in the dragon's blood in the medieval *Nibelungenlied* epic. Hagen's ability to manipulate this vulnerability ultimately arises, in Levin's contention, from a will to power, where "power in the *Ring* and over the ring means the power to produce — and control the production of — narrative information" (p. 27).

That Levin's marshalling of evidence is highly selective will be apparent to anyone possessing even a basic familiarity with the *Ring* in its entirety. Since his argument is centered on a clear-cut distinction between "good" and "bad" uses of language, Levin cannot account for the many instances in which the presumably "Aryan" characters practice deception — whether in a mode of narration or *Darstellung*. It is, after all, Wotan's trickery of Alberich to gain possession of the ring that engenders the curse to begin with, and the god's great monologue in *Die Walküre* catalogs the extent and dilemma of his self-deception with overwhelming impact. (Levin's analysis throughout reads as if the *Nibelungenlied* were Wagner's only source, indeed as if Siegfried never yielded his place to Wotan as the central character of the *Ring*, taking no notice of the significant evolution in Wagner's thought about what he was hoping to accomplish as his work progressed throughout a quarter-century span.)[5] What are we to make of Brünnhilde's betrayal of Siegfried, motivated as it is by the urgency of vengeance? Or of Siegfried's willingness to deceive Brünnhilde in the guise of Gunther? Although his memory of their love has been erased under Hagen's manipulations, he eagerly takes part in the deception. Nor is there any mention of the ambivalent character of Loge, whose verbal cunning would seem to make him a principal exemplar of the "linguistic corruption" of modernity Levin so carefully circumscribes.

In short, far from attributing evil in the *Ring* to an easily identifiable, "egoistic" scapegoat, Wagner seems quite clearly to emphasize the widespread extent of corruption in the world of the cycle. It's worth noting that Brünnhilde, in her final narrative, does not blame Hagen for what has befallen the hero but instead draws attention to the culpability of Wotan. Indeed, the violence and aggression that are unleashed repeatedly cannot be pinned down to Mime's or Hagen's manipulations, as Levin would have it (nor to Alberich's, although his role remains largely unaccounted for in the analysis). After Siegfried brutally kills his foster parent, he shows himself quite willing to strike down his actual grandfather when he encounters the Wanderer in one of the cycle's most resonantly powerful scenes (an encounter that the book simply ignores).

Even on the level of close reading of paradigmatic scenes, Levin neglects important aspects of their surrounding context. What is the significance of the Wanderer's largely narrative and reiterative colloquy with Mime between the two scenes of the dwarf's interaction with Siegfried? And what of the passage immediately following Siegfried's murder by Hagen (not, as Levin misstates, with his sword [p. 29] but with his spear, an object of obvious metaphorical implication in the *Ring*)? The transfigurative state that Siegfried here momentarily experiences, to the music of Brünnhilde's awakening, seems to embody a conflation of narrative and enacted elements and bears enormous implications for the hero's own belated awakening to a new level of consciousness, the poignant, failed hope of finally escaping from the *Ring*'s ineluctable pattern.

Perhaps most damaging to the hermeneutic straitjacket into which Levin tries to fit Wagner's aesthetic preoccupations is the role of the orchestra as both protagonist and narrator in the drama. Aside from a reading of the *Rheingold* prelude as an allegory of the origins of language (rather than of the world), Levin leaves the musical part of the equation in the *Gesamtkunstwerk* untouched. But the orchestra's alternately prophetic and retrospective commentary would seem to invite precisely the kind of conscious involvement from the audience that Levin claims Wagner would so assiduously avoid. In fact, the orchestra itself seems at times to be an agent of narration, whether in moments of transition such as the descent into Nibelheim and Siegfried's *Rhine Journey* or, most crucially, in the cycle's concluding passage of evocative summation.[6]

The rest of the book applies a similar method of argument to Lang's *Die Nibelungen*, the first of a two-part cinematic treatment of the *Nibelungenlied*, and is illustrated with stills from the film (many of which have a curiously campy resonance). Levin isn't interested in the significance of the director's marked disdain for Wagner, nor does he take the opportunity here to discuss the influence of operatic dramaturgy on the mode of narration in silent film. Instead, he interprets *Die Nibelungen* as an allegory of the dangers of an inferior kind of viewing, which leaves the spectator susceptible to the gaudy, superficial attractions of Hollywood cinema.

Here, Siegfried represents the "naive viewer" whose uncritical identification with the image renders him vulnerable. The scapegoat or "bad object" in this case is Alberich, who enthralls Siegfried with a spectacle that is "a perfect condensation of the nationalist critique of Hollywood with the fantasmatic terms of Jewish cultural aspirations" (p. 125).[7] Hagen, by contrast, here embodies a kind of critical, disengaged viewing that Levin argues is the preferred mode Lang wished to inculcate in the too-easily-influenced German audience of the Weimar period. The book then concludes with a look at Michael Verhoeven's 1989 film *The Nasty Girl*, which Levin celebrates as an ironic inversion of the dramaturgy of disavowal he believes he has unveiled in Wagner and Lang.

In many ways, Levin reads like an epigone of such studies as Paul Lawrence Rose's *Wagner: Race and Revolution* and Marc A. Weiner's *Wagner and the Anti-Semitic Imagination*,[8] which, for all their considerable flaws, are far more passionately argued and thought-provokingly original in insight. Levin's book, moreover, betrays its genesis as a dissertation in its pretentiously academic style, marked by constant stops and starts as the author hovers over a point. In a telling passage from the preface, Levin defines the role of the dramaturg as being "responsible for developing a reading of a work and then, during rehearsals, lobbying the director on its behalf, attempting to insure that the production remains true to that reading" (p. ix). At least so far as his analysis of Wagner is concerned, Levin demonstrates that remaining true to a particular reading need not guarantee remaining true to the evidence of the work itself.

Thomas May

NOTES

1. W. H. Auden, "The Greatest of the Monsters," in *Forewords and Afterwords* (New York: Vintage Books, 1974), pp. 244–55.

2. An admittedly convoluted topic, Wagner's aesthetic epistemology receives a remarkably tendentious treatment throughout. For a different perspective that attempts to integrate Wagner's claim in *Opera and Drama* that the audience should become "participant witnesses of this organic process," see Hilda Meldrum Brown's *Leitmotiv and Drama: Wagner, Brecht, and the Limits of "Epic Theatre"* (Oxford: Clarendon Press, 1991), p. 43 and throughout (reviewed by the present writer in *The Opera Quarterly*, vol. 9, no. 3 [spring 1993], pp. 153–55).

3. Levin fails to differentiate between the different modes of narrative that Wagner classifies in *Opera and Drama*, that is, the

narrative of the novel or that of specifically circumscribed historical drama. The composer's privileging of mythos over historical fact obviously has much in common with Aristotle's formulation in the *Poetics*. Moreover, several scholars have discussed the larger structure of the *Ring* tetralogy in terms of Greek play cycles, noting Wagner's predilection for the putative Promethean trilogy of Aeschylus as well as his own discussion of Sophocles' Oedipus plays in *Opera and Drama*. See Michael Ewans's interesting but flawed theory of the *Oresteia* as model in *Wagner and Aeschylus: The Ring and the "Oresteia"* (London: Faber and Faber, 1982).

4. A fascinating example of how directors have tried to deal with the challenge of staging the long-suspended stretches of

monologue can be seen in Sergey Eisenstein's production of *Die Walküre* in Moscow in 1940, in which choruses of actors performed in mime downstage. See Mike Ashman's "Producing Wagner," in *Wagner in Performance*, ed. Barry Millington and Stewart Spencer (New Haven: Yale University Press, 1992), pp. 38–39.

5. In addition to the well-known polarity between the "optimistic" (Feuerbachian) and "pessimistic" (Schopenhauerian) *Ring*, another important perspective on the cycle's conceptualization can be seen in Wagner's own lengthy, "pre-Schopenhauerian" letter of 25/26 January 1854 to August Röckel. There, the composer writes that "the remainder of the poem [following the first scene between Wotan and Fricka] is concerned to show how necessary it is to acknowledge change, variety, multiplicity, and the eternal newness of reality and of life, and to yield to that necessity" (*Selected Letters of Richard Wagner*, trans. and ed. Stewart Spencer and Barry Millington [New York: W. W. Norton, 1987], p. 307).

6. Wagner's decision to let the music have the final (narrative?) word also raises the question of the extent to which the "bad aesthetic practices" formulated in the composer's earlier theoretical writings had shifted. Levin's insistence on the problematics of *Erzählung* leaves him blind to such other issues from *Opera and Drama* as the "narcotizing melody" of Rossinian opera, the desiccating effect of Christian polyphony, and, most importantly, the subservience of dramatic effect to musical means in Wagner's singular run-through of the history of opera.

7. In a recent biography of Fritz Lang (unmentioned by Levin), Patrick McGilligan describes the director's denial of accusations of anti-Semitism in the *Nibelungen* films. Interestingly, according to McGilligan, during the Nazi era the second part of the film "was not made available to the public, because its all-out nihilism conformed even less to Nazi ideology—though the first half, without the payoff, was essentially meaningless" (*Fritz Lang: The Nature of the Beast* [New York: St. Martin's Press, 1997], p. 103).

8. Paul Lawrence Rose, *Wagner: Race and Revolution* (New Haven: Yale University Press, 1992); Marc A. Weiner, *Wagner and the Anti-Semitic Imagination* (Lincoln: University of Nebraska Press, 1995). The latter was reviewed by the present writer in *The Opera Quarterly* vol. 12, no. 4 (summer 1996), pp. 87–91.

Leonora's Last Act: Essays in Verdian Discourse

Roger Parker

Princeton, New Jersey: Princeton University Press, 1997
187 pages, $32.50

The remarkable swell of scholarly interest in Verdi has coincided not only with growing attention to other non-German composers but also with new approaches to opera as a whole. Some of these developments are due to academic fashion, some to market forces (the demand for acceptable works to study and write about), and some to a convergence of what scholars write about in books and articles and what actually happens on the stage in opera houses around the world. Roger Parker emerged in the 1980s as one of the most important young voices in opera scholarship. Coeditor of two challenging, multi-authored essay collections[1] and founding coeditor of *Cambridge Opera Journal*, which quickly became a vibrant forum for interdisciplinary explorations, Parker has helped to move discussions of the genre in new directions.

It is certainly no coincidence that these activities have occurred alongside fundamental changes within the discipline of musicology, changes that have both broadened what is studied and substantively altered the methodologies scholars employ in their investigations. Parker professes a deep "sympathy with many of the aims (perhaps fewer of the methods) of the 'new' musicology" (p. 5), and this new collection of his essays on Verdi offers sustained testimony to that approval. We witness his sympathies in action through eight chapters that address a wide range of operas and issues. Although two have appeared in similar form elsewhere, the rest started life "either as a conference paper or in much abbreviated form as a program book for a recording or performance" and have undergone major revisions (p. xi). Presented in roughly chronological order, the essays chart some of the changes in the author's own interests and display an admirable methodological eclecticism. Parker has given broader unity by weaving several larger themes throughout the book.

While some chapters focus on a single Verdi work, Parker generally tries to use an opera, or a group of them, to scrutinize an overarching issue, such as revisions, sketches, staging directions, and reception. This provides another of the book's notable strengths. For as often as scholars and commentators have written about the revisions of *Macbeth*, *Stiffelio/Aroldo*, *Simon Boccanegra*, *La forza del destino*, and *Don Carlos*, rarely has anyone stood back to reflect on the larger aesthetic and critical issues that revisions raise from a postmodern perspective. In the first of two chapters invoking the book's title, Parker uses the 1862 and 1869 versions of *Forza* to scrutinize familiar but uncritical notions of organicism and growth. He questions the view that "a 'great' composer is one who manages most completely to determine every aspect of his creation, to wed every detail to some Gestalt" (p. 61). Another piece of threadbare common wisdom is that composers "mature artistically as their careers unfold" (p. 61). These ideas seemingly "collide" when Verdi revised a work, unless, of course, one sees revision as an act that makes the work even more unified and whole and is possible exactly because of the greater wisdom and mastery the more mature composer brings to bear.

Through keen examination of Verdi's changes, especially to Leonora's final moments in the opera(s), Parker shows how various connections to earlier scenes were either sacrificed or strengthened. His aim is not to turn conventional wisdom on its head by asserting that the revision weakens the work but to support a more discerning point: the revisions present Verdi's "reinterpretation of the opera," which "encourages us to accept his opera as protean and malleable: its surfeit of signifiers, its excess of meaning and expression will continue to defy unitary or even remotely comprehensive expression" (p. 100). If we consider revisions as a sort of musical music criticism, new interpretive windows are opened.

Other essays also broach wide-angle issues. A fascinating chapter on the famous "Va pensiero" chorus from *Nabucco* draws on research Parker did while preparing the opera's critical edition and which he elaborates in a forthcoming monograph.[2] One concern is Verdian mythmaking, specifically with respect to his early career and the true extent of his engagement with political causes. Through careful investigation of the reception of this chorus, Parker convincingly shows that its nationalist baggage came only at the end of Verdi's life, culminating at his 1901 funeral. Not quite the artistic epiphany Verdi was so at pains later to claim for its genesis, the chorus musically is intimately bound to Zaccaria's ensuing *Profezia*. Parker ponders how and why the chorus gradually became separated from its context and evolved into a "vehicle of nostalgia" (p. 39).

Although the chapter on *Falstaff* concentrates on a single work, Parker again tries to make a larger point about Verdi's own self-representation and cultural conservatism in the face of contemporaneous trends in Italian opera. Wanting to go beyond the idea of Verdi's last opera as an "old man's toy," Parker sees the work as a sort of manifesto. While many fertile ideas race by, the discussion here lacks focus. It may not be so naive to take Verdi at his word that he was writing the piece "merely to pass time," "for my own amusement," "for myself and my own pleasure" (pp. 105–6). The more important question to ask is how and why. The musical allusions to *Il barbiere di Siviglia* and *Die Meistersinger* that Parker points to and the countless affectionate references to and literal quotations from his own earlier operas (*Aida*, *La traviata*, *Otello*, etc.) that others have noticed find larger retrospective and generic resonances throughout the opera. Parker mentions Verdi's flirting with sonata form at the opening and his use of a comic fugue at the conclusion. This engagement goes much further. The entire opera is a miraculous aesthetic, musical, and cultural commentary that works through subtle allusions to the composer's own past and to the opera world of his present. Verdi provides a wise and loving deconstruction of the conventions of the genre — the exit scene, letter reading, lovers' duets, finales, and so forth. The idiosyncratic hermeneutics that often attend late or last works are rarely so evident as in Verdi's incomparable comedy and require unusual sensitivity to special features.

Parker is always alert to what is considered the text of an opera, especially to what is included and excluded. He notes that the *disposizioni sceniche* and *livrets de mise-en-scène* that minutely documented original and early productions of certain Verdi operas — and which seem clearly, if not unproblematically, to record various levels of authorial intention — are often ignored in critical editions and scholarly studies. As a case study Parker considers *Les vêpres siciliennes*, but once again the implications go well beyond this specific work.

Parker's concerns also include the reception of these "texts" and how they are viewed over time. Parker's investigations go well beyond merely accumulating early reviews, discussing various performances, or comparing critical assessments. He knows that if we no longer cling to the notion of an autonomous work of art as being self-identical over time, if we now recognize that significance accrues and changes through history, then the history of reception assumes considerable importance and value.

One chapter examines some current trends in Verdi criticism, especially how (and why) Abramo Basevi's rather obscure study of Verdi from 1859 has come to assume such authority in recent decades. Another explores Philip Gossett's rich discovery that Gilda's "Caro nome" in *Rigoletto* recycles material originally sketched for Lina in *Stiffelio*. The contexts, of course, could not be more different — Lina, the adulteress, in contrast to the virginal Gilda — yet Parker teases out not only hidden symmetries but also more weighty aesthetic concerns.

I have enjoyed reading Parker's book and am writing this review while sitting in Vienna's Wahring Cemetery, now called the "Schubert Park," in front of the original graves of Beethoven and Schubert, savoring a welcome respite from Schubert scholarship as I look to more southerly concerns, and relishing the chance to think daily about Verdi while experiencing nightly productions at the Staatsoper of *Jérusalem* (miserably sung) and *Vespri* (superb), as well as of more familiar Verdi fare.

Why I am telling you all this? In part so as "to position [myself] within the academy" (p. 43) and the Schubert Park, but more importantly to enact a rather self-indulgent stance that I find a frustrating feature in much of the "new" musicology. Although the personal tone is most evident in Parker's first and last chapters, such moments appear throughout. Chatty personal parts — where we are asked to share an author's experiences — draw support both from identity politics (in which Parker, as a living white male writing from the "center," does not much engage) and from a performative subjectivity that in the hands of a Roland Barthes can be extraordinarily beautiful and moving, but in less poetic hands can be irrelevant and annoying.

I do not want to overstate the problems here; many readers surely will appreciate Parker's disclosures and playfulness. Personal passages often serve as the opening gambit for a chapter — Parker musing over photographs of Verdi or listening to a Kathleen Ferrier recording — and act as a frame for more specific (and conventional) discussions. In some instances, a fairly traditional program book essay has been given postmodern performative garb, a strategy one does not usually encounter in Parker's earlier writings. Well written and expertly informed, the book reveals the author's authority and passion, while the range of concerns and methodological eclecticism gives it a wide significance. Some readers may appreciate the personal and trendy bits that others may wish had been avoided. I wonder how such scholarship and criticism will age.

As Parker notes, he tends to engage less in analysis in more recent essays, although even in the earlier ones the level of technical discussion is clear and not intimidating for readers without musical training. His sympathy with postmodern musicology is found more in the type of questions asked and the responses proposed than in a distracting use of jargon. Occasionally too clever, the many fresh insights are well worth some of the flourishes. Abundant musical examples and extensive quotations in original languages, as well as in translation, mean that the book can be read without constantly running to the library. (I am grateful for this sitting in the Schubert Park.) Given this generosity, the absence of a bibliography and index is curious.

Christopher Gibbs

NOTES

1. *Reading Opera*, ed. Arthur Groos and Roger Parker (Princeton: Princeton University Press, 1988); and *Analyzing Opera: Verdi and Wagner*, ed. Carolyn Abbate and Roger Parker (Berkeley: University of California Press, 1989).

2. *The Works of Giuseppe Verdi*, ser. 1, vol. 3 (Chicago: University of Chicago Press, 1987); "'Sull'ali dorate': The Verdian Patriotic Chorus in the 1840s," to be published by the Istituto Nazionale di Studi Verdiani.

Verdi's Theater

Gilles de Van

Translated by Gilda Roberts

Chicago: The University of Chicago Press, 1998
434 pages, $60.00 (cloth), $25.00 (paper)

Among the recent publications on Verdi and his operas, *Verdi's Theater* by Gilles de Van stands out for the fresh and illuminating perspective the author brings to the subject. This book is a translation and revision of the author's original study in French, *Verdi: Un théâtre en musique* (Paris: Fayard, 1992). While some previous studies of Verdi's operas have nominally approached Verdi as a man of the theater, they often resort to retellings of plot with some platitudes about the music. Those studies inevitably dissociate the text-related elements from the musical ones, often with a bias toward one or the other, and the result is an unsatisfactory and artificial separation of the elements that, in practice, interact dynamically to create opera. With his focus on Verdi's dramaturgy as it emerges in the operas' plots, librettos, characterization, and music, de Van avoids that pitfall and, instead, presents the composer and his works in a uniquely effective way.

De Van uses nineteenth-century melodrama as the basis for understanding Verdi's operas. By taking this tack, he shows how Verdi integrated text and music to create his operas and thus is able to discuss the composer's style in concrete terms. Had he focused, instead, on the librettos or on the music, he would have arrived at a less effective and provocative book. By taking the more difficult route of dramaturgy, he arrives at insights that challenge the reader into reconsidering some hackneyed images of Verdi and his music.

In discussing nineteenth-century melodrama, de Van begins with a more general explication of the cultural "rules" that guide this convention (see chap. 4, pp. 88–145). In doing so, he arrives at a typology of characters that is useful for his exploration of dramaturgy. Although the use of archetypes may seem Jungian and, to an extent, simplistic, they become a critical part of de Van's discussion of the conventional actions that take place in melodrama, especially in Verdi's hands. With this typology as the basis of his study, de Van is able to examine intelligently Verdi's use of characters and the way he manipulated them to respond to the demands of the libretto and the music.

Hand in hand with the discussion of archetypes is an exploration of the "grammar" of action and the "syntax" of plots in nineteenth-century melodrama as applied to Verdi's operas. While the use of alphanumeric codes for character types and plot elements seems aseptic, it helps to put the characters and plot elements in perspective. Such shorthand prevents the analyst from dwelling on plot and characters in order to concentrate on the harder and more important issues. It is then possible to focus on the motives behind Verdi's work and the ways he breaks away from some of the clichés of his time. However, as de Van makes clear, Verdi went beyond the conventions of melodrama to arrive at something new and more personally expressive. Had Verdi's operas not surpassed the theatrical conventions the composer inherited, they would be regarded by succeeding generations as curiosities and period pieces. In outgrowing the expectations of melodrama, Verdi found his own voice and style:

> Verdi's evolution went forward on two levels. At the deepest and aesthetically most important one, it led him to question, not the types and situations peculiar to this code [*melodrama*], but the laws governing it: he clouded the essential clarity of melodrama by creating characters that were increasingly complex and ambiguous; he challenged the law of moral plenitude by casting doubt on the monolithic coherence of characters; and, finally, he called into question the law of excess by showing up its destructiveness and absurdity. (p. 146)

Conventional melodrama did not need music for its successful presentation on stage. Yet by starting with melodrama, Verdi gave his audiences something familiar as the basis for his operas. In going further, though, the composer challenged his audiences by taking stock characters and situations in different directions, thus making his operas more music dramas than melodramas set to music (p. 55). The musical language he used allowed him to create unique and engaging characters and to juxtapose ideas in ways that would simply not occur in conventional theater.

In exploring the dramaturgy and aesthetics of Verdi's operas, de Van shares with his readers his own approach to Verdi's music. Analysis often fails when it only reduces a work into its constituent parts. Yet de Van succeeds analytically not only in reducing to their basic components various parts of Verdi's operas, but also in finding a way to restore them to their place in the works under discussion.

It is not enough to analyze an opera in terms of music alone. While it may be convenient to adopt the conventional modes of harmonic and melodic analysis, those elements are only part of the entire work. Rhythm, meter, texture, and timbre are all critical facets of Verdi's *tinta*; yet it is only when the analyst attempts to integrate the elements of drama with those of music that it is possible to understand more deeply how the numbers, scenes, and acts interrelate structurally.

In following this type of framework, de Van's book is not easy to read. He expects a thorough knowledge of Verdi's operas as well as those of his contemporaries. Additionally, de Van refers to secondary literature throughout his study, and the reader may benefit from the excellent bibliography (pp. 387–409). (The latter is organized by topic, including specific operas.) The reader who wants to grasp de Van's ideas immediately should start by reading the conclusion (pp. 337–44) and the chapter titled "Unity" (pp. 309–36) to gain an idea of the directions in which the author will go. When reread in context, those sections not only will be more meaningful, but also will have contributed a sense of the whole that the author explores in careful detail in the first half of the book.

In retrospect, the only weaknesses stem from the author's occasional odd choice of material. When it comes to understanding the complex issues involved in studying Verdi's style, it is best to draw on the finished works for solid examples of his accomplishments. In a book titled *Verdi's Theater*, references to unfinished works, like the projected adaptation of *King Lear*, are misleading; an impulse rather than a completed opus, *Re Lear* need not be considered even in light of the fleeting references that Verdi is known to have made to it. The space devoted to a section of the *Requiem*, although understandable in context, is also puzzling. The *Requiem*, for all its theatricality, is not a work for the theater; useful as de Van's discussion of it may be, the book as a whole would have benefited from a similar analysis of some of the more complex scenes in *Simon Boccanegra* or *La forza del destino*. At the same time, it is disconcerting to find a glossary (pp. 344–48) in a monograph that is clearly not an introduction to Verdi. While it may have been a feature of the French edition, the English version would have been better served by defining any technical terms when they first occur in the text. In some cases, definitions are unnecessary, since readers attracted to this book are likely to be familiar with such elements of opera. On the other hand, the more extended discussions of Verdi's music at the end of the book are extremely useful.

It is sometimes difficult to comment on the nature of a translation, but Gilda Roberts's is generally quite clear and readable. I can quibble with only a few places that betray an apparent lack of familiarity with the operas; for example, she refers to Elisabeth de Valois as Don Carlo's mother-in-law (p. 181). That kind of lapse is small in comparison with the larger task of rendering such a detailed and complex text into clear English. Roberts is also sensitive to the use of musical terms, which are retained in Italian as they should be. (The present reviewer has encountered other translations that render every word in English at the expense of obscuring musical terminology best left in the original language.)

This book will not replace any of the existing studies but, as the author himself anticipates (p. ix), rounds them out. With his fresh perspective on Verdi's work and informed discussion of melodrama, de Van has made a fine contribution to the literature. Those who wish to analyze Verdi's work in terms of text and music will benefit from de Van's model, which integrates these elements rather than segmenting them. In this excellent study general readers will find unique insights enabling them to return to the standard operas and even the less familiar ones with a deeper appreciation of their content.

James L. Zychowicz

Roman Monody, Cantata, and Opera from the Circles around Cardinal Montalto

John Walter Hill

Oxford: Clarendon Press, 1997
943 pages, 2 volumes, $150.00

[In 1587] Cardinal Montalto succeeded Cardinal Ferdinando de' Medici [as principal patron of musicians in Rome], and he delighted in music no less than the latter, because he moreover played the harpsichord very well and sang in a sweet and affecting manner and kept in his household many of the profession, . . . to whom he gave large salaries. And . . . the cultivation of music was revived. . . . Indeed, all the *maestri di cappella* had to undertake to train various castrati and other boys to sing with embellishments and in expressive new styles.[1]

Alessandro Peretti (1571–1623) became Cardinal Montalto in 1585, two weeks after his uncle was consecrated Pope Sixtus V. In 1589 he was named vice-chancellor of the Church, a lifetime appointment, during which he served eight popes, resided in the huge Palazzo della Cancelleria, received an immense income, and supported "one of the most numerous and splendid households that was seen in Rome at that time."[2] Exactly a century later, another young cardinal/nephew, Pietro Ottoboni, began his illustrious years as vice-chancellor (1689–1740), during which he lavishly commissioned and produced oratorios and operas (some of them based on his own librettos), welcomed one and all to his weekly chamber concerts, and employed librettists, singers, instrumentalists, and composers (such as Corelli). Hill's excellent work makes us aware that "the circles around Cardinal Montalto" may have been even more influential than those around Ottoboni. Previously this had not been suspected, because Montalto exhibited none of Ottoboni's ebullient flair. He was instead rough in appearance, "grave in personal comportment, . . . quite reticent in speaking and full of a certain external melancholy, . . . almost entirely converting day into night and night into day [which] made it extremely difficult to deal with him and made him even more distant from worldly affairs, towards which his nature little inclined him."[3] Owing to his personality traits, he "hoarded" (1:299) and "so jealously guarded" (1:140) the musical repertory written for or performed at his chamber concerts that it remained virtually unknown to us until our brilliant puzzle-master, John Walter Hill, identified and united the surviving pieces. In his second volume, he publishes them, while in his first he categorizes them, discusses their ancestry, describes the great difficulty with which singers learned to embellish them, and then places some within dramatic works, one of which is a Roman opera of 1614 consisting of "approximately twenty-nine closed, lyrical segments, connected by dialogue recitative" (1:291).

The musical sources that Hill assembled are discussed in chapter 5, and his complete inventories of them (including concordances with other sources) are placed in twenty tables in appendix B. The four main sources were copied by a Roman, Francesco Maria Fucci, who perhaps obtained access to Montalto's library shortly after the cardinal's death. Four other manuscripts are collateral sources, while the remaining two manuscripts contain guitar intabulations. The other ten sources are Italian prints (published at Venice, Orvieto, or Rome in 1618–23), only one of which is closely related to the Fucci copies. At the end of chapter 5, Hill lists almost one hundred monodies composed by Orazio Michi dell'arpa (1594–1641), who was employed by Montalto in 1613–23 and became the cardinal's favorite musician (1:35). Perhaps Michi notated his works after Montalto's death, since they do not appear in any of the twenty sources identified with Montalto's circles.

Volume 2 includes transcriptions of 147 pieces of Roman monody from the main and collateral sources, seventeen additional works composed by five of Montalto's employees (Ippolito Macchiavelli, Giovanni Bernardino Nanino, Giuseppino Cenci, Pellegrino Mutij, and Michi), and twenty-seven examples from Nanino's models for improvising a part above a basso continuo. Because of the felicitious division into two volumes, a reader can view Hill's transcription of any piece as he reads Hill's comments upon it. The observations given below will focus on the forty-eight pieces found in Torrefranca 250, which is "by far the longest, largest in format, and most elaborately decorated of Francesco Fucci's manuscripts" (1:180).[4] Hill classifies its works as eighteen madrigals in reduced polyphony, in which the bass line has a vocal character[5]; four recitational madrigals and recitatives, in which the "speaking in music" is occasionally interrupted by bursts of florid melismas or cantillation passages (which are often in 3/2); and twenty-six strophic variations and verse forms. In all of these works, the largest vocal range is a twelfth (usually c^1–g^2 or c–g^1), the final pitch is usually g (but f, a, and d are also found), and the chords delightfully meander modally.

The discussion of music in chapter 6 culminates with a discussion of the variations applied to four verse forms: the canzonetta, terza rima, ottava rima, and sonnet. Their settings include three to eight musical strophes, but four is by far the most common number. Their texts are usually pastoral, and Montalto's response to each may have resembled that of Jacques to the performance of the first strophe of "Under the greenwood tree" in Shakespeare's *As You Like It* (c. 1600): "More, I prithee, more. I can suck melancholy out of a song, as a weasel sucks eggs. More, I prithee, more" (2.5). In Montalto's repertory, when "more" means subsequent strophes, it usually elicits ones that become ever more ornate;[6] and when "more" means another piece, it always brings forth a unique work, based on the layout and meaning of its words, which are substantially different from those in any other piece. One should therefore analyze the text (as Hill does) in order to understand, for example, why no. 1 in Torrefranca 250 has a strophic bass that "walks" through the piece, why no. 3 has a bass that is through-composed except for the five-measure refrain that marks the end of each strophe, why no. 8 has recitational bass and vocal lines, and why no. 47 has a bass with the unusual form of a/b/c/b/ac.

The ancestry of strophic variations is discussed in chapter 3. Since it is impossible to date more than a few extant monodies, some of those in sources stemming from Montalto's circles may have been notated before any of those found in Florentine sources were written. Giulio Caccini (1551–1618) has often been credited as the first to exhibit his performance and compositional skills by notating and thus refining improvised embellishments. But Caccini was trained in Rome, then—after he moved to Florence in 1565—by Scipione del Palla, who had mainly been active in Naples (1:60). Because of this and other sound reasons, Hill posits a Neapolitan/Roman origin for the unwritten practice of embellishing afresh over each repetition of a strophic bass. Such improvisation must have still been practiced by Montalto's singers, because forty-seven pieces in his musical sources provide only a single musical strophe for two to five text strophes.[7] Much of the brilliant thinking about unwritten traditions in medieval to Baroque Italy was done by Nino Pirrotta and Howard Mayer Brown, who are the dedicatees of Hill's study. Both Hill and I were students of the former at Harvard University, where he memorably brought even the simplest strophic settings to radiant life by evoking various contexts for their improvisational performances in magnificent courts, such as that of Isabella d'Este. Since Pirrotta died on 22 January 1998, he may not—alas—have had time to observe the many ways in which Hill has explored, explained, and enriched his enduring legacy.

If you were trained as a "classical" vocalist or instrumentalist and were asked to "sit in" with a jazz group, you may well have found the experience totally bewildering. Hill relates in chapter 4 that similar problems were faced around 1600 by singers who had been trained to sight-read all the subtleties of Renaissance notation, but had never participated in the unwritten tradition of spontaneous embellishment. Hill gleaned his primary evidence from passages in the 112 letters that he prints in appendix A. Thirty-seven of them were written to

Marquis Enzo Bentivoglio of Ferrara by Cesare Marotta, a composer, theorist, and singing teacher employed by Montalto in 1604–23. His wife, Ippolita Recupito, who was one of the four best women singers then in Italy, likewise served the cardinal, and Cesare—not surprisingly—lived largely in her shadow (1:25-33).[8] His letters stress that he taught the new style by rote rather than note in order to tailor each embellishment to each singer's current abilities, and that oral instruction was needed in order to ensure that young pupils produced and preserved the proper affect and technique for each passage.

In each of his last three chapters, Hill discusses a dramatic production planned or produced by Montalto. The first was Guarini's *Il pastor fido*, which was planned for the marriage of his brother in spring 1696, then aborted when the marriage contract was canceled. Since Cardinal Odoardo Farnese, who was within Montalto's circle of friends, did produce the work at Ronciglione in September 1696, Hill hypothesizes that one or more of the five settings of texts from *Il pastor fido* in Montalto's musical sources might have been written for the aborted production, then utilized in Farnese's. The second work, produced in March 1612, was a set of intermezzi, performed within a spoken comedy. Their texts consisted of Guarini's reworkings of three episodes from Tasso's *Gerusalemme liberata*. These intermezzi were subsequently recast for productions at Ferrara in 1613, 1614, and 1616. One or more of the four monodies that survive from the 1616 intermedi for *Bradamante gelosa* may have first been heard in the 1612–14 productions. The remaining drama was the opera *Amor pudico*, which was staged for the second marriage of Montalto's brother during carnival 1614. Its text was by the Florentine Jacopo Cicognini, and its music was by Nanino (sixteen choruses), Marotta (parts I–II and a bit of V), Mutij (III), Macchiavelli (IV–V), and the six singers who performed texts by Italian poets (in IV). Settings of three poets' texts are the only extant pieces from this opera.

The five monodies based on narrative texts from *Il pastor fido* are all through-composed madrigals or recitatives. One is by Cenci (no. 33), one is by Rontani (no. 41), and the others are anonymous. No. 35 has lavish melismas that tellingly picture the active verbs. A far richer palette of expressive devices is utilized in "Cruda Amarilli, che col nom'ancora,"[9] another setting of which opens Monteverdi's fifth book of madrigals. Two further narratives performed within dramas are found in Montalto's manuscripts: no. 20 is Monteverdi's "Lasciatemi morire" from *Arianna* (Mantua, 1608), and no. 14 is Ottavio Catalani's lament for Erminia in *Gerusalemme liberata*. The latter was sung by Olimpia Saponara in an unidentified "comedia" sponsored by Cardinal Savelli in February 1719. Its bass-line has the unusual form of ab/cb´/ab´/ca. Above its b sections the voice is gently lyrical, while above a and c it is passionately recitative-like.

The monodies heard in the dramas of 1612–16 are all in strophic variation form. Those in the intermedi of 1612–16 are based on one canzonetta and three ottave rime. Macchiavelli composed the first (no. 11), Marotta the next two (nos. 22 and 48), and Nanino the last (no. 91). Extravagant melismas are featured in the last three, which were sung by Fortune (portrayed by Ippolita Recupito), a Fury in hell, and a magical bird. Aspiring singers who encounter these pieces today should heed Jacques' command in *As You Like It*: "Come, warble, come," because many of us hope to experience the affective qualities of their scintillating passages. In *Amor pudico*, Dante and Sannazzaro perform terze rime, while Petrarch has a sonnet. By far the most fascinating of the three is Dante's piece, which was composed and sung by the baritone Domenico Puliaschi (range G–d^1); its first and third tercets are recitational and closely related, while its second and fourth are lyrical, yet quite different from each other. When Marotta in 1614 described one of his monodies that alternated recitation and cantillation, he termed it a *Romanesca bastarda* (1:222). Marotta's piece resembles Puliaschi's (1:223), Catalani's (no. 14), and twenty-one of the works composed by Michi (1:227) — some of which "conform to the most narrow and restrictive definition of the term *cantata* that can be found in recent scholarship" (1:232). These hybrids are all enthralling works, and well deserve revival today.

In the past, the origin of opera has often been traced to Florence around 1600, when Peri and Caccini set *Euridice*, presumably after inculcating some of the dramatic ideals of the local *camerata*. After you have read Hill's book, you may well be convinced that opera began instead as an outgrowth of the embellished singing of fine strophic verse by improvising soloists in Naples and Rome, who apparently foreshadowed similar developments in Florence. In support of this revised view, Hill provides ample evidence as well as thought-provoking hypotheses concerning the significant roles played by Montalto and those within the circles around him. Performers will welcome Hill's transcriptions of 164 monodies, which are, however, not free from errors (there are, for example, textual problems in no. 33, mm. 23–25, and no. 122, mm. 26–38, as well as incorrect pitches in no. 15, m. 28, and no. 42, final chord). Scholars will welcome the publication of 112 letters and the inventories of monodies found in twenty musical sources, but should note that the "Index of Pieces" at the end of volume 1 unfortunately does *not* include references to the many monodies listed on twelve tables printed within the text. Italianists will enjoy reading the letters and the song texts (a few of which are translated into English as they are discussed in volume 1). And we can all refresh our knowledge of analytical terms, such as "aposiopeses" and "cataplexal epizeuxis" (1:186–87), as we consider how "the peroratio grows out of the exordium" (1:221).

All things considered, Hill's traversal of "the circles around Cardinal Montalto" takes many giant steps (some of which are gigantic leaps based on reasoned hypotheses), and thus makes an immense contribution to our knowledge of the forerunners and early history of music drama.

Lowell Lindgren

NOTES

1. Vincenzo Giustiniani (1564–1637), *Discorso sopra la musica* (1628), as translated in Hill, 1:108.

2. Cardinal Guido Bentivoglio (1577–1644), *Delle memorie* (1640), as translated in Hill, 1:20.

3. Ibid.

4. Venice, Conservatorio di Musica "Benedetto Marcello," Fondo Torrefranca 250, is described in Hill, 1:141–51 and 359–63, and transcribed in 2, nos. 1–48.

5. Three madrigalesque works are for more than one singer (no. 30 is for soprano and bass, while nos. 10 and 13 are each for three sopranos). These are the only pieces in Torrefranca 250 for more than one singer. One of the other four main manuscripts has four further duets (one for two sopranos and three for two basses). Other duets are found in collateral and printed sources.

6. No. 2 is a five-strophe and no. 7 is an eight-strophe example.

7. Nos. 50–77, 99–100, 104–6, 109–10, 112–14, 116–17, 148, and 156–61.

8. On the dust jacket of each volume is reproduced a painting (c. 1611) that might represent Ippolita and Cesare.

9. Hill identifies no. 102 as a madrigal (1:255, 371) written in florid arioso style, which is "the most common in early Florentine solo madrigals" but is entirely lacking in the Fucci manuscripts (1:190).

Opera in Context: Essays on Historical Staging from the Late Renaissance to the Time of Puccini

Edited by Mark A. Radice

Portland, Oregon: Amadeus Press, 1998
410 pages, $44.95

In law and medicine the casebook, a collection of illustrative instances, is well established as a means of study and a repository of information. Now comes *Opera in Context*, which is at heart a historical casebook in the field of operatic staging. Its ten authors deal with the initial productions of works dating from 1600 (*Il rapimento di Cefalo*) to 1910 (*La fanciulla del West*), and, whether from clear editorial guidance or an authorial meeting of minds, remarkably consistent treatment prevails throughout.

The materiality of opera production is central in every chapter, with each at some point focusing on the design of the stage itself; precise measurements and information as to racking, trapdoors, placement of the proscenium, and use of a front curtain—such matters are almost invariably covered. The same is true for the scenery in its varied aspects: its planning and manufacture, its positioning and how it was moved about, as well as the illusions it produced. Moreover, descriptions of the hall or opera house in which a work was staged are included, with an eye on seating capacity, along with topics like acoustics, sight lines, and the presence of balconies or boxes. The contributions of celebrated stage designers and architects like Giacomo Torelli, Karl Friedrich Schinkel, and Gottfried Semper are occasionally introduced. All these subjects are thoroughly documented, most effectively through seventy-five illustrations showing floor plans, cross sections, and contemporary depictions of performance. And where the text gets into the technical arcana of stagecraft, the authors helpfully explain the important terms of the art.

One area of ever-changing equipment, namely lighting, attracts deserved attention, for of all the mechanical components of opera staging it has been the most steadily responsive to the setting and action of the drama (this quite aside from the audience's need for artificial light). Helen M. Greenwald's essay, "Realism on the Opera Stage," studies the prevalence, even the structural significance, of twilight moments in Puccini's operas; she especially delves into the techniques for achieving the "California sunset" that opens *Fanciulla*. Belasco-influenced subtleties in lighting are of course a far cry from the elaborate makeshifts of an earlier day. In Purcell's time, footlights might consist of a trough filled with oil in which floated "circular pieces of cork through which holes had been punched. A metal or glass collar was anchored in each hole, and a wick was run through it" (p. 81).

Whenever opera betrays its settled tendency to overwhelm or astonish, human as well as mechanical resources can of course be enlisted. On-stage masses of people, whether as disorderly crowds or regimented processions, have often been called for, and nowhere more methodically than in French grand opera. The chapter by Karin Pendle and Stephen Wilkins on the Salle Le Peletier looks at this management of crowds from the appropriate backstage vantage point. A hundred years earlier in Paris, machinists had already accommodated crowds, even on would-be clouds that could "hold 300 performers at once" (p. 54).

Similarly amazing scenic transformations and mythological marvels were a customary feature in seventeenth-century opera, as the chapters by Massimo Ossi and Barbara Coeyman attest. But perhaps the most notorious operatic instance of hocus-pocus is that described in E. Douglas Bomberger's essay: the Wolf's Glen scene in Weber's *Der Freischütz*. He details the working of the offstage noise-making machines and likewise specifies what chemicals were to be burned to create different-colored flames. (The combination called Bengali fire would give off so strong a stench that later productions were advised: "all the backstage windows . . . must immediately be opened at intermission" [p. 167].)

A pair of contrasting topics with respect to the music in opera repeatedly comes to the fore in *Opera in Context*. The first is an architectural problem: where is the orchestra to be situated? Among various actual locations the most striking may be, on the one hand, that seen at the Bayreuth Festspielhaus (six levels descending below the forestage) and, on the other, that which is presumed for the seventeenth-century Dorset Garden Theatre (a "musick room" placed above the proscenium, as explicated in Mark A. Radice's essay). The second, more complex musical question concerns the relations between the staging and the musical content of an opera. Sometimes the interaction involves merely an awkward moment in putting a work together such as occurred during the first *Parsifal* rehearsals when, for the transformation scene in act 1, the unreeling of the scrolled drops outlasted the time that Wagner had envisaged in his music. More frequently a natural give and take occurs between the mechanical or scenic possibilities and the dramatic intentions embodied in the musical score. A veritable lexicon of such relations could be formed from the examples given in this book.

Besides *Parsifal*, *Freischütz*, and *Fanciulla*, operas whose staging is investigated in detail include *Le prophète*, *La Juive*, and *La muette de Portici* (written up by Pendle and Wilkins), Handel's *Rinaldo* ("Handel's Haymarket Theatre" by Mark Stahura), and Lully's *Psyché*, Luigi Rossi's *Orfeo*, and Cavalli's *Ercole amante* (Coeyman). The earliest work, dealt with by Ossi, is *Il rapimento di Cefalo*, which was given at the same time as Jacopo Peri's landmark opera, *Euridice*.[1]

Opera lovers may feel especially drawn to the chapters on Mozart, Verdi, and Wagner. Malcolm S. Cole goes beyond his assignment by deftly sketching Viennese operatic life around 1790 as it affected Mozart; in emphasizing the elements of casting, patronage, and audience expectations, he rounds out a more generous notion of context than do his fellow authors. As to Verdi and Wagner, Evan Baker chooses for each a crucial aspect of the career, which guides his discussion. The focal point for Verdi is the composer's collaboration with Giuseppe Bertoja, the scenic designer at the Gran Teatro la Fenice in Venice with whom he worked off and on from 1846 (*Attila*) until 1857 (*Simon Boccanegra*). The hands-on Verdi, the engaged man of the theater, comes fully to life in this chapter. Baker's "Richard Wagner and His Search for the Ideal Theatrical Space" traces the idea of Bayreuth through its inchoate conceptual beginnings to its final realization, grounding the master's thinking in his early opera-house experience. In these essays Baker's keen organizing powers enable him to select from a flood of relevant information the most telling details, the most revealing quotations.

Opera in Context should reward both generalists and specialists among its readers. It fulfills its scholarly obligations not only through abundant endnotes but with a separate bibliography for every chapter as well. (The skimpy index will be of less use, limited as it is to proper names and titles.) While this volume is not actually "a comprehensive history of staging techniques that have been used for opera production over the centuries," as the Introduction would have us believe it is (p. 13), Mark A. Radice as editor has here supervised a novel and well-thought-out project. The result is a series of individually authoritative essays, each the more valuable because of the themes it shares with the rest.

Christopher Hatch

NOTE

1. Ossi's essay carries the subtitle "Bernardo Buontalenti's *Il rapimento di Cefalo* at the Medici Theater in 1600," thus associating the work with its stage director rather than the composer or the librettist. The music, little of it now extant, was written by Giulio Caccini, and the poem by Gabriello Chiabrera. On page 18, though not elsewhere, the poet Ottavio Rinuccini is wrongly named in Chiabrera's stead.

American Aria: From Farm Boy to Opera Star

Sherrill Milnes
with contributions by Dennis McGovern

New York: Schirmer Books, 1998
288 pages, $30.00

"Oh no," I hear you cry, "not another listing of 'and then I sang . . .'" Fortunately, this book is considerably more than that. It is a well-thought-out, well-written autobiography, recounting Milnes's life from his childhood on a farm near Downers Grove, Illinois, to his triumphs as *the* Verdi baritone of his generation, to his acrimonious split with the Metropolitan Opera in 1997.

Growing up just outside suburban Chicago meant that he and his older brother Roe were about the only farm boys in their school. Fortunately, they lived on the right side of the school district line and attended schools with excellent music programs. Their mother, Thelma, was a church organist and choir director as well as a piano teacher, so music, both classical and religious, was an integral part of the boys' lives.

Milnes does not hesitate to tell the naughty parts of his growing up along with the good bits. Blowing up mailboxes, taking potshots at the neighbor's barn, and losing his virginity, thanks to a false I.D., in the ironically named town of Godly, Illinois, were as much a part of his life as of that of any rambunctious boy. Yet through it all he sang, played violin, piano, and tuba, and eventually enrolled at Drake University, known for its music program, intending to be a music teacher. After being expelled and readmitted, Milnes settled into a serious track in music, but opera was the furthest thing from his mind.

Milnes traces his career from dance-band crooner and jingle singer, through Tanglewood and Northwestern, to Margaret Hillis and Boris Goldovsky, fleshing out his chronology with anecdotes and personal reminiscences. The reader learns of his failed first marriage and the deaths of his parents as well as the amusing gender-bending problems of being named "Sherrill."

In 1965 Milnes made his debut at the Met and "the rest," as they say, "is history." Again, however, this book is not just a list of his triumphs throughout the 1960s and 1970s. It is also a recounting of operatic stories, most of which involve Milnes, although some seem to have been put into this book because he had heard them rather than been personally involved.

In Milnes's own words, the 1980s were "A Decade of Panic" because of vocal problems that began with episodes of having little or no voice and not knowing what to expect when he opened his mouth and ended with two laser surgeries and no further recurrences of the problem. Yet rumors were rife of his career being over and even of his suffering from cancer (NOT true). His second marriage was failing, and he saw his career going down the drain. About the time this was all clearing up, his relationship with the Met fell apart, and his next contract was unceremoniously not offered, with no explanation.

Although bitter, and rightly so, about his treatment after thirty-one years of service, which included several new productions and opening nights, Milnes ends the book on a positive note. He looks forward to continuing to sing as long as he can and sharing his life with his new wife, Maria Zouves.

In many ways, this book should be required reading for all aspiring opera singers. It gives a good account of the steps Milnes went through to reach the top. It tells both the good and bad sides of being a "star." It can make the reader laugh, cry, wince with pain, and sympathize. Although some of the stories are thirdhand, they are all interesting. Needless to say, James Levine, Bruce Crawford, and the rest of the management of the Met do not come out smelling like roses. However, in general, Milnes does not downgrade his colleagues and does provide much insight into the care and feeding of an opera star.

The book includes two appendixes. The first is a chronology of debuts and key dates in Milnes's operatic career and an alphabetical listing by opera of first performances and other key events of his career with the Met. The second is a discography/videography of his recordings.

Catherine E. Campbell

The Four Voices of Man

Jerome Hines

New York: Limelight Editions, 1997
227 pages, $23.00

Professional advice based on fifty-plus years of business success will certainly pique any reader's interest. If this success happens to be in the music profession, it is especially remarkable — and even more so if the career is in vocal performance. The author's extraordinary list of performance credits includes a record-breaking history as a singer for the Metropolitan Opera: 41 consecutive seasons, 24 major roles, 830 performances, and 50 radio broadcasts. Metropolitan Opera basso Jerome Hines's new book, *The Four Voices of Man*, could be appropriately subtitled "How to Develop and Maintain a Career in Opera Performance," or "Everything You Wanted to Know — and More — about Performing in Opera." While the title refers to one of the author's general pedagogical perspectives, the book is indeed a career development text with a strong dose of pedagogy, unarguably fundamental to achieving and maintaining success and longevity in this or any field. The author gives the reader an overflowing cup of reality that may make an aspiring singer think twice about attempting an operatic career.

Hines considers himself a troubleshooter for professional-level singers, and prior to the table of contents, he in fact gives this word of caution: "If you are not at an advanced level of training, please keep this book on the shelf until your teacher recommends that you read it" (p. v).

Approximately half of the book's pages, as well as chapters, deal with aspects of vocal pedagogy. Following "Vocal Axioms" in chapter 1, the author continues with a methodical discussion of breath support, vocal physiology, and placement and registers. Five chapters then deal with the book's title, a reference to the author's belief that the human voice has four components corresponding generally to range. A chart in the second of two appendixes (p. 227) lists the First Voice as the "chest voice" (male) or "belting/raw chest" (female); the Second as the "middle voice" (male) or chest voice (female); the Third as "high voice" (male) or middle voice (female); and the Fourth as "falsetto" (male) and "high voice" (female). His premise is: "Yes, men's and women's voices are basically the same, but we have confused the terminology when discussing their registers" (p. 86). Hines attempts to analyze the four voices in detail and describes the manner in which the four may work as one.

The second half of the book is devoted to practical advice and valuable tips to the singer aspiring to a performance career in opera. The chapters explore topics ranging from vocal health, diets, and stage fright, to dealings with other opera personnel, such as "Choosing a Teacher," "The Conductor and Coach," "The Impresario," "The Manager," and "The Critic." The chapter titled "The Critic" should be recommended reading for all opera critics. Indeed, this book would help many critics gain a better understanding of the challenges involved in opera performance. Hines also underlines a performer's need for philosophy, self-discipline, and motivation in performance. He poses important questions, such as "What drives you?" and "Why sing?" (p. 216), as he examines the philosophy and motivation behind the creative urge found in every form of art.

There are frequent references to Hines's earlier book, *Great Singers on Great Singing* (Doubleday, 1982), and he acknowledges that these interviews gave him much to ponder (p. ix) and inspired his current writing. "I learned more about vocal technique in the writing of that book than I had learned in all my previous years of study and I feel it has added many years to my vocal life" (p. xiv). The Acknowledgments section, where he lists persons and their contributions to his career, is an impressive list of "who's who" in voice teaching and opera over the past sixty years.

Hines is uncompromising in his pedagogical views, and readers will respond positively to many of his opinions. He is especially successful in describing the physical feelings of singing, often a daunting task in pedagogical discussions. For instance, his description of how to use the image of "drinking the tone" is very clear. It "prompts the diaphragm to more strongly resist the support muscles" (p. 23). Hines gives many personal examples, including his own experiences with a particular laryngeal approach referred to as the "Melocchi School" (pp. 65–66) and with "trauma" or broken blood vessels (pp. 144–49).

While many of Hines's tips and comments will be applauded and cheered

("At last, someone has put this in writing"), some readers may be offended or at least put off by his opinions and frequent assumptions. His approach to pedagogical discussion seems to be one that attempts to correct misconceptions, in contrast to most authors who simply present their views of the "correct" concept. While the author allows for human differences, whether of gender or age, he frequently repeats, "If I can do it, so can you" (p. 69) or "Be patient and follow my example: I have survived at least three generations of critics" (p. 210). His statement that "half the students I hear today are singing the wrong repertoire, and many are actually in the wrong voice category" (p. 116) will certainly ruffle the feathers of a few vocal coaches, and a few of his comments on types of voice teachers, as well as his discussion of art song's place in training for opera, may make some voice teachers bristle. Controversy is not new in the voice-teaching profession. Unashamedly biased, Hines pulls no punches and must be admired for his uncompromising beliefs. Teachers and students alike will listen seriously to his sound advice regarding the importance of solid technique and practice; for example: "As you add new ideas, constantly return to the things you were always able to do and make sure they still work for you" (p. 58).

The writing style is generally a personal one. The language is frequently conversational and informal, even within a scientific discussion, thus reminding the reader that this is less a scholarly book than it is a career help text. Still, footnotes (there are none), more specific dates, and more consistent terminology (early references to "c′" switch to "middle c" in subsequent chapters) would clearly enhance its value and usefulness. All too frequent editing errors, whether misspellings (e.g., "Cornell MacNeal" on page xxi, "principle muscles" on page 17) or printing gaffes (words run together, missing punctuation, font changes), tend to weaken the professional impression of the vast amount of important information presented.

Hines asks the tough questions, poses the challenges, and identifies the sacrifices necessary for developing and maintaining a career in opera performance — without holding back. The book is highly recommended for the advanced singer who is considering a career in operatic performance. With the aforementioned exceptions, voice teachers and coaches will find it enjoyable reading, often informative, and occasionally enlightening. One cannot help but admire Hines for his professional longevity, for his convictions, for sharing so much of his personal experience, and for tackling the subject matter in such a straightforward way. *The Four Voices of Man* makes a strong and unique contribution to the literature for the singer-actor.

Linda June Snyder

Fritz Reiner

Philip Hart

Evanston, Illinois: Northwestern University Press, 1994
330 pages, $30 (cloth), $14.95 (paper)

Priest of Music: The Life of Dimitri Mitropoulos

William R. Trotter

Portland, Oregon: Amadeus Press, 1995
495 pages; $29.95

Herewith a pair of biographies, each of a podium giant who has been neglected in that respect. Fritz Reiner's lifespan (1888–1963) somewhat exceeds that of Dimitri Mitropoulos (1896–1960); however, both found parallel careers and greater acceptance for their work in America than in their homelands. Different sorts of politics motivated their respective hegiras, but each would confront very similar challenges in his adopted nation.

How they coped with these hurdles would determine the trajectories of their posthumous reputations: Reiner's steadily high (a recent RCA recoupling of his "Living Stereo" *Also sprach Zarathustra* and *Ein Heldenleben* recordings has sold over 16,000 copies — a mega-blockbuster in the reissue market, where 1,000 sales marks the break-even point), Mitropoulos's enduring a long period of opprobrium, but latterly curving upward, with no sign of this newfound appreciation's peaking yet.

Although one of these volumes is significantly closer to "definitive" than the other, they're both eminently worth buying — I return to each one frequently — so I'll spare readers lengthy résumés of the Reiner/Mitropoulos career. The former made history early on by leading the public-domain performance of *Parsifal*, a midnight affair in Budapest on 1 January 1914. In short order, Reiner was handed major responsibilities at the Saxon Court Opera, though, on the death of general music director Ernst von Schuch, Schuch's formal title would be withheld from Reiner.

Mitropoulos's breakthrough came at a 1930 Berlin Philharmonic *Gastspiel* in which (*vice* a reluctant Egon Petri) he elected to double as soloist and conductor in Prokofiev's Third Piano Concerto. The resultant success, combined with word of Mitropoulos's enormous technical facility and prodigious memory, soon made him greatly in demand as a guest conductor. This gradually freed him from the snakepit of musical politics in his native Greece, where the constant infighting and machinations were in inverse proportion to the amount of durable concert music emerging from the Hellenic realm.

Ironically, Mitropoulos's American career moved more smoothly than Reiner's. The latter would hold three benchmark tenures: first, with the Cincinnati Symphony (1922–31), then the Pittsburgh Symphony (1938–48), and—most enduringly for posterity—with the Chicago Symphony (1953–62). In each case, Reiner would be driven from his post by a recurring nexus of factors, in which personal indiscretions and political meddling usually played large roles. If Mitropoulos couldn't play musical politics to (literally) save his own life, Reiner's attempts at them were more maladroit than Machiavellian.

Thus, Reiner periodically found his career becalmed, sustained by a teaching stint at the Curtis Institute, the *Ford Sunday Evening Hour*, and peripatetic work as Wagnerian-for-hire in American and English opera houses. It's a very telling thought that, for all of Hart's access to Reiner (in Hart's erstwhile capacity as the Chicago Symphony's associate manager), the portrait that emerges is unsympathetic, despite Hart's diligent efforts to show Reiner's better side. The conductor's warmer instincts were too often overcome by those paranoiac, stingy, or mercenary qualities that dominated the personality of his third wife, Carlotta. She, in turn, would fan similar flames in Reiner's nature, eventually prompting some crisis or other. In everyday work, these would manifest themselves in the desire to conduct as little of the subscription season as possible, an absolute abhorrence of out-of-state touring, demands for extra remuneration for recording, and a tendency to harken after whichever recording or guest gig would scare up some extra cash.

Ultimately, the Reiners' porcupine-like tendencies would prompt his downfall at the Chicago Symphony (hastened, as was Mitropoulos's at the New York Philharmonic, by recurrent heart trouble). When the State Department offered to facilitate what would be the Chicago Symphony's first-ever European tour (proposed for 1959), the venture fell through thanks to the inability of the three crucial parties to communicate: the orchestra's patrician president, George Oldberg; its hard-headed manager, George Kuyper; and the Reiners, largely insulated from the other parties (and from Chicago itself) at the best of times. As the State Department kept adding dates and destinations to an already arduous tour itinerary, neither Oldberg nor Kuyper was prepared to put his foot down, with the latter particularly unwilling to put the orchestra's money where his mouth was. As for Reiner, the eventual fall-guy, he earned his scapegoat role by (a) endlessly dilly-dallying when he should have been assembling tour programs; (b) refusing an invitation to the prestigious Venice Biennial; and (c) planning to skip out on most of the orchestra's planned Lucerne Festival dates (the proposed crown jewel of the tour), so he could make records with the Vienna Philharmonic instead.

Like Caesar at the Forum, Reiner was done in by one of the closest in his small circle of friends: Claudia Cassidy. The justly infamous music critic—to stretch the term to its breaking point—of the *Chicago Tribune* wielded a powerful and vindictive verbal blade, which she used to shorten the American careers of Rafael Kubelik, Desiré Defauw, and Jean Martinon. Reiner was, for many years, one of the chief beneficiaries of her dizzy-dame prose (sentences without verbs, tangential gush, etc.), along with Carol Fox's Lyric Opera. These weren't cultural institutions, they were causes — and Cassidy's cheerleading was seconded in a more sophomoric tone by Roger Dettmer, at the *American*.

Cassidy and her husband were the most frequent dinner guests *chez* Reiner. Yet, when the European tour collapsed, with its consequent affront to Chicago prestige (Leonard Bernstein and the New York Philharmonic swiftly picked up the gauntlet, in one of their most famous accomplishments), Cassidy was swift to spearhead the Reiner-must-go faction. Given the conductor's failing health, how much longer he could have stayed at the CSO's helm is open to debate, but the rapidity with which the glory and visibility he had given the band were disregarded was a shameful denouement.

Mitropoulos was Reiner's antipode in just about every respect. Dionysus/ Apollo, Romantic/Classicist, spontaneous/control-freak, generous-to-a-fault/ tightwad, loquacious/epigrammatic, workaholic/self-disciplined — any broad generalization you want to apply would probably work, although it is disservice to both men to reduce them to Categories A and B. Mitropoulos was forever doling out money to others, while Reiner watched every dime, and the former adored giving concerts on the road and mixing with "his men," while the more class-conscious Reiner found it a chore.

By all accounts, Mitropoulos was likely to give a seat-of-the-pants kind of performance, while Reiner was meticulous, his technique (superbly detailed by Hart) leaving no room for ambiguity while assuring precision. Frequent repetition bored Reiner (more of a problem in the opera house), while some of Mitropoulos's documented off-nights are pretty helter-skelter affairs. Mitropoulos's musical technique has defied verbal description (and he did not encourage its emulation, while Reiner's Curtis tenure produced several noteworthy pupils), but its aim was not unlike Furtwängler's, which was to empower the orchestral players to give something of themselves, even more than they knew they had.

After his 1936 Boston Symphony debut, Mitropoulos took the American concert scene by storm, snaring the directorship of the Minneapolis Symphony (now the Minnesota Orchestra) within weeks of his first appearance with the ensemble. From 1937–49, he achieved a level of execution/interpretation from the MSO that, as a longtime Minneapolitan, I can confidently assert has not been matched since. This is attested by such recorded souvenirs as a Mahler First Symphony or a Tchaikovsky Fourth that are remarkable not simply for when and where they were made, but as compared with anything done since. Both through his programming at the symphony and in his work with Ernst Krenek in chamber concerts, Mitropoulos gained for the Twin Cities a reputation as the new-music mecca of the United States.

All good things, however, come to their inevitable end, and Mitropoulos succumbed to the siren song of the New York Philharmonic. Although the Philharmonic was in the throes of a troubled period (following the Barbirolli and abortive Rodzinski directorships), Mitropoulos felt that the challenge was too prestigious to decline. Fatalistically, he would stick it out at Carnegie Hall to the bitter (and it was very bitter) end, even though escape routes onto podiums in San Francisco, Rome, Monte Carlo, and Vienna presented themselves.

Although Reiner managed to shrug free of the manipulative pull of Columbia Artists' impresario Arthur Judson (who also held controlling influences with the New York and Philadelphia orchestras and CBS radio) and Rodzinski had made a brave, but ultimately futile, stand against Judson's crass cross-pollination of his assets, Mitropoulos was no match. Wearing his CAMI hat, Judson would program new soloists with the Philharmonic to test their market appeal. The Philharmonic's Sunday afternoon broadcasts (which often required program changes from the back-breaking subscription series) provided an even bigger platform for Judson's soloists to appear with Judson's Philharmonic, over Judson's radio network.

Mitropoulos's Franciscan nature made him an easy mark for Judson's "enforcer," Bruno Zirato, to say nothing of the peculiarly ill-disposed and divisive Philharmonic players, many of whom offered rank insubordination in the face of the unwillingness of Mitropoulos (as opposed to a Szell or Boulez) to crack the whip over them. Add in an ailing subscription base, Mitroupolos's jumbled programming tendencies, and an ornery circle of critics—of whom Virgil Thomson offered the most erudite commentary—and you had a situation not unlike an unarmed man walking into a tiger cage.

In a city where one review can still make or break a Broadway show, the *New York Times*'s chief music critic wielded particular power. When the ambitious Howard Taubman (eventually to succeed to the plum Broadway beat) drew this duty, anti-Mitropoulos sentiment was building, and Taubman seized the chance to deliver an ultimately fatal blow: an article slugged "The Philharmonic—What's Wrong With It and Why." This blast, and the untimely death of Guido Cantelli eight months later, paved the way for the accession of Leonard Bernstein to the Philharmonic's podium.

Bernstein figures in both narratives, having been Reiner's finest pupil. To both Reiner and Mitropoulos he would swear copious fealty, hare off abruptly when a greener pasture presented itself, then be brought smartly to heel by his mentor, at which point Bernstein would offer up even more copious apologies. It is a pattern of opportunistic behavior that Humphrey Burton also ruefully notes in his authoritative Bernstein biography.[1]

Unlike Joseph Keilberth and Fausto Cleva, neither Reiner nor Mitropoulos died while actually conducting opera, but their ends were similar. Reiner's weakened heart succumbed to pneumonia between rehearsals for *Götterdämmerung* in his final return to his old Metropolitan Opera harness. Mitropoulos's own overtaxed heart literally burst during a rehearsal of Mahler's Third Symphony, on the stage of La Scala.

Given Mitropoulos's pioneering championship of Mahler (particularly those symphonies Bruno Walter backed away from), it was a fitting end. Ironically, for all of Reiner's typecasting as a Wagnerian, *Carmen* was the opera he conducted more than any other. If Mitropoulos is identified more closely with the advocacy of new music, Reiner was no shirker. Indeed, the establishment of Bartók's music in the standard repertory is principally Reiner's achievement (plus that of allies like Rudolf Serkin, who counted collaborations with both conductors high among his musical experiences). Invaluably, Hart provides an exhaustive listing of Reiner's repertory — and a discography of equal thoroughness — and one notes the considerable place that Hindemith, Prokofiev, Shostakovich, and Stravinsky occupy. The hard-to-please Stravinsky regarded Reiner as one of the best interpreters of his music (along with Pierre Monteux), although American composers were likelier to get a hearing from Mitropoulos.

The latter's more catholic sampling of the new and obscure encompassed a fair amount of trivia, along with works that tested the limits of the most tolerant performer. (Ralph Shapey's intractably thorny methods and personality, though, forced Mitropoulos to admit defeat.) For most of his career Mitropoulos aligned himself with the serialist movement — Berg, Schoenberg, Krenek, Sessions, etc. — although disillusion and a sense of futility set in toward the end, which may partly explain his embrace of composers like Morton Gould and Erich Wolfgang Korngold.

Both men's recorded legacies suffered from the priorities of their respective labels (Mitropoulos would move from Columbia to RCA and back again, while Reiner jumped from Columbia to Victor permanently). Reiner's desire to set down his versions of the complete Beethoven symphonies and much else of his core repertory was constantly being put on hold by RCA's desire for another Dvořák "New World" or more Rossini overtures.

At least Reiner and the CSO were RCA's "first team." Mitropoulos and his orchestras were constant back-benchers, and suffered accordingly in recording priorities. Just as he could not impose his will on the Philharmonic's musicians, Mitropoulos failed to stand up against Columbia's insanely overscheduled marathons of recording, and his reputation has suffered from the results. While Reiner's Pittsburgh and Chicago recordings have offered powerful testimony to what he was after, musically, Mitropoulos's redemption has come largely through the issue of European airchecks and (more recently) Minneapolis Symphony recordings.

The cursory, highly subjective, and gushily uninformative discography appended to William Trotter's Mitropoulos book is nearly as serious a failing as the absence of any catalogue of his repertory. One must try to deduce the scope of these anecdotally. Although Hart sets aside a whole chapter for delving into the methods, goals, and stylistic orientation of Reiner, nothing so coherent is attempted with Mitropoulos. Indeed, such descriptions of Mitropoulos's music making that pepper the text make one doubt that Mitropoulos, although a great man, was anything more than a minor conductor. (Fortunately, the recordings that exist refute such an impression.) One reads frequent allusions by Trotter to excessive rhythmic vehemence, spasmodic hyperemphases, metallic orchestral tone, and a predominance of forward motion over sensuality. Could Trotter have been listening to Toscanini records by mistake? More seriously, the hard-edged, angry orchestral sound that Trotter attributes to Mitropoulos can be heard quite clearly in Eugene Ormandy's Minneapolis recordings but softens and blooms audibly in subsequent Mitropoulos shellacs.

In fairness, Trotter inherited this project from the late Oliver Daniel (author of the comprehensive *Stokowski: A Counterpoint of View*),[2] who did the body of the research and lived to write one chapter. At conjecture, that would be the one prefacing Mitropoulos's New York tenure, sketching the musical scene of the day and the forces Mitropoulos would have to contend with. In scheme, execution, and elegance of style, it stands apart from the remainder of the book.

Elsewhere, as vivid as Trotter's prose can be —"Mitropoulos would have been alienated by that hollow triumph, by the spectacle of a hundred tenured Babbitts launching salvo after ideological salvo at the empty seats in the auditoriums where concerts of their increasingly ugly and in-bred music was performed" (pp. 432–33) — he relies heavily on the cut-and-paste method of biography, often printing several consecutive paragraphs of review or transcript at a go. Chronology (even after three readings) is difficult to follow, and factual detailing is sloppy: Italy's RAI network is always referred to as "RIA," and the *Boston Globe*'s current music scribe, Richard Dyer, is somehow present (under the auspices of the *Boston Herald*) at Mitropoulos's 1936 BSO debut. The latter gaffe led one of Dyer's friends to ask him, "Who are you, Methuselah?"

Also, Trotter's book becomes an extension of the pro/con Bernstein war whose opening salvos were fired by Joan Peyser a decade back. Each side has settled scores with each other, through subsequent Bernstein chroniclers such as Meryl Secrest and Burton. Both Peyser and composer David Diamond use Trotter as a firing platform in the continuing battle over how Bernstein's image will be seen by posterity.

Hart's methodology is as tidy and economical as that of his subject. Quotations are rarely allowed to run on for more than two consecutive sentences, and the author manages to package a detailed and vivid narrative of a busy musical life into fewer than 250 pages that nevertheless speak with absolute authority. That the name of the venue where Reiner conducted his last *Carmen* performances (Naples's Arena Flegrea) escapes the author illustrates the lengths one must go to find nits to pick with Hart.

Both authors had to work under considerable handicaps. Much of Mitropoulos's correspondence has been either destroyed or sequestered by acolytes, while Columbia University continues to sit, Fafner-like, on an invaluable cache of Reiner communiqués to and from the composers of his day. Hart spent about eleven years bringing his Reiner quest to fruition, a task made no easier by Carlotta Reiner's scattershot (and scatterbrained) dispersal of the conductor's estate.

Trotter's book is generously and splendidly illustrated. Northwestern University's treatment of the photographs collected by Hart displays a stinginess worthy of Carlotta Reiner herself: printed on cheap, blurry paper stock, with a whole page often allotted to a 1/6 page or so of picture. Inexcusable.

Still, Hart's book is so thorough and enlightening a labor of love, a love that does not accede to myopia, that it should be the defining work on Reiner for some time to come. If Reiner himself doesn't jump lovably off its pages — well, he wasn't that kind of man but given to a certain "just the facts" circumspection that informs his not-inconsiderable music making. One could scarcely find a more accessible, outspoken, and endearingly vulnerable subject than Mitropoulos, and Trotter conveys the man with such immediacy that one follows Mitropoulos's story like a familiar tragic narrative, knowing that what makes him so embraceable is what will ultimately strike him down.

There may well be yet another Mitropoulos book to be written, one that defines the importance of his musicianship better, but Trotter plugs an important gap, though not so impregnably as Hart does his. For now, how about Szell, Monteux, Rodzinski, and some of the other neglected greats of the American orchestral scene?

David McKee

NOTES

1. Humphrey Burton, *Leonard Bernstein* (New York: Doubleday, 1994).

2. Oliver Daniel, *Stokowski: A Counterpoint of View* (New York: Dodd, Mead, 1982).

Recordings

From Bourbon Street to Paradise

The French Opera House of New Orleans and Its Singers, 1859–1919

VAI Audio VAIA 1153 (1 CD)

New Orleans traces its operatic tradition to at least 1796; by the first decade of the nineteenth century the city could boast of annual winter operatic seasons. Between 1828 and 1831, in 1833, and again in the following decade the resident New Orleans troupe toured to cities on the east coast, where they introduced works of Spontini, Rossini, and Auber to audiences in New York, Philadelphia, and Baltimore.[1] Ironically, for years these east coast stagings have been cited erroneously as "first United States performances" when in fact the scores had been in repertory in previous seasons in the Crescent City.

From 1819 until the outbreak of the Civil War the Théâtre d'Orléans mounted productions praised for their decor and the quality of the singers who formed the resident operatic troupes. These were supplemented by guest appearances by such noted singers of the nineteenth century as Luciano Fornasari, Celestino Salvatori, Anna de la Grange, Laure Cinti-Damoreau, Henriette Sontag, Pauline Colson, Felicita Vestvali, Mario Tiberini, Maria Piccolomini, and Erminia Frezzolini.

On 1 December 1859 a new theater, the French Opera House, opened, and there, for the next sixty years, the operatic tradition was nurtured until that theater was consumed in flames on 4 December 1919, shortly after the resumption of a regular season following World War I.

This VAI compilation of operatic arias and songs, lovingly assembled by record collector Lewis M. Hall, an authority on singers of the late nineteenth and early twentieth centuries, illustrates some of the most important artists who appeared at the French Opera House during its long history, beginning with Adelina Patti, who sang there during the 1860–61 season, prior to the beginning of her international career.[2] Patti's rendition of "La Calesera," a song dedicated to her by the composer, Sebastián Yradier, was recorded in 1906 when

French Opera, New Orleans

the soprano was sixty-three. Her voice comes through clearly, although at times with something of a pinched sound and some overload.

More thrilling is the example of Lillian Nordica, heard here in an excerpt from Erkel's *Hunyady László*, "Ah! rebegés." Although limitations in the recording process are responsible for some distortion of her top tones, her extraordinary trill is a clear demonstration of a fabulous technique. When she appeared in New Orleans during the final weeks of the 1906–7 season it was felt that her best years were behind her, but this selection, recorded in 1907, shows a voice in radiant condition.

Even more exciting are the act 1 aria ("Je suis encore") and the Fabliau from Massenet's *Manon*, both done to perfection by Lucette Korsoff, a member of the French Opera troupe during the 1901–2 season, during which she was heard as Lakmé, Lucie, Gilda, Ophélie, and Marguerite de Valois, among other roles. Korsoff's *fil de voix* and *piano*, rapid trills and brilliant top notes, clear as a bell in both arias, easily explain her popularity.

But while these examples are representative of overall vocal excellence, it is the male artists here assembled who are an absolute revelation. Some of these — Florencio Constantino, Andrés Perello de Segurola, and Léon Escalaïs — are well known to record collectors. But the majority, singers whose careers were confined largely to France and Belgium, except for these seasons in New Orleans, and who are not often encountered, display a level of singing and interpretation that, in this era of frequently bland, media-hyped performance, is rare indeed.

Constantino, who made his United States debut in New Orleans during the 1906–7 season as a member of a touring Italian company, demonstrates a solid upper register in a song by Richard Barthélemy and Enrico Caruso, "Adorables tourments." And in the *Rigoletto* duet "E il sol dell'anima" the notorious ascending line holds no terrors for him. He is partnered here by the American soprano Alice Nielsen, no better and no worse than many Gildas. During that New Orleans season she and Constantino were paired in *Rigoletto*, and she was heard in several other roles, to mixed reviews. (After an unsuccessful Lucia one critic mused "one wonders what she will attempt to sing next").[3] On the other hand, although frequently criticized for hogging applause meant for others and for his general lack of involvement in the onstage drama, Constantino drew raves for his singing of Don José (debut), Turiddu, Rodolfo, Almaviva, Enzo, and Edgardo. On 5 January 1907 Constantino sang Maurizio when Cilea's *Adriana Lecouvreur* was given its United States premiere in the French Opera House.

De Segurola, another member of the 1906–7 troupe, was also a participant in the *Adriana* premiere (Prince de Bouillon). Although at the time the press commented on a certain weakness at the bottom of his range, his smooth delivery and aristocratic vocalizing won him notices as Colline, Escamillo, Barnaba, and Méphistophélès. Here he is heard in an excerpt from Donizetti's *Lucrezia Borgia*: Alfonso's aria and a slightly truncated version of its cabaletta, in which one admires his flexibility and panache.

Perhaps the most famous member of this trio in New Orleans was Léon Escalaïs, whose feat of singing Manrico's "Supplice infâme!" (*Le trouvère*) five times — with fifteen high Cs — on the evening of 11 November 1909, became part of the lore and legend of the French Opera. Some twenty-two years after his 1883 operatic debut, Escalaïs recorded this version of the cabaletta with piano accompaniment. The brilliant *fort ténor* top is readily apparent, but to my taste his voice is shown to even better advantage in the Sicilienne from Meyerbeer's *Robert le diable* (recorded during the same period, 1905–6), in which Escalaïs scales down the voice to great effect and demonstrates both a command of florid singing and an impressive trill.

Tenor Georges Régis is represented by two arias from *Mignon*, an opera that received its first United States staging at the French Opera House in 1871. Although his brief career at the Met (1909–10) was in supporting parts, on the strength of these tastefully performed selections Régis would be singing leading roles there today. His is a lovely, mellow voice with an agreeable timbre. During the 1905–6 season in New Orleans he sang over a dozen roles in both opera and opérette, including Wilhelm Meister, and was Prince Alexis in the first United States staging of Giordano's *Siberia* at the French Opera on 13 January 1906.

Yet another light tenor, Francisco Nuibo, was cast, like Régis, for the most part in important tenor supporting roles — Ruodi in *Guillaume Tell*, Léopold in *La Juive*, but also Jean in the first New Orleans staging of Massenet's *Le jongleur de Notre Dame*. Here he is represented by "Anges du paradis" from *Mireille*, a recording made in 1905 but not first released until the 1950s. And in an aria from Massenet's *Le mage*, another important tenor, Auguste (a.k.a.

Henri Albers as Rigoletto. (Courtesy of the reviewer.)

Agustarello) Affre, clearly demonstrates the type of *squillo* sound so beloved of creole audiences of the day.

The voice ranges most favorably captured in the acoustical process are the baritones and basses; the examples herein make this release an absolute must for collectors. In an aria from Gounod's *Cinq Mars* the Dutch baritone Henri Albers displays dramatic flair and an evenly produced voice with a richness throughout its registers. His wide repertory during his New Orleans season (1896–97) included Nélusko, de Nevers, Guillaume Tell, Alphonse XI (*Favorite*), and Rigoletto.

During the 1902–3 season François Mézy also starred in the role of Tell. His recording of "Sois immobile" is notable for a sense of style now virtually lost, an impressive way with the text, and a voice floated with excellent support. Mézy returned to the French Opera in 1905–6, where he sang Gleby in the U.S. premiere of *Siberia*, as well as other roles. He again was the *baryton de grand opéra* during the 1913–14 season, when his roles included Scarpia, Athanaël, Telramund, and Caoudal in *Sapho*.

Three basses complete the picture. Fernand Baer (another *Siberia* premiere principal — Walitizin) was *deuxième basse* during the 1905–6 season. The center of his voice is a true bass, rather than a struggling bass-baritone, as demonstrated in a rarely encountered aria from Saint-Saëns's *Henry VIII*. Jean Vallier, one of the most remarkable voices featured here, was the *première basse noble* that season. Despite some surface noise in this selection, Vallier's clarity of enunciation and a fine trill make his rendition of "Si la rigueur" a special treat. His voice is even in scale throughout its range, and there is no change in quality from top tones to the bottom low E. In addition to Cardinal de Brogni, Vallier's roles that season encompassed Marcel in *Les Huguenots*, Ramfis, Hagen in Reyer's *Sigurd*, Claudius in *Hamlet*, and Balthazar. Finally there is Albert Huberty, *basse noble* during the 1909–10 and 1910–11 seasons. What a remarkably beautiful instrument, the voice of a solid basso, warm and powerful! His rendering of Flégier's "Le cor," a song that, incidentally, he performed at a French Opera benefit on the evening of 3 March 1911, is irresistible. Equally fine is his version of "Pauvre martyr obscur" from Paladilhe's *Patrie!*, an opera that was promised during the 1910–11 season but never produced. (That season Huberty did create Maître Pierre in *Le chemineau*, when Xavier Leroux's opera was given its first U.S. staging at the French Opera on 11 February 1911.)

In sum, this is an indispensable collection for anyone interested in French opera and song interpreted by some of the finest voices, many little known, who specialized in this repertory early in this century. With only one or two exceptions, reproductions of the original acetates, transferred by Russ Hornbeck, are clean and free of excessive surface noise. So clear, in fact, are some of the reproductions that one can scarcely believe their age. For example, the two *Mignon* arias by Régis from 1908 could pass easily for recordings from the electrical era.

The informative notes by Mr. Hall in the accompanying booklet are supplemented by photographs of the artists, many in costume. Let us hope that he may be persuaded to begin work soon on a second volume.

Jack Belsom

NOTES

1. See Sylvie Chevalley, "Le Théâtre d'Orléans en tournée dans les villes du nord, 1827–1833," *Comptes rendus de l'Athénée Louisianais* (New Orleans: Athénée Louisianais, 1955).

2. See Jack Belsom, "En Route to Stardom: Adelina Patti at the French Opera House, New Orleans, 1860–1861," *The Opera Quarterly*, vol. 10, no. 3 (1994), pp. 113–30.

3. *New Orleans Daily States*, 2 December 1906.

Tito Schipa: The Early Years

The Complete Gramophone and Pathé Recordings, 1913–1921

Arias and duets from *Arlesiana, Barbiere di Siviglia, Bohème, Cavalleria rusticana, Don Pasquale, Falstaff, Faust, Gioconda, Lucia di Lammermoor, Manon, Pagliacci, Rigoletto, Sonnambula, Tosca, Traviata, Zazà*, and zarzuelas
Songs by Barthélemy, Bizet, Caccini, Cottrau, Franck, Schipa, Tate, Tosti
With sopranos Giuseppina Baldassare-Tedeschi, Nina Garelli
Marston (distributed by Harmonia Mundi) 52008-2 (2 CDs)

Tito Schipa (1889, Lecce–1965, New York) is one of that group of singers that also includes Peter Dawson, Giuseppe De Luca, Lucien Fugère, and Adelina Patti, whose careers of fifty years and more bear testimony to careful husbandry of well-schooled voices. Schipa's operatic debut occurred when he was twenty, and he was still giving concerts when over seventy. In his heyday, (approximately 1920–35) his operatic repertoire included *Adriana Lecouvreur, L'amico Fritz, L'Arlesiana, Il barbiere di Siviglia* (both the Paisiello and the Rossini scores), *Don Giovanni*, Wolf-Ferrari's *Le donne curiose, Don Pasquale* (which he recorded on commercial discs in 1932), *L'elisir d'amore, Falstaff, Fedora, Fra Diavolo, Lakmé, Linda di Chamounix, Lodoletta, Lucia di Lammermoor, Madama Butterfly, Manon, Martha, Il matrimonio segreto, Mignon, Rigoletto, La sonnambula, La traviata*, and *Werther*. He traveled widely: two years of performances in the Italian operatic provinces led to appearances in the principal theaters of Milan, Rome, and Naples. Barcelona, Berlin, Brussels, Buenos Aires, Chicago, Copenhagen, Lisbon, London, Moscow, New York, Paris, Rio de Janeiro, Stockholm, Vienna, and Zurich knew him in opera or concert. In between these activities he composed songs (some of which he recorded), a mass for four voices, a mass for chorus, some piano pieces, and the three-act operetta *Principessa Liana* (Rome, Teatro Adriano, 22 June 1929). His films included *Tre uomini in Frak* (1932), *Vivere* (1937), *Canto alla vita* (1937, featuring music by De Curtis, Giordano, Liszt and Schubert), *Chi è più felice di me?* (1938), *Terra di fuoco* (1939), *In cerca di felicità* (1943), *Rosalba* and *Vivere ancora* (1945), *Il Cavaliere del sogno* (1946), and, with Bechi, Caniglia, Gigli and Gobbi, *Follie per l'opera* (1948). Latterly, he took up teaching, his pupils including Cesare Valletti and, interestingly, Joan Crawford, who studied with him in 1938. His financial fortunes fluctuated widely and, evidently, unwisely: the present reissue's booklet provides the fascinating sidelight that the tenor once became the owner of 45,000 automobile heaters after the Continental Automotive Corporation of Chicago defaulted on a loan.

Schipa was, without doubt, the greatest purely lyric operatic tenor of the period 1920–40 and has been described by Rodolfo Celletti as, in an absolute sense, one of the greatest singers of our time.[1] And yet he was not without vocal shortcomings; perhaps more than any other tenor he brings to mind the tag *multum in parvo*. As Michael Scott has observed, "The skill with which he presented limited natural resources to their best advantage to give full expression to his attractive personality makes him unique."[2] Notwithstanding his assertions in some letters that he always sang everything in the original keys, his range was never extensive: even in his youth he rarely ventured above B natural, and his lower notes were weakly developed. But between these extremes the recorded voice is attractive, distinctive, and instantly identifiable, and his diction — even on acoustic recordings — crystal-clear. While we do not hear from him the flamboyance or the ornaments that characterize Mattia Battistini or Fernando De Lucia, his singing appears effortless, the art that conceals art. Where he is peerless among his successors and scarcely approached even by recorded predecessors is in the delicacy, the transcendent grace, and the fastidiousness of his singing: his floated notes and *filature* must have been the despair of his contemporaries. No later tenor has so combined a flawless (if small) lyric voice, innate musicality, interpretative charm, and the refined taste that can be displayed only when the vocal technique is equal to the intellectual challenge, and when the voice is a compliant instrument of the singer's intention. Dorothy Kirsten, who made her Chicago debut as Flora in *La traviata*, wrote of Schipa's Alfredo: "Though his voice was somewhat small and not really beautiful in quality, his vocal technique was extraordinary and his style so impeccable that one forgot the limitations of his instrument. During the third act where he chastises Violetta and the singing becomes quite dramatic, the manner in which he used his light voice to show his anger was a fine lesson. He never forced, but obtained with his beautiful phrasing all the necessary dramatic effects. His lightest pianissimo sound, so perfectly projected, reached into the farthest corner of the opera house and was the envy of all tenors."[3]

Subtle taste is, of course, ever at the mercy of crude technique, which modern audiences and critics would never tolerate in instrumentalists but readily ignore in singers. For at least three centuries critics have bemoaned falling vocal standards: however, unlike them, we need not rely on fallible memories, for Schipa's many gramophone records clearly document his charm and considerable abilities. His first commercial discs were made in 1913, his last a Durium LP in 1953, and unofficial recordings exist from as late as 1964. These last show a voice dilapidated in places but a still impressive technique: his phrasing, in items such as his warhorse "Che se nne scorda cchiù" (of which the present set includes his earliest recording, from 1919), is nothing short of astonishing. These early records were largely of operatic material; later he recorded many of what have been termed "Italian café songs," which amply display his enchantingly joyful style and preserve for us much of the ambience of the interwar years. There are many, including this reviewer, who decline to regret that Schipa did not, instead, record Debussy and Hugo Wolf.

The present issue includes thirteen published sides made for the Gramophone Company in 1913 and thirty-four sides (two of them unpublished) made for Pathé in Milan (1916 and 1919) and New York (1921), in a total of forty-four musical selections, some recorded for both companies, and some (the *Lucia* and

Faust pieces, for example) heavily cut to fit on to a 25 cm record. Some three-quarters of these selections are operatic or zarzuela: in the general context of historical reissues on CD, it is important to state that the pitch of thirty of them has been tested and found correct to score and, when transposed, to the accompanying booklet. That not only Schipa's top notes but also his range was restricted is demonstrated at numerous points in this set, for example in the 1913 "Salve dimora" and in both the 1913 and 1919 versions of "Che gelida manina." All three are — correctly, I believe — reproduced here, transposed by a semitone to avoid the high C, though it then presents him with difficulties in the lower register: in the 1913 version of the *Bohème* solo he sings both syllables of "belli" on A, thus avoiding the low D. In the 1919 version this stratagem proves unnecessary, but, perhaps to arouse our interest in this much-recorded aria, instead of remaining on the opening G in the first phrase he sings instead the rising orchestral line exactly as, with a semitone heavier transposition, De Lucia had in his 1917 recording for Phonotype. (In mentioning individual notes the presumed transposition has been taken into account.)

Schipa's grace, elegance, and musicality are to be found throughout this release. The mood is established in the very first track, Des Grieux's "Ah! dispar vision" (Ah, fuyez douce image), from *Manon*, in his melting delivery of "Vision, ah, dispar" at the end of the first section of the aria, and in the final note, which demonstrates that, in his singing at least, the tradition of the *messa di voce* still survived. In the *Traviata* duet his ravishing reentry on "Amore, misterioso" is at once a relief from the squeaky Nina Garelli and a thing of beauty in its own right, worthy of being placed alongside Melba's feat when, in the duet with Germont *père* (Brownlee), she glides into the reprise of "Dite alla giovine."

Notwithstanding occasional solecisms, such as his liberties with "Che gelida manina," fastidious taste was another Schipa characteristic. A role he made his own was that of the Duke in *Rigoletto*, and he would doubtless have defended vigorously, as exactly in the *a piacere* spirit of the times in which it was written, the modest decoration that he adds to "Questa o quella," where he interpolates an unwritten C between the D-flat and B-flat of "una" in the phrase "meglio ad una" and repeats the device in the second verse, on the second syllable of "amor."

It is often the songs that bring to us the delightful, the inimitable Schipa. His "Che se nne scorda cchiù" has already been mentioned as a notable achievement, the 1919 "Granadinas" displays astonishing purely vocal management, and those familiar with his singing of Barthélemy's "Pesca d'ammore" only in the 1923 or 1926 recordings should be prepared to be bewitched all over again by this 1919 Pathé — of which Ward Marston has evidently used a superb copy — where the tenor's exquisitely floated high notes can surely never have been shown to better advantage.

As Marston points out in the accompanying booklet, five of Schipa's acoustic Gramophone Company records were not issued in the red label series and are difficult to find. Even more difficult must have been the task of assembling a complete set of his Pathés, and the fact that this set has done so, with added unpublished material, will make it irresistible to Schipa enthusiasts. The problem with complete issues, however, is that they sometimes confront us with performances that we would rather avoid. But perhaps we need reminding that even Homer nods, and this service is performed by Schipa's Pathé of Almaviva's first serenade: in the andante his graceful singing brings forgiveness for an evident lack of virtuosity, but the allegro cruelly exposes his deficiencies in this particular piece of florid music. "Amarilli" and "Panis angelicus," by contrast, suffer from an unnecessarily funereal tempo.

The set's booklet documentation is excellent, supplying matrix and issue numbers, transposition information, recording dates, and an informative essay by Robert Baxter. (It is gratifying to note among the list of credits that the term "audio conservation" has replaced the clearly inappropriate "audio restoration.")

Many transfers of historic material have been processed half to death, the vocal timbre becoming a victim of a perceived commercial need to reduce rumble and scratch to a level deemed acceptable to the modern listener, who is accustomed to a complete absence of nonmusical noise. More than forty years ago, Desmond Shawe-Taylor, reviewing the five-LP set of historical reissues *Fifty Years of Great Operatic Singing*, wrote that

> a good many of the acoustic recordings, especially the earliest, have gained their new smoothness at the expense of some of their original brilliance, colour and individuality. In the process of transfer to LP they have no doubt been subjected to a heavy cut of higher frequencies so as to reduce surface noise. Engineers always overestimate the extent to which this can be done without loss of those overtones which give immediacy and life to the voice; their graphs "prove" that nothing could in those days be recorded above some very low frequency ceiling, and . . . their ears do not tell them when their graphs are wrong.[4]

Today, of course, transfer engineers do not resort to the crude high-frequency filters once used to tame the sound from noisy pressings. However, I know of *no* method of removing extraneous noise lying within the frequency range of the music recorded without simultaneously—and detectably—losing musical overtones, especially those of female singers. No amount of amplifier adjustment can replace such losses, which usually become obvious only when a side-by-side comparison is made with the original.

Since many purchasers may be unable to make such a comparison, a limited evaluation has been undertaken, and it is a pleasure to report that, so far as it was possible to verify, Marston's transfers have not denatured Schipa's voice. A side-by-side comparison of the CDs was made with direct pressings of eight of the items, four Gramophone Company and four Pathé, at a carefully adjusted equivalent volume level. In four of those items (two of each make), a marginal, but only very marginal, loss in vocal quality was detectable. In the other cases the CD sound was quite as good as that from the direct pressings. The Pathés, in particular, as well as being rare, are very difficult to reproduce to this standard. Hence this set can be recommended wholeheartedly.

Michael E. Henstock

NOTES

1. Rodolfo Celletti, *Enciclopedia dello spettacolo*, vol. 8 (Rome: Casa Editrice Sadea, 1954), pp. 1672–73.

2. Michael Scott, *The Record of Singing*, vol. 2 (London: Duckworth, 1979), pp. 98–100.

3. Dorothy Kirsten and Lanfranco Rasponi, *A Time to Sing* (Garden City, N.Y.: Doubleday, 1982), p. 81.

4. Desmond Shawe-Taylor, *The Gramophone*, vol. 34, no. 404 (January 1957), pp. 285–87.

Kirsten Flagstad, Volume 3: Live Performances 1948–1957

Songs by Grieg, Strauss, Wagner, and "Ah, perfido!" (Beethoven)

Arias and duets (with Ferdinand Frantz, Max Lorenz, Set Svanholm, and Günther Treptow)
from *Tristan und Isolde, Der fliegende Holländer, Die Walküre, Götterdämmerung, Dido and Aeneas, Elektra, Alceste*
Various orchestras, conducted by Wilhelm Furtwängler, Geraint Jones, Erich Kleiber, Johann Hye-Knudsen, Gaetano Merola, Sir Malcolm Sargent, Georges Sébastian, Sir Thomas Beecham, Alfred Wallenstein
Simax (distributed by Qualiton Imports) PSC 1823 (3 CDs)

There are many reasons to listen to recordings of aging singers. The noblest one is to savor the artistic maturity, insight, and wisdom gained over a lifetime of experience. The basest one is the perverse delight in a voice so mauled by time, abuse, or faulty production that it is most suited to party tapes or cautionary lectures in vocal pedagogy classes. There is also the pleasure that great singers, like ancient monuments, can provide even in decline. A characteristic turn of phrase, a signature inflection or feat can trigger a lovely reminder of years of enjoyment provided and triumphs achieved.

In the case of the legendary Norwegian soprano Kirsten Flagstad (1895–1962), a top reason to play her late recordings is to marvel at her durability. The first of the reasons outlined above does not apply because her interpretations did not mellow or deepen appreciably over time. Her direct, patrician approach to the music she sang remained virtually unchanged during her forty-five-year career. One turns in vain to the postwar Flagstad for examples of the shifts in approach or emphasis that mark, say, the half-dozen or more recordings of Schubert's *Winterreise* that Dietrich Fischer-Dieskau made over the years. Furthermore, although she did make some twilight-period recordings that document some strain or diminution of powers, her immense discography[1] is virtually free of embarrassments and entirely devoid of the disasters that operatic ghouls dote on. No, the allure of the recordings that Flagstad made after age fifty is the diva's amazing ability to defy time.

Flagstad's almost unparalleled preservation of the radiance, clarity, solidity, effulgence, amplitude, and ease that her singing displayed in her youth is apparent in every track in this album, which is the third volume of the five-album, fourteen-disc survey of her "most important" discs released by Norway's Simax label in honor of the one-hundredth anniversary of her birth. I reviewed the first volume (PSC 1821, 3 CDs) in these pages about two years ago (see endnote); this invaluable collection contains her earliest recordings, including some from her teens. Volume 2 (PSC 1822, 3 CDs) was not distributed in the United States, because it contained live recordings of performances given at the Metropolitan Opera as well as in Norway. So did the original pressings of volume 3, but it has been specially remastered just for the American market to remove the lone Met item ("Abscheulicher!" from the 10 March 1951 performance of *Fidelio* conducted by Bruno Walter). Volume 4 (PSC 1824, 2 CDs) and Volume 5 (PSC 1825, 3 CDs) are devoted to songs by Beethoven, Schubert, Schumann, Brahms, Wagner, Strauss, Wolf, Sibelius, Foster, Bridge, Scott, Carpenter, Barber, Ronald, Hagemann, Rogers, Watts, Bax, Elgar, Head, Delius, and Grieg (including the latter's *Haugtussa* cycle, which Flagstad recorded three times between 1940 and 1956).

Some of the material in the present album comes from the opera house, some from the concert hall. The very first item, the *Tristan* love duet with Set Svanholm and conducted by Erich Kleiber, was captured in the Teatro Colón in Buenos Aires but was part of an orchestral program. Svanholm's plangent tenor and liquid legato suit this rapturous music perfectly, and Flagstad's expansive tone spreads like honey to fill every nook and cranny of the auditorium with no trace of effort. Elsewhere, her healthy Senta is a far cry from the haunted creature immortalized by Leonie Rysanek, but she gives a handsome rendition of the ballad in a San Francisco concert conducted by Gaetano Merola.

Flagstad's 1950 La Scala Brünnhildes with Wilhelm Furtwängler are well known to collectors, and the three snippets presented here — the battle cry, the Todesverkündigung (with the solidly baritonal Günther Treptow), and an eight-and-a-half-minute chunk of act 3 beginning with "War es so schmählich" (with Ferdinand Frantz) from *Die Walküre*, plus the prologue duet (with Max Lorenz, her preferred heldentenor partner) and Immolation Scene from *Götterdämmerung* — are sterling examples of the exalted standard she maintained in this demanding repertory for decades. The passionate intensity or verbal shading that distinguished the work of Frida Leider, Astrid Varnay, Martha Mödl, and Lotte Lehmann were never part of Flagstad's vocal and artistic personality, but the cannon-shot high B and the joyous portamento down off it that lead into the battle cry's middle section prove that she could be a very stirring and characterful singer, and she makes the solo's final high B especially big and strong to prove that she still had plenty of vim and vigor despite being just four months shy of her fifty-fifth birthday.

The most historically important selection in this album dates from only two months after her Scala *Ring*: the premiere of Strauss's *Four Last Songs*, in London, with Furtwängler conducting the Philharmonia Orchestra with a briskness one doesn't always associate with him. Flagstad doesn't follow the published order of the songs, and she omits a high B in "Frühling," but the high tessitura of the music doesn't faze her, and she sings with wonderful freshness and pliancy. Unfortunately, the recorded sound is lamentably dim and scratchy. If only this incomparable team had made a studio recording!

Flagstad's ability to lighten her immense voice allows her to float long, high-lying phrases in Strauss's "Befreit" and Beethoven's concert aria "Ah, perfido!" with ease and, in the latest items in this collection, to trip through ten Grieg songs with a friskiness and grace that any lyric soprano half her age would envy. (All the songs, including Wagner's *Wesendonck* conducted by Sir Thomas Beecham in 1952, are accompanied by orchestras rather than pianos, which makes the sonic mix that much more sumptuous.) In the Beethoven, recorded in 1951, her voice commands the same delicacy and girlish purity that it did in the 1937 version in Simax's volume 1. Her vibrato is a bit loose and sluggish at first, but the firmness of yore returns within two minutes. Flagstad's pianissimo is also on ready call in her regal reading of Dido's lament, recorded in London's tiny Mermaid Theatre. A momentarily under-pitch high note mars her noble concert performance of Elektra's Recognition Scene solo (she refused to sing the entire role, and presumably the monologue as well, because she was incapable of giving voice to their murderous emotions), but she bangs out a string of Olympian top B-flats in Alceste's "Divinités du Styx" (sung in Norwegian) without batting an eye in 1957, shortly before she turned sixty-two!

Young or old, Kirsten Flagstad was truly a singer for the ages.

William Albright

NOTE

1. In my review of volume 1 of Simax's series in *The Opera Quarterly*, vol. 13, no. 4 (summer 1997) I quoted the program note's statement that Flagstad made more than 900 recordings and noted that it was an amount that "surpasses by three, four, five, even eight times the number of recordings made by Lauritz Melchior (her most frequent Wagnerian costar . . .), Caruso, Dame Nellie Melba, or Luisa Tetrazzini; it tops even the prolific John McCormack, of whom 791 recordings exist" (p. 175).

Médée. Luigi Cherubini

Médée: Phyllis Treigle
Jason: Carl Halvorson
Néris: D'Anna Fortunato
Créon: David Arnold
Dircé: Thaïs St Julien
Femme de Dircé: Jayne West
Autre femme de Dircé: Andrea Matthews

Le coriphée: John Ostendorf
Brewer Chamber Orchestra
Chorus Quotannis
Bart Folse, conductor
Newport Classic (distributed by Allegro
  Corporation) 85622 (2 CDs)

Luigi Cherubini (1760–1842), a native of Florence and a pupil of Sarti, completed eleven operas before settling permanently in Paris in 1788. There, leaving behind the traditions of Italian *opera seria* and *buffa* and somewhat influenced by Gluck, he began developing a new dramatic style that eventually established him as a key figure in the nascent movement of Romanticism. Winton Dean describes Cherubini as "a Classical artist dragged willy-nilly into a Romantic age, from which, after supplying it with the technical means of expression, he retired into silence."[1]

But before that "retirement" in 1821, when he became the revered—if not universally admired—director of the Conservatoire, Cherubini wrote a number of important French operas (*Démophon*, 1788; *Lodoïska*, 1791; and *Elisa*, 1794). These were works in a characteristically austere style, massively constructed, displaying orchestral effects and ensemble writing that were to influence Beethoven and Weber. (Beethoven was a great admirer of Cherubini and assured him of that fact.)

Médée, which followed in 1797, was somewhat different. Outwardly it followed the form of the *opéra comique*, with spoken dialogue separating the musical numbers. In this respect it may be regarded as a model for Beethoven's *Fidelio* (1805), but what was readily accepted in German theaters found a rather cool reception in France. It is not surprising that *Médée* achieved only a few performances at the Théâtre Feydeau, after which it disappeared from view until the mid-1850s, when Franz Lachner replaced the spoken dialogues with recitative and incorporated certain musical revisions for a production of *Medea* in German. It was this version that served as basis for the 1909 La Scala revival of *Medea* (in an Italian translation by Carlo Zangarini). A powerful dramatic momentum was generated in 1953 when Maria Callas assumed the title role and subsequently performed it under the batons of such *maestri* as Vittorio Gui, Leonard Bernstein (substituting for the ailing Victor De Sabata), Tullio Serafin, and Nicola Rescigno.

There have been several recorded versions of the Callas *Medea*, but now we have the first studio recording of *Médée* minus the Lachner alterations and (as conductor Bart Folse assures us in the accompanying booklet's essay) "with all of the music and all of the spoken dialogue." This is a classic *tragédie lyrique* to which the *mélodrame* (spoken declamation over music) adds yet another dimension. I doubt that present-day audiences would embrace Cherubini's original design any more readily than the baffled Parisians did way back in 1797, because classical declamation does not easily coalesce with the modern concept of opera as music drama. Today's more informed ears, however, must respond to Cherubini's own brand of theatricality and dramatic energy while reluctantly agreeing with Dean's observation that "the want . . . of a certain creative warmth . . . kept him out of the front rank of opera composers."[2]

This estimable new recording falls short of total success in various respects. The period-instrument orchestra (thirty-three players, with 5-5-4-3-2 strings) performs very well, and the Chorus Quotannis is quite effective when the overall balances are right. Phyllis Treigle has the makings of a formidable Médée, passionate in her pleading and vengefulness, but her tone is unsteady and she reveals a limited emotional range in her important second-act duet with Créon. Carl Halvorson's cultivated tenor is at least one size too light for the demands of Jason's music, and David Arnold's smoothly placed basso also lacks kingly authority. D'Anna Fortunato is the most assured of the principal singers, and her account of the aria "Ah! nos peines" is effective, but the role of Dircé lies beyond her interpretive grasp. The entire American cast handles the French text well, following the outstanding example of producer John Ostendorf in the spoken role of Le Coriphée.

If one can imagine French counterparts in dramatic talent and vocal weight to Callas, Vickers, and Zaccaria (the cast of the 1958 Dallas *Medea*), such might be the ideal cast for Cherubini's somewhat problematic opera. Over the years, the Lachner recitatives have been rather maltreated by scholars; even though the eminent Edward J. Dent admitted that they "are a good deal better than one might expect," Dean later qualified that remark by ruling that "they seriously distort Cherubini's design, which employs a graded method of dramatic expression . . . with striking originality, notably in the finale of Act II."[3] This finale, incidentally, is convincingly done in the Newport Classic recording. Unfortunately, it is ill served by a boxy-sounding acoustic that proves a weakening force in the entire enterprise.

Let me play the devil's advocate for the maligned Lachner: He was no hack but a thoroughly accomplished musician who was Generalmusikdirektor in Munich from 1852 until his death in 1890 at age eighty-seven. He rescued a forgotten classic from limbo in 1855 and correctly regarded its spoken element as something of an albatross at a time when Wagner's enormous impact loomed over German stages. He provided *Medea* with recitatives befitting the spirit of his era and turned it into a stageable Romantic opera — the kind Cherubini envisaged in 1797 but, lacking the compositional daring, failed to realize.

George Jellinek

NOTES

1. Winton Dean, "Opera under the French Revolution," *Essays on Opera* (Oxford: Clarendon Press, 1990), p. 113.

2. Winton Dean, "French Opera," in *The Age of Beethoven, 1790–1830*, ed. Gerald Abra-

ham (London: Oxford University Press, 1982), p. 38.

3. Edward J. Dent, *The Rise of Romantic Opera*, ed. Winton Dean (Cambridge: Cambridge University Press, 1976), p. 82, 82n.

L'inganno felice. Gioachino Rossini

Isabella: Annick Massis
Ormondo: Lorenzo Regazzo
Duke Bertrando: Raúl Giménez
Batone: Rodney Gilfry
Tarabotto: Pietro Spagnoli

Le Concert des Tuileries
Marc Minkowski, conductor
Erato (distributed by Atlantic Classics)
0630-17579-2 (1 CD)

In his *Vie de Rossini*, Stendhal singles out *L'inganno felice*, the composer's fourth opera, as a breakthrough score, a herald of great things to come. Although he dismisses the roughly contemporary *Cambiale di matrimonio* as a "joli petit succès," the author of *Le rouge et le noir* declares rapturously of *L'inganno felice*: "Here genius bursts forth from all quarters." A *farsa* by Giuseppe Foppa, written for the 1812 carnival season in Venice, *L'inganno felice* tells of the "happy deception" whereby Isabella, the gentle wife whose virtue has been impugned by members of her husband's household, is recognized as innocent and reunited with her spouse, Duke Bertrando, after being abandoned at sea and living in hiding for ten years. As Damien Colas points out in the informative notes to the Erato recording, *L'inganno felice*, with its emphasis on reconciliation and the unmasking of evil, harks back in many respects to the *lumières* and the eighteenth-century sentimental comedies, while also anticipating (in the "trionfo dell'onore e dell'innocenza" evoked by Isabella) the moral concerns of such later Rossinian masterworks as *La Cenerentola, ossia La bontà in trionfo*.

Musically, too, *L'inganno felice* looks both backward and forward, and its richness is well served by the sprightly playing of Le Concert des Tuileries under the direction of Marc Minkowski. From the whimsical meanderings and deliciously tart harmonies of the *sinfonia* (reminiscent of Cimarosa) to the shimmering, *Tancredi*-like scoring for strings and winds that introduces the finale, Minkowski and his musicians bring to life the wit, grace, and splendor that characterize Rossini's music even at this earliest stage of his career. (Incidentally, recordings of, say, *Il signor Bruschino* and *Le comte Ory* by these same forces would make most welcome additions to the catalogue.)

The vocal soloists perform at a similarly high level. Soprano Annick Massis is a lovable Isabella, striking just the right balance between plaintiveness and determination, and pouring forth bright, cultivated tone and beautifully tapered phrases. As Batone, Isabella's chastened tormentor, Rodney Gilfry gives an impressive performance — rather broad at times, but astonishing for the fearlessness with which he attacks the role's dizzying range and intricate *fioritura*. (Not surprisingly, Gilfry's vocal agility and splendid diction have made him a much-admired Dandini in *La Cenerentola*, whose musical idiom is foreshadowed by Batone.) Pietro Spagnoli, as Isabella's rescuer Tarabotto, delivers the text with comparable relish and offers up a vibrant, lightly burnished *basso*: his nimble exchanges with Gilfry in "Va taluno mormorando" are a highlight of the recording. Lorenzo Regazzo is appropriately sinister in the role of Ormondo, the opera's chief villain.

Rounding out the cast is tenor Raúl Giménez as the nostalgic, heavy-hearted Duke. While singers with more boisterous personalities and more dogged handlers have drawn greater attention, Giménez has quietly established himself as today's most distinguished interpreter of early *ottocento* opera, a worthy heir to Tito Schipa and Maria Callas in this repertory. The comparisons are not arbitrary: like his illustrious predecessors, Giménez is a vocal aristocrat, making up for less than effulgent tone with delicacy of expression, supple phrasing, and a keen sense for the overarching shape of a musical period. (Witness, for example, the airy grace he brings to Elvino in the Naxos *Sonnambula*, or his "Pegno adorato e caro" in the Teldec *Cenerentola*, all silk and honeyed tenderness.) *Pace* the prophets of operatic doom—and the numerically challenged, who in matters tenorial can count no higher than three—Giménez's singing, in this set as elsewhere, is the stuff of which "golden ages" are made, no less compelling in the terzetto "Quel sembiante, quello sguardo" than in his lavishly embellished entrance aria, "Qual tenero diletto." How lucky we are to live at a time when this admirable musician has committed to disc so many of Rossini's wickedly difficult tenor roles—and when the ongoing "Rossini renaissance" brings forth such an accomplished recording of *L'inganno felice*, showing Stendhal's "new Napoleon" taking his earliest triumphant strides.

Marion Lignana Rosenberg

Il turco in Italia. Gioachino Rossini

Fiorilla: Cecilia Bartoli
Don Narciso: Ramón Vargas
Selim: Michele Pertusi
Don Geronio: Alessandro Corbelli
Poet: Roberto De Candia
Zaida: Laura Polverelli

Albazar: Francesco Piccoli
Orchestra and Chorus of Teatro alla Scala, Milan
Riccardo Chailly, conductor
London (distributed by Universal Classics)
   289 458 942-2 (2 CDs)

Along with *Le comte Ory* and *La pietra del paragone*, *Turco* belongs to that sterling trio of sophisticated Rossini works that stand, in opera companies' and audiences' affections, a step below the "big three" (*Il barbiere di Siviglia*, *L'Italiana in Algeri*, *La Cenerentola*). Of the "little three," *Turco* is perhaps the most consistently inspired, thanks not only to its musical values but also to the dramatic originality: the presence of the Poet and his detached observation of the events, in which he finds the material for his next comedy. In addition, Fiorilla is perhaps Rossini's most charming role for lyric soprano. The music ideally characterizes a woman who is teasing, flirtatious, and spitfire-like by turns, before her husband turns the tables on her in the final scene. Thanks to that episode, in which the duly chastened wife earns back the audience's sympathy, Fiorilla takes on rather more dimension than the better-known comic and *semi-seria* Rossini heroines.

Rossini saves the most exciting solo passage for the last scene: Fiorilla's memorably vaulting, adventurous scena, boasting exciting fioriture and tremendous musical variety throughout. The other individual numbers do not invariably convey such specificity of character; Narciso's music, in particular, fails to take fire, but the libretto is partly to blame for that. The crucial duets, however — Selim/Fiorilla, Fiorilla/Geronio, Geronio/Selim — communicate an enchantment and an exhilaration equaling anything the "big three" can offer. Take note of the extraordinary finale of the ball scene, in which Geronio ("affannato e disperato" says the libretto) is left onstage alone, convinced that he must be going mad.

This London set presents Margaret Bent's critical edition, prepared under the auspices of the Rossini Foundation, which restores various numbers written by Rossini's unnamed collaborator(s) for the premiere but deleted in the composer's 1815 revision for Rome. The Roman production also included a new second-act aria for Geronio, restored here. Also not by Rossini are the recitatives and the second-act finale, which Bent retains. Further details are outlined in the booklet's invaluable essay by Philip Gossett, whose assistance as artistic advisor must have been an enormous boon to the artists taking part in this splendid recording.

While Cecilia Bartoli may be the performance's raison d'être, its driving force is certainly the conductor. Riccardo Chailly's reputation and experience as a Rossinian has grown considerably since he recorded this opera with Montserrat Caballé and Samuel Ramey more than a decade ago. What strikes one immediately are his well-chosen tempos; thankfully, he never lets the proceedings turn frantic, no matter what degree of vigor may be required. Chailly also takes advantage of every opportunity for an effective change in atmosphere; for example, following Fiorilla's effervescent opening solo, his superb La Scala players simply ravish the ear with the sober-but-buoyant string accompaniment for the smooth approach of Selim's ship. While high spirits are never far away (the Geronio/Narciso/Poet trio is an especially scintillating moment), Chailly balances them with the affecting seriousness of certain key episodes, such as the reunion between Selim and Zaida. The conductor constantly reminds us that Rossini labeled this work a *dramma buffo*, rather than a *commedia* like *Barbiere*.

In most cases, Chailly has assembled a fine team of artists — and they are as much a team as the legendary group that recorded Rossini for Glyndebourne under Vittorio Gui in the 1950s. Chailly's singers play off each other with real flair, no one pushes for exaggerated effects, and all share a remarkable ease in florid passages (one need only compare the Selim of Michele Pertusi with that of Nicola Rossi-Lemeni in 1954 to realize how far we have come in this respect). All are wonderfully fleet in patter as well; Pertusi and Alessandro Corbelli execute theirs with especially winning panache in the very tricky finale of the Selim-Geronio duet. The voices also blend excellently in the ball scene's a cappella quintet. If Chailly has erred, it is in using a supporting mezzo and tenor who are unworthy of the occasion, and in choosing two baritones — Corbelli and

Roberto De Candia (the Poet) — whose similar timbres often make it tough to differentiate the two.

Fiorilla has been recorded by four ladies of highly contrasting vocal weight and tone. Only Sumi Jo strikes one as an expected choice in this role, yet she ranks next-to-last in persuasiveness. Her accomplished, technically admirable performance is in many ways generic, lacking interpretive originality and sufficient vocal variety. Vocally and temperamentally miscast, Caballé seems to sight-read her way through her portrayal, sinking her recording in the process (one pities her colleagues Chailly, Ramey, and Enzo Dara). Maria Callas, on the other hand, is a delight — considerably more appealing than in her more celebrated Rosina, and in almost invariably steady voice. Throughout one can scarcely believe that the same singer was also at the time a Norma, Gioconda, and Tosca.

And now we have Bartoli, another surprising choice for Fiorilla, and ultimately the most successful of the four. Hers is in many ways a standard-setting performance for future Rossini singers on disc. Bartoli deemphasizes her mezzo-oriented vocal colors, sounding here simply like a fairly dark-timbre lyric soprano. Her command at the top extends as far as an easy trill on high A, an interpolated D in her big second-act scena, and pianissimo B-flats emitted with ease. She plays with the coloratura, always to apt expressive purposes. One tends to take her unique rhythmic vitality for granted, but listeners should be grateful for the special excitement and dash it brings to her work. As an utterly complete singer of Rossini, she also manages legato passages with mesmerizing control, and, as is her wont, all her ornamentation grows naturally out of Rossini's original lines.

What brings the greatest joy, however, is Bartoli's irresistible involvement in this role. Her vibrant portrayal radiates a joie de vivre that explodes through one's speakers. Frequently she imbues her tone with a beguiling smile (something that Callas, for all her brilliance in the role, never quite managed). When Bartoli's Fiorilla first beholds Selim, her curiosity in "Che bel Turco!" is adorable. As she welcomes the Turk to her home, even a single word of recitative — "Sedete," for example — displays devastating sexiness without going overboard. She doesn't have Callas's hilarious way of sobbing into the acciaccature in the Fiorilla-Geronio duet, but she manages that passage endearingly nonetheless. She gets her claws out for the quarrel with Selim's wife, Zaida, but also plumbs depths of emotion in the long scena in which Fiorilla learns that her husband has rejected her. Although Bartoli leaves nothing to chance, her delivery seems absolutely spontaneous throughout. Small imperfections (near-inaudibility in various whispered phrases, occasional shrillness and loosening of focus on high) are forgivable. Where sheer artistic intelligence is concerned, this is Bartoli's most impressive Rossini singing on disc, and it bodes well for her future investigations of soprano roles.

As with Bartoli, there appear to be no limits in the technique of her Selim, Michele Pertusi. Onstage and on disc, his Alidoro (to Bartoli's Cenerentola) has confirmed his position as the most important Italian bel canto bass of the past several decades. This artist's command of Rossinian fioritura is as dazzling as that of most coloratura sopranos. His timbre offers an ideal middle ground between, say, the massive Rossi-Lemeni (EMI) and the comparatively slender-voiced Simone Alaimo (Philips). Pertusi's only vocal weakness is a peculiarly airy *mezza voce*, which will surely improve with time. While not the last word in seductiveness, he is well in the picture dramatically; his approach is unfailingly elegant—princely, indeed.

The two baritones have good-not-great instruments, but both are fine vocal actors. As Don Geronio, Corbelli relishes the text with unfailing gusto; a line like "Quanti bocconi amari" is a detail that instantly brings the put-upon husband to life. However, even at his character's most pathetic (in the ball scene), Corbelli never indulges in the vocal mugging one dreads in Rossini *buffo* parts. Although the grainy top of De Candia's voice makes for a few passing moments of concern, he has the measure of the Poet. The role's sine qua non—not just a sympathetic manner, but the feeling of taking the audience into his confidence—is vividly present throughout.

Don Narciso, the larger of the two tenor roles, offers fewer rewards than a Ramiro, Lindoro, or Almaviva. Ideally, Narciso needs a voice whose natural tessitura sits a tone higher than Ramón Vargas's. This marvelous young Mexican artist (whose Edgardo in Lucia is the finest bel canto tenor portrayal I have witnessed in a theater) cannot "sit" constantly in the upper fourth of his voice. A pervasive sense of strain produces an occasional—and quite atypical—roughness of tone in Vargas's singing here. Still, even in a less than congenial assignment, he provides much that is admirable, for example, splendid fioriture and expressive *mezza voce* in his tough act 2 aria. Vargas also manages a spot-on imitation of Pertusi upon greeting Fiorilla while disguised as Selim at the ball. He projects a positive presence, even if he achieves no more success than his recorded competition (Raul Giménez, Ernesto Palacio, and the young Nicolai Gedda) in making something substantial out of Rossini's lovesick cicisbeo.

Zaida is no mere comprimaria, for she must exude a sex appeal that rivals Fiorilla's, along with lush tone and an easy upper register. Laura Polverelli gives an average performance, confident but in no way memorable, and making very little of the words. She is certainly no match for Marriner's Susanne Mentzer, by quite a distance the finest recorded Zaida. As for the Albazar, his fine coloratura notwithstanding, the hard-toned Francesco Piccoli does not fill the bill, and listeners are advised to fast-forward through his aria.

Any lover of this opera will surely have either the EMI or the Philips set already. The former can be savored for Callas, Mariano Stabile's lovable poet, and the characterful (if vocally often awkward) Rossi-Lemeni. Philips has the always invigorating Marriner at the helm, along with a fine cast, made more enjoyable if one can accept Jo's light-soprano limitations. London's new entry, however, displays an interpretive authority and a boldness—from Bartoli, above all—that allow it to take the field as the recorded *Turco* of choice.

Roger Pines

Oberon. Carl Maria von Weber

Oberon: Deon van der Walt
Rezia: Inga Nielsen
Fatime: Vesselina Kasarova
Puck: Melinda Paulsen
Hüon von Bordeaux: Peter Seiffert
Scherasmin: Bo Skovhus

Mermaids: Heidi Person, Hermine May
Deutsches Symphonie-Orchester Berlin
Rundfunkchor Berlin
Marek Janowski, conductor
RCA Victor Red Seal (distributed by BMG
Classics) 68505-2 (2 CDs)

Over twenty years ago, John Warrack observed that *Oberon* is "better known by repute than in performance."[1] Today, at least in America, Weber's last opera is still rarely performed, and recordings of it are few and far between. Nevertheless, *Oberon* contains some excellent music, and this RCA Victor recording conducted by Marek Janowski gives a good representation of it.

This fairy-tale opera is unique among Weber's works in that it was originally set to an English-language libretto by James Robinson Planché, for London's Covent Garden. After the composer's death, the writer Theodor Hell (the pseudonym of Carl Gottfried Theodor Winkler) translated the text into German, and his became the standard version of *Oberon*. So far as is known, there has been no complete recording of the original English version. Janowski uses Hell's German text for his recording.

From the outset *Oberon*'s libretto was considered weak, and much of the criticism of the opera concerns this element. Some of the problems may be traced to the story, which is based on C. M. Wieland's eighteenth-century poetic retelling of a medieval *chanson de geste*. The opera combines human events with fairy-tale elements and exoticism. The elf-king Oberon vows not to return to Titania, queen of the fairies, until he encounters a truly faithful pair of lovers. In helping an exiled knight from Charlemagne's court, Oberon eventually finds those lovers in the persons of Reiza (Rezia in the German libretto) and Huon of Bordeaux, a quest that also involves a magic horn, the threat of slavery, shipwreck, and ultimately the prospect of execution.

Despite the fantastic elements thrown into the plot, Planché's libretto seems strangely artificial and banal. It is no wonder, then, that two previous recordings of the opera use a narration in lieu of the original spoken dialogue (Raphael Kubelik's, on Deutsche Grammophon; and James Conlon's, on EMI, which is based on Gustav Mahler's revision).[2] In contrast to those two earlier efforts, Janowski's recording has the virtue of including the dialogue between the musical numbers. This contributes a sense of dramatic pacing and avoids the pedantic tone associated with narrated recordings. (Narration certainly assists in clarifying operas in unfamiliar languages, like the Hungarian of Zoltán Kodály's *Háry János*, but it is not always convincing.)

The popular notion of Weber as a precursor of Wagner often causes performers to treat his operas too heavy-handedly. Janowski, however, approaches *Oberon* with a lighter, more idiomatic touch. For once, the opera sounds like a Romantic fantasy instead of a dark tragedy. After all, it was composed at a time when Rossini held the stage and the vocal style was not yet dominated by the larger voices that would later come into vogue. Janowski's Italianate way with the score is reminiscent of the approach taken by Richard Bonynge and Joan Sutherland, for example, in their performance of Agathe's "Und ob die Wolke" (on the *Age of Bel Canto* set, London 448 594-2 [2 CDs]). This tack is apparent in Huon's aria "Von Jugend auf in die Kampfgefild" (act 1, no. 5), which Peter Seiffert sings with agility and nuance. Even more revelatory is Inga Nielsen's lighter touch in Rezia's "Ozean, du Ungeheuer!" (act 2, no. 13), an aria that Warrack anachronistically deems to require "the voice of a Brünnhilde."[3] The rest of the cast is uniformly excellent, and the finely balanced work of the chorus and orchestra adds to the high quality of the recording.

The accompanying booklet contains the libretto in German (with English and French translations side-by-side) and period illustrations. Essays by Thomas S. Grey, Frank Ziegler, and Matthias Lehn (in English, German, and French, respectively) offer useful insights into the work, with Ziegler's providing a clear and concise discussion of the context in which *Oberon* was composed.

Along with his other Weber recordings (*Euryanthe*, Berlin Classics 0011082BC [3 CDs] and *Der Freischütz*, RCA 62538-2 [2 CDs]), Janowski's *Oberon* is a standard-setting performance. Those who already know the piece should find this set a fresh and rewarding listening experience; those seeking it out for the first time should start with this recording.

James L. Zychowicz

NOTES

1. John Warrack, *Carl Maria von Weber*, 2d ed. (Cambridge: Cambridge University Press, 1976), p. 342. Warrack devotes an entire chapter to an analysis of *Oberon* on pages 321–44.

2. The CD transfer of the Kubelik/DG recording omits even the narration.
3. Warrack, *Carl Maria von Weber*, p. 343.

Lohengrin. Richard Wagner

Lohengrin: *Peter Seiffert*
Elsa von Brabant: *Emily Magee*
Friedrich von Telramund: *Falk Struckmann*
Ortrud: *Deborah Polaski*
Heinrich der Vogler: *René Pape*
Herald: *Roman Trekel*
Noblemen: *Peter Bindszus, Andreas Schmidt, Bernd Riedel, Bernd Zettisch*

Pages: *Minjou Choi, Konstanze Löwe, Ileana Gunescu-Booch, Christiane Berghoff*
Staatskapelle Berlin
Chor der Deutschen Staatsoper Berlin
Daniel Barenboim, conductor
Teldec (distributed by Atlantic Classics) 21484-2 (3 CDs)

A new *Lohengrin*, though not exactly a top priority (it's about time for some brave record company to give *Rienzi* another chance, for starters), is still welcome—particularly when the performance is as good as this one.

The box claims "Complete Version," without elaboration. Naturally, the stage cuts that can be heard on some recordings (not only the "live" ones but some of the older studio versions, as well) are not made here. There is, however, ample precedent for this sort of "completeness" on disc. By "complete," Teldec means that this performance has restored a section of Lohengrin's Grail Narrative, deleted by Wagner before the opera's Weimar premiere but printed as an appendix in some scores (e.g., the one published by Broude Brothers). The only other recording that offers this full version of the Grail Narrative is the 1966 RCA set conducted by Erich Leinsdorf (recently reissued as RCA Opera Treasury 50164-2).

For those who do not have access to a score with the appendix, what happens in the original version is (roughly) as follows: After Lohengrin sings "Sein Ritter ich — bin Lohengrin genannt," instead of the loud orchestral outburst topped off with a cymbal clash familiar from abridged performances, there is a statement (beginning *mf*, swelling to *ff*, then quickly diminishing to *p*) of the so-called Grail Motif (the fact that it was originally played by the orchestra after the revelation of Lohengrin's name suggests that, in Wagner's mind, it was a "Lohengrin Motif" as well). The King and the chorus react (their music is similar to that heard in act 1, after Lohengrin's entrance).

Lohengrin then explains ("Nun höret noch . . .") how, when word reached Monsalvat that a maiden (Elsa) was in distress, he was chosen for the mission. At the same time, the swan had sought refuge at Monsalvat; Lohengrin's father, Parzival, realized that the swan was the victim of a magic spell. Because those so afflicted can be freed from enchantment after serving the Grail for a year, Parzival took the swan under his protection. (All this is sung to a passage of typical "early Wagner" declamatory music, with a predictable reprise of the Swan Motif. The diaphanous orchestral accompaniment is remarkably beautiful, even by this opera's standards.)

In the final section of the omitted passage (beginning with the words "Durch Flusse und durch wilde Meereswogen") Lohengrin describes how the swan ferried him to Brabant; the music is a reprise of the marchlike theme that accompanied his initial appearance, in act 1 (and that will accompany his departure, at the end of act 3). It starts out delicately but builds rapidly to an exciting climax — the big orchestral crash already alluded to, at which point the original and the abridged versions converge. (Thus, in the original, the passage for the King and the chorus *after* the crash is a commentary on the narrative as a whole, not just on the revelation of the knight's name.) The restored music consists of fifty-six bars and takes a little over four minutes to perform, so its inclusion does not significantly increase the opera's running time (although it obviously adds to the burden on the tenor!). Still, one can see why Wagner felt that, at a point so late in the opera's action, something had to go. The mystery is why tenors who perform "In fernem Land" out of context (in concert or on records) never opt for the fuller version. In a booklet note (p. 18), Daniel Barenboim describes the restored passage as "indispensable," which is surely an exaggeration. (After instructing Liszt to make the cut prior to the opera's premiere, Wagner never seems to have contemplated reinstating the passage.) But Barenboim and Peter Seiffert make an even better case for these extra bars than did Leinsdorf and his Lohengrin, Sándor Kónya.

Barenboim's is a distinguished reading, on the same high level as Kempe's or Kubelik's. The Solti and Abbado recordings demonstrate that it's possible for a performance to be exceptionally well executed but still have little to say about the work. Barenboim clearly sees *Lohengrin* as a drama, and not at all as an old-fashioned opera. His tempos can be quite fast, and yet even when they are broader the overall impression is of a steady forward motion, because the rhythms are so sharply defined. As a result, even though Barenboim favors rich, weighty orchestral sonorities, his performance never bogs down. The act 3 prelude is taken very quickly—justified by the *sehr lebhaft* marking—and has a light, playful quality that is delightful to hear: for once, the wedding festivities sound like the kind of party one would want to be invited to. And it is followed by a lovely rendition of the Wedding Chorus—Barenboim, his chorus, and his orchestra seem to have agreed to pretend that they had never heard this number prior to the recording sessions: they encourage the listener to approach the piece afresh, too.

Barenboim's cast is unusual because it contains no weak link. The Elsa, Emily Magee, is a singer new to me—I hadn't caught up with her previously, live or recorded. She has a large, lush, but convincingly youthful-sounding soprano that fills out the music with room to spare. Magee is also an extremely accurate singer. Interpretatively never less than effective, she is at her best in the Bridal Chamber scene, where there is a real sense that this Elsa is being driven by subconscious impulses to steer the conversation toward the Forbidden Question. The role has been well done on records, but Magee need not fear the competition. One looks forward to hearing her again.

The role of Ortrud holds no terrors for Deborah Polaski, an experienced Brünnhilde and Elektra. The part is often taken by a mezzo, but in my opinion a dramatic soprano voice such as Polaski's is more appropriate. Although forceful, Polaski is an unusually young- and seductive-sounding Ortrud; she realizes that the character does not have to shout all of the time, and in fact her attention to legato and other niceties of phrasing puts some Elsas one has heard to shame. As a result, the act 2 duet for the two women (i.e., the section beginning "Ha, dieser Stolz") is exceptionally well sung here. (It can take a bruising in performances that feature an Ortrud of the brute-strength school.)

Seiffert resists the temptation to turn Lohengrin into a plaster saint: he always sounds fully human and involved in the action. The voice, appealing in quality, suggests a full lyric tenor rather than a true heldentenor: the baritonal color that Seiffert summons in his lower register can seem artificially grafted onto the rest of the instrument. On this recording, there is one chink in Seiffert's technical armor: when he tries to play around with dynamic levels on sustained tones, his vibrato can cross the line and become a waver (audible on two exposed phrases: "Elsa, ich liebe dich" in act 1; and "Heil dir, Elsa! Nun lass vor

Gott uns gehn" in act 2). One hopes that these instances of unsteadiness are the result of a temporary indisposition and not the first symptoms of premature decline.

Falk Struckmann is so incisive, so rhythmically on the mark, and makes so much of the words, that it's almost possible to overlook how well he actually sings the part of Telramund. His voice has a lean, pointed timbre and narrows at the top instead of expanding grandly. As a result, Struckmann might not be one's first choice for Wolfram von Eschenbach or similar parts in which richness and beauty of timbre are desirable. He is extremely musical, though (his consistent accuracy of pitch is unusual to hear in this role, and satisfying in itself).

René Pape is an excellent King Henry, warm and full of voice, eloquent with the text. Good as he is, though, he still has healthy competition on records. Karl Ridderbusch, on the Kubelik set, is still unique for the ease with which his velvety bass encompasses the part's high tessitura. Gottlob Frick, on the Kempe recording, makes the most of an instrument that is far less beautiful than either Ridderbusch's or Pape's: Frick manages to sound both larger-than-life and intensely personal. (His interruption of Elsa's Dream—"Elsa, verteidge dich vor dem Gericht!"—is unique in its anguished urgency; one can almost visualize this King seizing Elsa by the shoulders and giving her a good shaking to "snap her out" of her reverie.)

Roman Tekel, a vivid Herald, completes the group of principals, and the Noblemen and Pages are entirely satisfactory (the Noblemen include baritone Andreas Schmidt, which is certainly luxurious casting).

The recording brings out a lot of subtle orchestral detail. The solo singers tend to be closely miked, with the chorus positioned much more distantly—a rather old-fashioned balance, evocative of opera sets made in the early days of stereo. (When Pape sings along with the chorus in act 3, his voice is given an unreal prominence.) By fair means or foul, the engineers have managed to make all of the individual vocal lines audible during the ensemble that ends act 1 ("O, fänd ich Jubelweisen," etc.). The sound doesn't open up as excitingly as I had hoped it might at the end of act 2, where the off-stage organ and brass fanfares seem too close. On the whole, though, this is a solid production that should give continued satisfaction from a sonic standpoint.

The three-CD format, increasingly common for *Lohengrin*, is not ideal: it requires a disc break during the Ortrud/Telramund scene at the beginning of act 2. (I own a CD reissue, several years old, of the EMI/Kempe set, on which act 2 is—absurdly—spread across all three discs, with *really* bad breaks at the beginning *and* the end of the act. If the Kempe recording ever reappears on CD at reduced price, I hope this will be corrected.) If and when some sort of extended-play digital audio disc appears on the market, it would, theoretically, allow us to hear this and other Wagner operas without interruption—a mind-boggling prospect. In the meanwhile, *Lohengrin* is better served by allotting two CDs to act 2. In addition to Barenboim's note about the performed text, the booklet contains a good essay on the opera, photos and biographies of the singers, and a full libretto in German, English, and French. Many of Wagner's stage directions are either shortened or eliminated, though — an annoying economy, and unfair to any purchaser who might be new to this opera.

In sum, the Teldec set is as good a studio recording of this opera as we have ever had at full price. Those unfamiliar with the work, or those who wish to replace an older version, can buy with confidence.

Roland Graeme

Cox and Box, or The Long-Lost Brothers. Burnand and Sullivan

James John Cox: Leon Berger
John James Box: Ian Kennedy
Sergeant Bouncer: Donald Francke

Kenneth Barclay, pianoforte
The Divine Art (in association with the Sir
*   Arthur Sullivan Society) 2-4104*

The names of W. S. Gilbert and Arthur Sullivan have come to be inextricably linked in the history of musical theater, but when they first appeared on the same London playbill they were not linked at all. On 29 March 1869, the Gallery of Illustration gave the premiere performance of Gilbert's *No Cards*, pairing it with another one-act piece called *Cox and Box*, by F. C. Burnand and Arthur Sullivan. Later that year, *No Cards* was replaced by another Gilbert libretto, *Ages Ago*, with music by Frederic Clay, who, during rehearsals, introduced the dramatist to his friend and fellow composer Sullivan. Although the first fruits of that meeting would not be served up on stage for several years — *Thespis*, the first Gilbert and Sullivan opera, opened in 1871 — the seed had been sown.

Burnand seems never to have forgiven Gilbert for stealing his collaborator: in the years he served as drama critic and (after 1880) editor of *Punch*, reviews of the Gilbert and Sullivan operas were full of praise for the latter but rarely had a kind word for the former. But Burnand had squandered his own opportunities to solidify a partnership with Sullivan: in 1867 they jointly produced a full-length operetta, *The Contrabandista*, which failed, and in 1894 they revised and revived it as *The Chieftain* — which also failed. Sullivan's biographer, Arthur Jacobs, says that "the clumsy scansion" of the verses written in response to the composer's stipulations for *The Chieftain* makes it "obvious . . . that Burnand had not grasped the musical point very well."[1] And it is equally clear that his forte was not the construction of original plots; rather, Burnand's dubious distinction as a Victorian dramatist lay in burlesques of the work of others. The titles of such pieces as *Robbing Roy* (1879) and *Faust and Loose* (1886) painfully indicate their pun-ridden content.

Indeed, one of the chief reasons for the success of *Cox and Box*, the sole hit spawned by Burnand and Sullivan, is that very little of it derives from Burnand himself. Rather, the piece is an adaptation of John Maddison Morton's *Box and*

Cox, the 1847 farce that had been one of the great comedic triumphs of the earlier nineteenth-century stage. Just as Alan Jay Lerner later did in turning Shaw's *Pygmalion* into *My Fair Lady*, Burnand had the good sense to appropriate not only plot but prose from his more talented predecessor; indeed, there is scarcely a line of dialogue in *Cox and Box* that is not borrowed verbatim. His only important contributions were the lyrics (called "funny" by the *Tomahawk* and "idiotic" by the *Daily Telegraph*)[2] that furnished a pretext for Sullivan's music, and the transformation of Morton's Mrs. Bouncer, proprietor of the lodging house in which the action transpires, into Sergeant Bouncer, a bamboozling basso much given to military reminiscences.

Bouncer's bunco consists in renting the same room to two different tenants: Cox, a hatter, who is only home at night, and Box, a printer, who returns from work in the morning. Inevitably, when the former is given an unexpected holiday and comes back to the room, the lodgers discover the deception and angrily agree to share the same space only until Bouncer finishes preparing the little back second-floor room for occupancy by one of them. Their initial hostility, however, eventually dissolves into amicable conversation, through which they discover the remarkable coincidence that Cox is now engaged to the same unappealing widow once betrothed to Box, who escaped the bonds of matrimony only by leaving false evidence of suicide behind him. The two now quarrel over Penelope Ann, with each holding her to be the intended of the other — but when word subsequently arrives that the rich woman has drowned and left a will bequeathing all her property to "my intended husband," both Cox and Box lay claim to that title. After unsuccessfully attempting to settle their dispute by tossing loaded dice and two-headed coins, they receive a letter indicating that Penelope Ann is alive, well, and on her way to their room. But she never actually appears, instead sending up yet another letter, which liberates the two protagonists by announcing her union with Mr. Knox. Relieved, they turn to each other for the farce's crowning joke. To quote from Morton (just as Burnand did):

> BOX: You'll excuse the apparent insanity of the remark, but the more I gaze on your features, the more I'm convinced that you're my long lost brother.
> COX: The very observation I was going to make to you!
> BOX: Ah — tell me — in mercy tell me — have you such a thing as a strawberry mark on your left arm?
> COX: No!
> BOX: Then it is he! (*They rush into each other's arms.*)[3]

This magnificent spoof of the recognition scenes of melodrama became famous in the Victorian theater, with later writers adapting and embellishing it. Indeed, the denouement of Gilbert's *La Vivandière* (1867), a burlesque of Donizetti's *La fille du régiment*, occurs when Tonio establishes his claim to be the true Earl of Margate, and thus socially qualified for Maria's hand, by pointing out that he has no strawberry marks at all.

It seems unjust that Morton's minor masterwork has now become a rarely exhibited museum piece, while Burnand's more than derivative libretto has held the stage throughout the twentieth century. But the latter was graced with Sullivan's music, as piquant and propulsive as that which he later supplied for the more mature scores of the Savoy operas. The survival of *Cox and Box* was assured in 1921, when the D'Oyly Carte Opera Company trimmed it down to twenty-five minutes for use as a curtain-raiser and paired it in performance with the shorter full-length Gilbert and Sullivan operas, such as *The Sorcerer*, *HMS Pinafore*, and *The Pirates of Penzance*. This version was twice recorded on vinyl by the company (on London OSA 1323, where it rounds out a five-sided recording of *The Gondoliers*, and on London OSA 1171, as the flip side for *The Zoo*, a one-act operetta that Sullivan wrote nine years later with B. C. Stephenson) and has made its way into the repertoire of many an amateur company of Savoyards.

Now comes the Divine Art Record Company, which, in association with the Sir Arthur Sullivan Society, has issued on compact disc its 1984 recording of "the original full-length version of 1866." The version in question was first tried out at Burnand's house on 23 May 1866 and repeated a few days later at a larger private party at Moray Lodge in Kensington. The author George du Maurier was Cox, and Sullivan himself played piano, "pounding out an extempore accompaniment," as "he had not bothered to write one down."[4] However, he not only finalized but orchestrated the score by the time he conducted it a year later at a charity performance at the Adelphi Theatre. Other changes were eventually made: an overture was written, the melody for Box's lullaby to his breakfast ("Hush'd is the bacon on the grid") was entirely reworked, and a duet for Cox and Bouncer ("Stay, Bouncer, Stay!") was added.

"To achieve as musically complete a version as possible," Divine Art has included the late-arriving duet in its recording, but fidelity to the original is otherwise the rule. Leon Berger, who also plays Cox, proclaims in the liner notes that "this recording was made in a Victorian drawing-room with the performers using real doors, windows, curtains and all the appropriate domestic props—much as it would have been first given at the informal presentation at Burnand's house." And the pianoforte played by Kenneth Barclay is said to have been "manufactured a century before his birth." The Pre-Raphaelite painter Holman Hunt, who twelve years before *Cox and Box* had journeyed to the shores of the Dead Sea to paint *The Scapegoat* in exactly the same light that had bathed the beast described in the Bible, could scarcely have demanded a more earnest dedication to authenticity than this.

Unfortunately, Divine Art's sixty-three-minute restoration of the whole unintentionally confirms the wisdom of the D'Oyly Carte adapters who cut the piece in half. To be sure, a couple of the cuts were well worth opening: the Handelian tune for Bouncer's mock-martial song ("Yes, yes, in those merry days") is too good to be limited to just one verse (as it is in the scaled-down version), and the fuller finale is more appropriate to the spirit of comedy, as it has the entire cast on stage to join in the concluding celebration. But most of the additions add little. The gambling duet, in particular, is downright dull: both Cox and Box repeatedly sing the word "sixes" when throwing dice and "head" when tossing coins, without ever establishing much of a melody. And the original version of Box's lullaby lacks the sinuous line of its successor but goes on twice as long. Moreover, if the recording proves that less is more, it also demonstrates that more may be less, as this fuller *Cox and Box* lacks the cheerfully bellicose overture Sullivan later added to get the piece off to a brisk start.

Still, the cast is clearly committed to the project, and two of the three performances are a pleasure. Berger, as Cox, at first speaks his lines as if he knows that his elocution teacher is in the audience and wants to show her that he's been doing his assigned exercises, but he eventually settles into the dialogue and displays a fine, firm baritone in all his singing. Donald Francke snarls, sniffles, snorts, mutters, and grumbles his way through Bouncer's part and sings in so heavy a Cockney accent that those unfamiliar with the lyrics will find themselves reaching for the libretto; still, the overall effect of this actorly approach is genuinely funny, and there is rich musicality in his bass. Ian Kennedy's Box, however, displays a thin tenor that tends to whiten on top and paces the monologue leading up to his lullaby so slowly that by the time he declares "How sleepy I am to be sure," the listener can empathize.

Recording engineer David Lisle has done a superlative job with the very forward sound, which, during the dialogue, shifts frequently from channel to channel and thus creates the aural illusion of stage movement. But even the best engineering cannot make Barclay's piano sound like more than a piano, however agile and accurate his playing is. Listeners familiar with the D'Oyly Carte recordings will miss the vigor, variety, and wit of Sullivan's orchestration. And an orchestra is ultimately what the composer wanted for this piece; indeed, one of his chief reasons for refusing to sell the touring rights to Thomas German Reed, proprietor of the Gallery of Illustration, was Reed's failure to supply a full complement of musicians. "I am not arranging for it to go down in the country in the form of a drawing-room entertainment," Sullivan wrote to Burnand. "We must wait our time. Opportunity and orchestra will turn up some day."[5] Those who cannot get enough of *Cox and Box* will want to add this recording to their collections; others would do well to heed Sullivan's advice and wait for a musically richer version.

Alan Fischler

NOTES

1. Arthur Jacobs, *Arthur Sullivan: A Victorian Musician* (Oxford: Oxford University Press, 1984), pp. 353–54.

2. See Leslie Baily, *The Gilbert and Sullivan Book* (London: Cassell & Company, 1952), p. 62; and Alan Hyman, *Sullivan and His Satellites: A Survey of English Operettas, 1860–1914*

(London: Chappell and Company, 1978), p. 5, respectively.

3. John Maddison Morton, *Box and Cox*, French's Minor Drama, no. 21 (London: Samuel French, n.d.), p. 24.

4. Baily, *The Gilbert and Sullivan Book*, p. 62.

5. Quoted in Jacobs, *Arthur Sullivan*, p. 53.

Lakmé. Léo Delibes

Lakmé: *Natalie Dessay*
Gerald: *Gregory Kunde*
Nilakantha: *José van Dam*
Mallika: *Delphine Haidan*
Frederic: *Franck Leguérinel*
Ellen: *Patricia Petibon*
Rose: *Xenia Konsek*
Mistress Benson: *Bernadette Antoine*

Hadji: *Charles Burles*
Fortuneteller: *Alain Chilemme*
Chinese merchant: *Jean-Pierre Lautre*
Vagabond: *Yves Boudier*
Orchestra and Chorus of the Capitole de Toulouse
Michel Plasson, conductor
EMI Classics (distributed by EMD) 5 56569 2
(2 CDs)

It was time for a new recording of *Lakmé*. There have been several versions, both studio and "live," but for most collectors who are building a basic opera library, the choice until now has been between the London set conducted by Richard Bonynge and an earlier EMI release led by Alain Lombard. Both of those recordings have begun to show their age from a sonic standpoint, but they remain solid performances; choice between them will probably be dictated by one's response to their heroines. On London, Joan Sutherland can be heard at her most opulent — enough said — and she is ably supported by Alain Vanzo (Gerald) and Gabriel Bacquier (Nilakantha); since her recording is available on CD at a reduced price, it is the obvious pick for the collector on a budget.

My favorite version has been the EMI/Lombard because of Mady Mesplé's extraordinary performance in the title role. Mesplé's voice may be an acquired taste (many listeners find her tone too shallow and wiry and dislike its persistent rapid vibrato). For me, though, the French soprano's total immersion into the character outweighs these considerations. In the opera, Lakmé is often referred to or addressed as "enfant," and Mesplé is convincingly childlike — so much so, in fact, that there is something disturbing about Gerald's erotic interest in her and her eager response to it. The sound of her voice aside, Mesplé is wonderfully agile and accurate, unique among recorded Lakmés for her clear and pointed enunciation of the text.

The new recording is a typically strong EMI/Plasson production, with first-rate orchestral and choral work, good clear sound, and an idiomatic and well-schooled cast. Plasson understands that most of this score consists of delicate lyricism, and his reading flows; the opera, instead of breaking down into its individual formal numbers, seems more of a piece than usual. (Bonynge also responds to the music with affection and taste but doesn't have Plasson's pinpoint control, nor is his orchestra on the Toulouse ensemble's level. Lombard, by contrast, can occasionally be accused of hitting too hard, although his weighty, melodramatic approach pays off in places.)

Our new Lakmé, Natalie Dessay, is a worthy successor to Mesplé. The voice is clear and firm, and (again) as agile as one could wish; her tonal production is much straighter and steadier than Mesplé's, so that listeners who object to the latter's vibrato should find the perfect antidote in Dessay's singing. An intelligent artist, Dessay shapes the music with distinction and has her own ideas about the character. Her Lakmé is a willful teenager, innocent at first, but turning ever more sophisticated as the action unfolds.

My only reservation about Dessay's performance concerns, oddly enough, the Bell Song. Dessay sings it so effortlessly that it doesn't sound here like much of a display piece; it lacks the excitement of a vocal high-wire act — a silly criticism, perhaps, but after replaying this track several times, both in and out of context, I can't shake the impression. In the more lyrical sections of this number, I don't sense that Dessay is telling a story, let alone addressing it to a crowd. Both Sutherland and Mesplé (in their very different ways) are more vivid here, conjuring up the moonlit forest, the danger that the "lost stranger" finds himself in, and the awe that the pariah girl experiences when he reveals himself to be Vishnu. Still, there is probably not another soprano active today who could do this role better than Dessay (Sumi Jo is the only possible contender who comes to mind) and few who could do it this well. (Furthermore, with her slim physique and fashion-model features, Dessay even looks the part — so how about a video?)

Gregory Kunde is an ardent and elegant Gerald. His voice betrays a hint of lightness at the very top (where this role makes uncompromising demands), but on the whole his stylish singing is a pleasure to listen to.

Two of Lombard's singers reappear on the Plasson set. Charles Burles, who sang Gerald for Lombard, is here demoted to the small part of Hadji, which he does very well. And José van Dam repeats his Nilakantha. Perhaps "repeats" is the wrong word, for he has rethought the role. Van Dam's voice is simply not what it was on the earlier recording; he now has less power at his disposal, and his sound is narrower and more limited in color. Van Dam does not commit the classic error of singers in this situation — that is, inflate his tone and bluster his way through. Instead, he scales everything down, sings well within his current limits, and uses subtler means to convey the Brahman's fanaticism. The aria "Lakmé, ton doux regard," warmly sung but basically treated as an opportunity for vocal display on the Lombard set, is now an intimate, subdued moment, and thus far more convincing as the expression of a father confiding in his daughter.

The supporting roles are all neatly and stylishly sung, if rather anonymously. The only standouts are Franck Leguérinel (a strong Frederic) and Bernadette Antoine (who, like her counterparts on the earlier recordings, has a lot of fun with Mistress Benson, the English governess).

The booklet's background essay on the opera is not particularly interesting and stiffly translated into English. The essay does, at least, remind us that Delibes composed other stage works besides *Lakmé* and his ballets: *Le roi l'a dit* (1873), *Jean de Nivelle* (1880), and *Kassya* (left incomplete, but performed posthumously in 1893, with orchestration by Massenet). Perhaps some enterprising label will investigate them.

EMI also provides libretto and translation — the latter an excellent version by Hugh Graham. Unfortunately, Graham's work has been sabotaged by his editor and proofreader. Many of the opera's stage directions, some of which are crucial to an understanding of the action, have been omitted. For example, it is not made clear that Lakmé has removed her jewels and left them behind when she goes to bathe; the Britishers seem to stumble across jewelry that has appeared out of nowhere. Elsewhere, readers unfamiliar with this work have to guess which characters are on stage at a given time. And the libretto contains an unfortunate misprint on page 79 of the booklet, where the French text is printed in both columns, with no English. Hopefully this will be corrected in future printings.

Those new to *Lakmé* who have no prior attachment to either the Sutherland or the Mesplé versions should definitely investigate this release.

Roland Graeme

Mazeppa. Peter Ilyich Tchaikovsky

Mazeppa: Nikolai Putilin
Maria: Irina Loskutova
Andrey: Viktor Lutsiuk
Lyubov: Larissa Diadkova
Kochubey: Sergei Alexashkin
Orlik: Viacheslav Luhanin
Iskra: Vladimir Zhivopistsev

Drunken Cossack: Nikolai Gassiev
Kirov Opera Orchestra and Chorus,
   St. Petersburg
Valery Gergiev, conductor
Philips (distributed by Universal Classics)
   462 206-2 (2 CDs)

The final three cantos of *Poltava*, Pushkin's epic poem of 1828, served as the dramatic source for *Mazeppa*, Tchaikovsky's eighth opera. The librettist, Viktor Burenin, intended it for Karl Davidov, the renowned cellist who in the early 1880s was head of the St. Petersburg conservatory. Davidov, however, had no time to compose the work and gladly yielded the text to Tchaikovsky. The composer began work on it during the summer of 1881 but was distracted by other assignments, including a celebratory cantata for the coronation of Tsar Alexander III. The writing gave him little pleasure; at one point he wrote to his benefactress, Nadezhda von Meck, "I have never yet experienced such difficulty in composing any large piece as with this opera."[1] The work's premiere occurred at the Bolshoi in February of 1884. Its reception was more positive there than in a St. Petersburg production a few days later, but in any case, it failed to establish itself in the public's affection.

Had Tchaikovsky been more committed to the work, it might have ranked with *Pique Dame* and *Eugene Onegin*. Certainly there was tremendous operatic potential in the real-life figure of Ivan Mazeppa, the ambitious Cossack ruler of Ukraine until his thirst for power led him to pit himself with Sweden against his former ally, Peter the Great (his defeat was catastrophic, forcing him to exile himself to Turkey, where he died). In the opera, the public Mazeppa is contrasted with the private one, a man deeply in love, at age seventy, with Maria, the young daughter of a wealthy landowner. The difficulties in Burenin's libretto (considerably revised by the composer) arise largely from the uneasy juxtaposition of public and private events. Pushkin achieved an effective balance in *Poltava*, but the opera does not. It comes to life most vividly in the scenes involving Maria's parents: Lyubov, desperate to save her daughter from Mazeppa's clutches and her own husband from execution, and Kochubey, implacable in his defiance of Mazeppa and noble in his death. One feels distanced from Maria's predicament (i.e., her family's strenuous objections to her loving Mazeppa) until her affecting final scene: she has witnessed her father's death, which had been ordered by Mazeppa; now, having gone mad, she is abandoned by him and sings a lullaby to the dead Andrey, her lovelorn suitor whom Mazeppa has just slain.

The title role remains a puzzlement. John Warrack expresses the problem thoughtfully: "Mazeppa himself is one of Pushkin's Byronic *âmes damnées*, a dark figure, devious and calculating yet a violent natural force, who is intended to excite our sympathy as well as our awe . . . [I]n portraying him the composer reflected not so much Mazeppa's dual nature as a bewildering inconsistency. The man who can on the one hand scheme his treacherous way to power and compass the torture and judicial murder of those who stand in his way, and on the other rhapsodize about the beauty of the night and his love for Maria, need not be beyond the understanding of music, as he is not beyond that of poetry; but a substantial act of creative sympathy is demanded. . . . [In the Maria-Mazeppa duet] there is little sense of where the key to this difficult, dark character is to be found."[2]

The music is highlighted by some exciting (if overlong) choral episodes, and all the dance music works predictably well, especially the effervescent Hopak in act 1. Of the opera's crucial relationships — Mazeppa-Maria, Andrey-Maria, Kochubey-Mazeppa, Lyubov-Maria — only that of mother and daughter rises to eloquence, in their hair-raising act 2 duet. In the many soliloquies, one occasionally glimpses Tchaikovsky's typical brilliance in revealing character through song, but the revelations come only fitfully. The ariosos of Mazeppa and Maria show the composer's usual feeling for expressive line (Mazeppa's first solo is also graced by superb writing for oboe), but how one wishes they were more emotionally penetrating and moving. Listeners need only compare Maria's opening arioso with any of Tatyana's important speeches in *Onegin* to hear what is missing. There are two solo episodes in which the composer fulfills himself: the shattering prison scene of Kochubey, which demands heavy declamatory singing and the textual intelligence of a great actor; and the extended mad scene for Maria. The demented heroine's appearance is set up rather conventionally (announced with trilling flute and soulful violin) and the scene takes a while to get off the ground dramatically. Still, its climax provides more excitement than anything one hears even from Lisa in *Pique Dame*, while the final lullaby provides the opera with an unexpectedly quiet, eerie ending. By the way, the events of the final act are preceded by a rousing six-minute symphonic introduction depicting the Battle of Poltava, appropriating the famous "Slave" theme from the Coronation Scene of *Boris Godunov*.

If *Mazeppa* is attracting new admirers today, much of the credit is due to Valery Gergiev, artistic director of the Kirov Opera, whose production was a great success in the company's recent visit to the Metropolitan Opera. Gergiev's new Philips recording captures a May 1996 Kirov performance in St. Petersburg. It faces stiff competition from Deutsche Grammophon's brilliant 1994 studio recording under Neeme Järvi, in which a Swedish chorus and orchestra collaborate with a predominantly Russian cast of principal singers.

Gergiev's Mazeppa is Kikolai Putilin, who has succeeded Sergei Leiferkus as the Kirov's leading baritone. Putilin exhibits unusually warm, rounded, Bastianini-like tone through much of the range. His low notes are frequently weak, and the top loses pitch (he sustains the A-flat of his demanding second-act aria through sheer willpower). More positively, he has a notably assertive manner, and the hard, cutting sound he brings to more aggressive passages is not at all inappropriate. One can certainly believe in his Mazeppa as a leader, but when the private Mazeppa sings of his longing for Maria, Pusilin cannot provide the yearning quality in his phrasing that Pavel Lisitsian brought to his unforgettable 1960 recording of Mazeppa's aria. Although Putilin manages fine legato in the duet with Maria, DG's Leiferkus is more sensitive overall, delivering the text with greater acuity and detail throughout. In Putilin one also misses Mazeppa's agony as he wonders how Maria will deal with her father's impending death. He makes his best showing in the opening of the third act, where he is in exciting vocal form while strongly projecting the defeated hero's desolation.

Mazeppa's opposite number, the hapless Maria, receives a frustrating performance from soprano Irina Loskutova. Hers is an excessively mature, almost matronly voice for this role, so dark that initially it seems as if she could manage the mother's role as easily as the daughter's. Her technique is undistinguished, betraying rattly sustained tones and frequent unsteadiness through the whole compass. It is much pleasanter at lower dynamics (there are some notably lovely quiet attacks in the first scene's big ensemble). A consistent harshness on high makes the finale of the Maria-Lyubov duet a particular trial. A few solid top notes in the mad scene hint at the improvement that might result from a better technical approach. Loskutova provides insufficient expressive variety, and only in the final mad scene does sufficient characterization emerge. The size of the role merits more attention than Loskutova is given in Philips's CD case and booklet (the company seems, wrongly, to consider Lyubov the more important role). All in all, she must take second place to DG's Galina Gorchakova, who — if not particularly imaginative interpretively — sings with magnificent warmth and radiance.

Poor Andrey, who pines in vain for Maria, is hardly more than the average ardent operatic lover, but he has a positive, energetic presence here in the voice of Viktor Lutsiuk. This man deserves an international career; even if DG's Sergei Larin has the more attractive timbre, Lutsiuk's tone is unfailingly strong and secure. He could phrase more feelingly, and he can't reveal dimension in his character where it doesn't exist. However, in more vigorous episodes — for example, Andrey's insistence that he be sent to Moscow in the opera's second scene — Lutsiuk verges on the thrilling, sounding as if he'd be terrific not only in *Pique Dame* or *Jenůfa*, but also in *Trovatore* or *Forza*. In act 3 he offers fine boldness and passion as he expresses Andrey's utter frustration at not having tracked down Mazeppa. His aria in that act is as difficult as it is ungrateful, with one tricky rising phrase after another; Lutsiuk copes manfully, if not easily.

Larissa Diadkova's Lyubov is the only portrayal common to both the DG and Philips sets. For the latter she sings with a bit more intensity, which of course can be expected in a live-performance recording, even though her vocalism shows less consistency than in the studio recording. Even when slightly under pitch, the top has an appealing soprano-like sheen, although her sound generally seems narrower and less ample than, say, Irina Arkhipova's. The voice loses a lot of beauty in heavy declamatory passages. Still, she generally sings impressively, her forcefulness extending to the treacherous arpeggio descent down to a confident G below the staff in the first-act finale (the role covers a range of more than two octaves). While taking it all in stride, Diadkova genuinely connects with her character's dignity and, above all, her agony in the scene with her daughter.

The bass voice of Sergei Alexashkin's Kochubey, particularly massive in the lower-middle, is also fairly rough-hewn in character — but velvety-smooth Ramey-style tone would be out of place here (DG's Kochubey, Anatoly Kotscherga, is even rougher in tone, but just as imposing in scale and equally persuasive dramatically). Alexashkin just gets by in awkwardly high-lying passages, and certainly his soft singing is not in the Kipnis or Reizen class. When singing full out, however, the voice is awesome (one can imaging him singing a splendid Dosifey or Pimen), his dramatic involvement considerable. He makes a particularly moving effect in the tour de force of the prison scene; even if the scene's climax taxes him, he really spills blood in it and its impact is one of the set's greatest strengths. Alexashkin also shows marvelous legato in his final lines before Kochubey's execution. The supporting players include a vibrant baritone, Viacheslav Luhanin (Orlik), who sounds as if he could sing a presentable Mazeppa himself.

A special asset of this recording is the Kirov chorus. Is there a more full-toned choral sound anywhere in the world? The women are delectable both in their lengthy number that opens the opera and in the second scene of act 1. The incomparably lusty and vigorous tenors give much pleasure as well. As one might expect, everyone's *piano* singing is consistently impressive. How inspired they must be by Gergiev, who is clearly devoted to the piece and has the technique and the theatricality to project it convincingly. He does not put a foot wrong, his orchestra responds with total unanimity, and the piece goes with an almost incredible dash and dramatic flair—but then, so does DG's performance, in which the conducting covers Järvi with glory (his 1979 *Onegin* broadcast from the Met remains the finest conducting of a Tchaikovsky opera that I can recall).

Philips's engineers have outdone themselves: the recorded sound is spectacular by any standards. Occasional stage movement is heard, as well as applause at the end of each act and after various individual numbers. The booklet includes the same brilliant essay by Richard Taruskin that accompanied the DG recording. Philips's printers deserve a black mark for a truly embarrassing blooper in the libretto of my review copy: twenty-five pages are missing, replaced by material from the recent Conlon/Voigt performance of Zemlinsky's *Eine florentinische Tragödie*, released by EMI!

So which *Mazeppa* should you buy if you want only one performance? Philips vs. DG presents one of the toughest choices in recorded opera for some time. DG's Gothenburg Symphony and Royal Opera/Stockholm Chorus may not have this opera in their bones, but the recording's vocal and musical standards are so consistently high that I would give it the prize, in spite of the many strengths offered by the indefatigable Gergiev and his Kirov colleagues.

Roger Pines

NOTES

1. As quoted in David Brown, *Tchaikovsky*, vol. 3: *The Years of Wandering, 1878–1885* (New York: W. W. Norton, 1986), p. 173.

2. John Warrack, *Tchaikovsky* (New York: Charles Scribner's Sons, 1973), p. 176.

Die toten Augen. Eugen d'Albert

Myrtocle: *Marianne Schech*
Arcesius: *Engelbert Czubok*
Aurelius Galba: *Wolfgang Windgassen*
Shepherd: *Franz Gehringer*
Reaper: *Ernst Grathwol*
Arsinoe/Shepherd Boy: *Lore Paul*
Mary Magdalen: *Hetty Plümacher*
Ktesiphar: *Alfred Pfeifle*
Rebecca: *Hanna Stolze-Fröhlich*
Ruth: *Liselotte Mann*
Sarah: *Anni Hackel*
Esther: *Else Blank*

Four Jews: *Helmut Zeckert, Kurt von Reimersdahl, Bruno Samland, Clythus Gottwald*
Old Jew: *Alfred Appenzeller*
Voice from the well: *Marianne Sauer*
Voice: *Harald Baender*
Echo: *Anneliese Weigel*
Radio-Sinfonieorchester Stuttgart
Südfunkchor Stuttgart
Walter Born, conductor
Myto (distributed by Qualiton Imports)
 MCD 982.185 (2 CDs)

Of Eugen d'Albert's twenty operas only two—*Tiefland* and *Die Abreise*—have been recorded. Now, Myto's CD release of a live 1951 performance of *Die toten Augen* (The Dead Eyes) extends the d'Albert discography to include what was once one of this composer's most popular stage works. After its premiere in Dresden in 1916, the piece made the rounds of other major European houses within and outside of Germany. By 1925 it had been performed in sixteen different cities in a dozen countries. The opera's triumphant progress slowed in the 1930s before coming to an abrupt halt during World War II. Apparently the only recorded mementos of its popularity were the composer's own rhapsodic piano transcription of the heroine's aria "Psyche wandelt durch Säulenhalle" and Lotte Lehmann's celebrated 1933 recording of the same excerpt.[1] This succulently melodic number became so closely identified with Lehmann that she often sang it as a recital encore. Recalling in her memoirs how her assumption of the role of Myrtocle put "the final seal" on her career in Hamburg, Lehmann describes the stunning visual effect Hans Loewenfeld's production created when she made her entrance "in the shimmering orange-colored robes of the blind Greek girl."[2] Despite her success in *Die toten Augen* in both Hamburg and Prague, Lehmann was never able to convince the directors of the Vienna State Opera to stage it for her there.

Hanns Heinz Ewers's libretto, derived from Marc Henry's play *Les yeux morts*, is set in Judea during the time of Christ; it combines myth and melodrama against the biblical backdrop. The title refers to the beautiful but blind Greek wife of the Roman legate Arcesius. Unaware of her husband's physical ugliness, Myrtocle longs to see the man she loves with such devotion. After an encounter with Jesus miraculously restores her sight, Myrtocle mistakes the handsome Roman knight Galba for her husband and throws her arms around him. Enraged, Arcesius strangles Galba. Thinking it is her husband who has been murdered, Myrtocle is horrified. When her maid privately reveals the dead man's identity, Myrtocle weighs her former happiness against her present misery and longs to be sightless again. By staring at the sun with open eyes (the magnetic Lehmann reportedly made the most of this pantomime), she blinds herself. After Arcesius returns, Myrtocle assures her husband that she never saw the man who murdered Galba.

The plot is filled out with genre scenes: Jewish women gossiping at the well, a comic turn for the Egyptian healer Ktesiphar, and Jews excitedly commenting on the offstage arrival of Jesus. Although Galba plays a pivotal role, he never asserts much of a dramatic presence, having to stand mute while Myrtocle pours out her love after seeing him for the first time. Arcesius and Myrtocle, on the other hand, are more convincingly drawn, the latter's radiant lyricism contrasting tellingly with the former's bluntness. The opera begins with a prologue in which a shepherd sets off to find a lost sheep, symbolic of Myrtocle's straying from her husband's protective embrace.

D'Albert clothes this hot-house story in late-Romantic music aglow with melody woven into a gorgeous orchestral fabric. The sumptuous score is imbued with the sound of Wagner and Strauss but carries d'Albert's unique stylistic stamp and flair for dramatic pacing. At least in this fervid live recording, *Die toten Augen* sounds like an important work. Walter Born leads a compelling performance, firmly paced yet expansive, with strong playing from the Stuttgart radio orchestra.

The big cast features singers associated with the Württemberg State Opera in the early 1950s. Ideally, the title role calls for the vocal glamour and soaring top that Lehmann undoubtedly brought to it. Marianne Schech lacks sufficient vocal polish and dramatic intensity but gives a heartfelt reading nonetheless. After her voice warms up, she sings fervently and with a certain refinement; her gleaming soprano opens up effortlessly on the high B-flats and Bs. Although she sounds unsettled in the aria, she rises to the challenge of the long duet with Arcesius and pours out golden tones after Myrtocle regains her vision. Engelbert Czubok (Arcesius), a Stuttgart veteran, displays a handsome but rather rough-hewn baritone that preserves its focus right up to high F, if not F-sharp, and he sings with sturdy conviction. Although the part of Galba gives Wolfgang Windgassen little to do, he manages it securely.

The supporting cast has no weak links. Lore Paul's bright-toned soubrette is apt for both the Shepherd Boy and Arsinoe. Hetty Plümacher's rich mezzo-soprano fills out Mary Magdalen's glowing tribute to Jesus with ample tones. Alfred Pfeifle's tenor incises the Egyptian healer's awkward vocal lines with deft comedic sense, and Franz Fehringer's Shepherd exhibits a blend of ardent lyricism and strength.

All in all, *Die toten Augen* is a fascinating opera that does not deserve the oblivion it has slipped into in recent decades. The performance on the Myto release makes a few nips and cuts in the score (the most serious being a two-page cut in the prologue), so there is still a need for a note-complete, digital version.

Myto fills out the second CD with excerpts from three other operas featuring Windgassen: Pedro's narrative from *Tiefland*; a duet from Hans Pfitzner's *Die Rose vom Liebesgarten* that unites the tenor with his wife, Lore Wissmann; and the *Siegfried* final duet, with Schech as Brünnhilde. These live performances from 1950 and 1951 capture Windgassen in firm if hardly ingratiating form. The long *Siegfried* extract documents what must have been one of Windgassen's earliest attempts at this arduous role.

Robert Baxter

NOTES

1. D'Albert's piano transcription, originally recorded in 1916, is available on Piano Library CD PL250. The Lehmann recording was once issued on an Angel LP (COLH 112) and on CD as part of the Metropolitan Opera's Centenarian series.

2. Lotte Lehmann, *Midway in My Song* (Indianapolis: Bobbs-Merrill, 1938), pp. 135–37.

Verlobung im Traum. Hans Krása

Marja Alexandrowna: Jane Henschel
Sina: Juanita Lascarro
Nastassja: Charlotte Hellekant
Barbara: Bogna Bartosz
Sofja Petrowna: Christiane Berggold
The Prince: Albert Dohmen
Paul: Robert Wörle

The Archivist of Mordasov: Michael Kraus
Deutsches Symphonie-Orchester Berlin
Frauenstimmen des Ernst-Senff-Chores
Lothar Zagrosek, conductor
London (distributed by Universal Classics)
289 455 587 (2 CDs)

This release is another noteworthy entry in London Records' laudable Entartete Musik series devoted to European composers whose creative activities were suppressed by the Nazi regime in the 1930s.

Hans Krása (1899–1944) was a native of Prague, a student of and later assistant to the Austrian composer Alexander Zemlinsky. He subsequently widened his horizons by repeated visits to Paris, where he studied with Albert Roussel. Although prodigiously gifted and signed up rather early by the prestigious Universal Edition of Vienna, Krása seems to have composed only a handful of works before embarking on his opera *Verlobung im Traum* (Betrothal in a Dream) in 1928. The work was introduced by Prague's Neues Deutsches Theater in 1933 under the direction of George Szell. After the outbreak of Nazism, Krása — who was deeply involved with Prague's young intellectuals — was either reluctant or unwilling to leave his native city until it was too late. He was deported and, along with thousands of his Jewish compatriots, died in a concentration camp.

Verlobung im Traum is in two brief acts, with a libretto by two of the composer's Prague colleagues, Rudolf Fuchs and Rudolf Thomas. Based on a short novel by Dostoyevsky (*Uncle's Dream*), the text is stamped by that author's characteristic contempt for the insular and hidebound conventions of nineteenth-century Russian society. Sina is an idealistic small-town girl in love with Fedya, a young revolutionary who is mortally ill. Yielding to her social-climbing mother's ambitious plan, Sina agrees to marry a senile Prince, hoping to save Fedya's life with her newly acquired wealth. Her intentions are thwarted by the Prince's nephew and one of Sina's relatives, both driven by their own selfish motives. Ultimately, the Prince is persuaded to leave town, Fedya dies, and the noble-hearted Sina, disillusioned, ends up in a loveless marriage. The two acts are framed by a prologue and an epilogue. The former is a stage-setting arioso delivered by the town archivist; the latter is a melancholy summation spoken by the archivist, who comments that, had it not been for *his* efforts to record the memory of these tragic events, poor Sina's entire life would have vanished without a trace.

Krása's music has links with the Second Viennese School, but it is distinctly tonal and accessible. Its sardonic, occasionally grotesque coloration is entirely appropriate to the subject matter. The opera is masterfully orchestrated, with a transparency that bespeaks French influences. Passages for piano, solo violin, and English horn occur with surprising effects, and the presence of saxophone denotes a jazzy element typical of 1920s Paris or the cabarets of Berlin in that period. In her excellent introductory notes in this recording's accompanying booklet Paula Kennedy remarks that "the range of influences displayed in *Verlobung* might seem bewilderingly eclectic" (p. 16). This is true, and the listener may be free to discover suggestions of Berg, Stravinsky, Weill, Les Six, and, perhaps, the cabaret songs of Schoenberg. Nonetheless, one is left with admiration for a truly original spirit and an all-pervasive sarcasm that anticipates the young Shostakovich.

Despite its good libretto and the compactness of its construction, the opera is only partially successful because Krása's orchestral mastery is not matched by his vocal writing. Unlike some of his contemporaries, he rarely takes his singers beyond the normal requirements of their range, but what Kennedy appropriately terms Krása's "heightened conversational style" leaves no memorable impression. Furthermore, the many ensembles rarely result in anything more than a self-defeating massive din. One particularly clever ensemble, however, deserves mention: in act 1, scene 3, Sina sings, for the benefit of the assembled guests, the melody of Bellini's "Casta diva" against a totally incongruous vocal and orchestral counterpoint.

The performance under the alert leadership of Lothar Zagrosek is an outstanding ensemble effort, and the recorded sound is excellent. Only the fine bass-baritone Michael Kraus is given solo prominence, but all the principals contribute laudably and with involvement. The second CD is filled out with a splendid account of Krása's three-movement *Symphonie* (1923). It opens with an eerie and delicate "Pastorale," continues with a sardonic "March" that seems to come from outer space, and concludes with a vocal treatment (well sung by soprano Brigitte Balleys) of a Rimbaud poem depicting the feelings of a child while his two sisters gently massage his hair in the process of delousing him — an unusual symphonic finale, indeed! The same Berlin orchestra, this time under Vladimir Ashkenazy, gives a splendid account of this weird but fascinating work, another testimony to Krása's eccentric yet indisputable gifts. Had he not died so tragically, he could have become the equal of Hindemith, Weill, and Korngold, his equally banished but luckier contemporaries.

George Jellinek

Moskva, Cheremushki. Dmitri Shostakovich

Bubentsov/Drebednyov: Andrei Baturkin
Masha/Vava/Kurochkina/Mylkina/Nervous
  lady/Lady construction worker 2: Irina
  Gelakhova
Baburov/Neighbor: Mikhail Goujov
Lidochka/Wife: Elena Prokina
Boris Koretsky: Anatoly Lochak
Sergey Glushkov/Kurochkin/Mylkin/Husband/
  Man in cap: Herman Apaikin

Lyusya/Neighbor/Lady construction worker 1:
  Lydia Chernykh
Barabashkin: Alexander Kisselev
Residentie Orchestra The Hague
Russian State Symphonic Cappella
Gennady Rozhdestvensky, conductor
Chandos (distributed by Koch International)
  CHAN 9591(2) (2 CDs)

Chandos has gone out on a commercial limb with this release: *Moskva, Chere-mushki*, a musical comedy first performed in 1959 in the Moscow Operetta The-ater, must be among Shostakovich's most obscure works. Initially well received, it dropped out of the repertory after a few years. The notes in the set's accom-panying booklet inform us that in 1961 the composer revised the work for a film version (titled simply *Cheremushki*) that "remained a regular New Year's Eve Soviet television-favourite for another decade or more" (p. 16) — in essence, the Soviet equivalent of *It's a Wonderful Life*. The mind boggles.

The title, which is in fact an address, might be freely translated as *Cherry Street, Moscow* — the name of a (fictitious, of course) new housing development for the working class. The complicated plot, which suggests a cross between the serials *Eastenders* and *Coronation Street*, but without the sex, almost defies synopsis, although Chandos gives it a shot in its thick booklet. The verbose libretto is tough going, at least in English; perhaps there are nuances in the original that simply don't survive translation. The anti-establishment satire is soft-edged, as might be expected in a stage work first performed during Khrushchev's regime and in the midst of the Cold War. The jokes are tired and obvious, on the whole; if an aspiring sit-com writer tried to submit some of this stuff, he'd be kicked out of the studio. The belated introduction of a fantasy element in the last act is most peculiar, given the cynicism of what has gone before.

The score consists of brief musical numbers separated by long stretches of spoken dialogue. The music is astonishingly conservative in idiom. It's easy to fall into the trap of judging a musical work by how innovative or forward-looking it is. Still, it's startling to hear a stage piece — written in 1959, set in what was then "the present," and ostensibly about the everyday concerns of ordinary folk — that sounds like a brashly orchestrated pastiche of a nineteenth-century operetta. There are marches, waltzes, and polkas, all rather foursquare: by com-parison, Lehár is rhythmically and harmonically radical.

On this recording, eight singers divide up no fewer than twenty-one parts among themselves (and conductor Gennady Rozhdestvensky takes on two addi-tional spoken bits). The demands of the vocal writing are relatively modest; the piece seems to call for performers who can switch back and forth between speech and song—an ensemble of singing actors, in other words. Chandos's cast consists of big-voiced opera singers who hit the music with ripe, confident tones. Better this, of course, than something thin and tentative; still, there are moments when the performance seems too large-scale.

Soprano Elena Prokina is charming in both of her roles. Irina Gelakhova, who portrays six different characters, has a typically plummy Russian mezzo-soprano. The men are good, though the preponderance of low voices makes it difficult to tell them apart. Tenor Herman Apaikan, who makes a pleasant sound, is pitted against a quartet of baritones and basses.

Rozhdestvensky conducts the piece as though it were *Prince Igor*, with deliberate tempos, weighty textures, bold instrumental colors. One suspects that much of the music would benefit from a lighter touch.

A recording of a work such as this would be useless without text and translation, and Chandos's booklet contains the libretto (in Cyrillic—no transliteration) with French, German, and English translations, all printed in adjacent columns in a mercifully legible typeface. The English appears to be accurate, but it is thoroughly British in tone. Thus a student, talking about studying hard at the last minute in preparation for an exam, uses the verb "swat"—whereas an American would say "cram" or "pull an all-nighter."

The sound is excellent, and Chandos's engineers have solved what might be called the Speech Problem. Here, the dialogue seems to have been recorded in the same space as the musical portions; all of the singers handle the spoken passages in an easy, natural manner, and the acoustics do not change drastically when switching from speech to song.

I suspect this recording will be of interest to Shostakovich specialists, those who must own every note the composer committed to paper. A single CD of musical highlights might be worth investigating, should Chandos choose to extract them from the complete set.

Roland Graeme

Contributors to This Issue

WILLIAM ALBRIGHT, freelance writer

ROBERT BAXTER, critic; radio commentator

JACK BELSOM, archivist, New Orleans Opera Association

CATHERINE E. CAMPBELL, professor of French, team-teacher of course entitled "Literature and Opera," Cottey College, Nevada (Missouri)

JACQUES CHUILON, Paris-based author; musicologist; vocal pedagogue; contributor to French opera journals

ALAN FISCHLER, associate professor of English at Le Moyne College

CHRISTOPHER GIBBS, assistant professor of music, State University of New York at Buffalo

ROLAND GRAEME, critic; author

CHRISTOPHER HATCH, former editor, *The Musical Quarterly*; former book review editor, *The Opera Quarterly*

MICHAEL E. HENSTOCK, author

CHRISTOPHER HEPPNER, recently retired professor of English, McGill University

GEORGE JELLINEK, author; critic; host of the nationally syndicated radio program *The Vocal Scene*

HARLAN JENNINGS, faculty member, School of Music, Michigan State University

TOM KAUFMAN, consultant in regulatory affairs; freelance writer; authority on performance history

LOWELL LINDGREN, professor of music, Massachusetts Institute of Technology

THOMAS MAY, classical music editor, Amazon.com; writer of music and theater criticism for the *Washington Post*, *Washington Review*, and *Opera News*

DAVID McKEE, managing editor, *Casino Executive* magazine, Las Vegas

ROGER PINES, program editor, Lyric Opera of Chicago

MARION LIGNANA ROSENBERG, author; translator; journalist; former broadcaster

LINDA JUNE SNYDER, professor of voice and opera, University of Dayton; member of board of directors, National Association of Teachers of Singing; former board member, National Opera Association

JAMES L. ZYCHOWICZ, musicologist; editor and director of sales, A-R Editions

Submission of Articles
and Instructions to Authors

1. The editor requests the submission of professionally donated articles on all aspects of opera, including history, composition, singing, conducting, staging, lighting, producing, and directing.

2. Articles must be original material. Three copies of the manuscript must be submitted; two of them may be machine-duplicated. The entire manuscript, *including endnotes*, must be typed in double space on one side only of 8 ½-by-11-inch heavy white bond paper. Erasable bond is not suitable for the publishing process. Number pages consecutively beginning with the title page. Please also submit a disk file of your article in a commonly used word-processing program, preferably Microsoft Word, on a 3-1/2-inch disk. If possible, consult *Merriam-Webster's Collegiate Dictionary* tenth edition, and *The Chicago Manual of Style*, fourteenth edition.

3. When creating the disk file, avoid automatic hyphenation, justification of right margins, and boldface type. Underline for italics rather than use an italic font.

4. The title page should contain a brief and meaningful title, the author's name and address, and a description of the author appropriate for the "Contributors to This Issue" page.

5. Endnotes with full source information, including specific page numbers, are necessary for all direct quotations and frequently should be used for information that has been paraphrased. (A bibliography should be included when there is no directly quoted or paraphrased material.) Number references consecutively, in the order in which they are first mentioned in the text, by arabic numerals. Ibid. is the only Latin abbreviation to be used (not op. cit. or loc. cit.), and "ibid." should not be underlined.

Endnotes (examples):

1. George Martin, *The Opera Companion to Twentieth-Century Opera* (New York: Dodd, Mead and Company, 1979), p. 104.

2. M. Owen Lee, "The Exasperated Eagle and the Stoic Saint," *The Opera Quarterly*, vol. 2, no. 4 (winter 1984–85), p. 80.

3. Martin, *Twentieth-Century Opera*, pp. 558–59.

4. Ibid., p. 311.

5. Lee, "Exasperated Eagle," p. 83.

6. We welcome any photographs or other art you might submit with your article, *but we require proper written permission for their publication*. (The author is responsible for any fees incurred in the acquiring of such permissions.) Only black-and-white photographs should be submitted. Each illustration or photograph should have a label pasted on its back, indicating the number of the figure, the name of the author, and the top of the figure. Do not make any marks on illustrations or photographs.

7. Musical notations may be included in articles. These notations may be hand drawn and will be typeset by the

publisher. Please place the musical examples at the end of the manuscript and include captions on a separate page.

8. The length of articles will undoubtedly vary. It is suggested that articles be 4,000 to 6,000 words in length.

9. All submitted articles will be reviewed by editorial consultants for suitability for publication.

10. Send articles to E. Thomas Glasow, *The Opera Quarterly*, 197 Oaklawn Drive, Rochester, NY 14617-1813.

11. It is a condition of publication in the journal that authors assign copyright to Oxford University Press. This ensures that requests from third parties to reproduce articles are handled efficiently and consistently and will also allow the article to be as widely disseminated as possible. In assigning copyright, authors may use their own material in other publications provided that the journal is acknowledged as the original place of publication and Oxford University Press is notified in writing and in advance.

The Opera Quarterly
Index to Volume 15

Articles

Authors

Books Reviewed

Carroll, Brendan G., *The Last Prodigy: A Biography of Erich Wolfgang Korngold*, reviewed by Stephen A. Willier, 2, 308–13

Chusid, Martin, ed., *Verdi's Middle Period (1849–1859): Source Studies, Analysis, and Performance Practice*, reviewed by James L. Zychowicz, 2, 294–97

Crespin, Régine, *On Stage, Off Stage: A Memoir*, trans. G. S. Bourdain, reviewed by William Albright, 1, 109–14

Della Seta, Fabrizio, ed., *La traviata* (Verdi), critical edition, reviewed by Aubrey S. Garlington, 2, 291–94

de Van, Gilles, *Verdi's Theater*, trans. Gilda Roberts, reviewed by James L. Zychowicz, 4, 727–30

Drake, James A., *Rosa Ponselle: A Centenary Biography*, reviewed by Joe Pearce, 2, 280–86

Girdham, Jane, *English Opera in Late Eighteenth-Century London: Stephen Storace at Drury Lane*, reviewed by Malcolm S. Cole, 1, 90–94

Gregor-Dellin, Martin, and Dietrich Mark, eds. *Cosima Wagner's Diaries: An Abridgement*, trans. Geoffrey Skelton, reviewed by Christopher Hatch, 1, 106–9

Gruber, Paul, ed., *The Metropolitan Opera Guide to Opera on Video*, reviewed by David McKee, 2, 286–90

Hall, Patricia, *A View of Berg's "Lulu" through the Autograph Sources*, reviewed by Graham H. Phipps, 2, 297–302

Hart, Philip, *Fritz Reiner*, reviewed by David McKee, 4, 742–48

Hill, John Walter, ed., *Roman Monody, Cantata, and Opera from the Circles Around Cardinal Montalto*, reviewed by Lowell Lindgren, 4, 730–35

Hines, Jerome, *The Four Voices of Man*, reviewed by Linda June Snyder, 4, 739–41

Jackson, Paul, *Sign-off for the Old Met: The Metropolitan Opera Broadcasts, 1950–1966*, reviewed by Bruce Burroughs, 2, 268–79

Kater, Michael H., *The Twisted Muse: Musicians and Their Music in the Third Reich*, reviewed by James L. Zychowicz, 1, 101–4

Küster, Konrad, *Mozart: A Musical Biography*, trans. Mary Whittall, reviewed by E. Thomas Glasow, 1, 94–97

Levin, David J., *Richard Wagner, Fritz Lang, and the Nibelungen: The Dramaturgy of Disavowal*, reviewed by Thomas May, 4, 718–23

Milnes, Sherrill, with contributions by Dennis McGovern, *American Aria: From Farm Boy to Opera Star*, reviewed by Catherine E. Campbell, 4, 738–39

Parker, Roger, *Leonora's Last Act: Essays in Verdian Discourse*, reviewed by Christopher Gibbs, 4, 723–27

Phillips-Matz, Mary Jane, *Rosa Ponselle: American Diva*, reviewed by Joe Pearce, 2, 280–86

Radice, Mark A., ed., *Opera in Context: Essays on Historical Staging from the Late Renaissance to the Time of Puccini*, reviewed by Christopher Hatch, 4, 735–37

Rosselli, John, *The Life of Bellini*, reviewed by Stephen A. Willier, 1, 98–101

Schnauber, Cornelius, *Plácido Domingo*, trans. Susan H. Ray, reviewed by Ronald T. Shaheen, 1, 114–17

Simpson, Adrienne, *Opera's Farthest Frontier: A History of Professional Opera in New Zealand*, reviewed by Tom Kaufman, 1, 105–6

Te Kanawa, Kiri, with Conrad Wilson, *Opera for Lovers*, reviewed by William Albright, 1, 109–14

Tommasini, Anthony, *Virgil Thomson: Composer on the Aisle*, reviewed by Victor Fell Yellin, 2, 302–8

Trotter, William R., *Priest of Music: The Life of Dimitri Mitropoulos*, reviewed by David McKee, 4, 742–48

Wilcox, Michael, *Benjamin Britten's Operas*, reviewed by Joe K. Law, 1, 117–20

Videos Reviewed

Recordings Reviewed

The following Statement of Ownership, Management, and Circulation is provided in accordance with the requirement as contained in 39 U.S. Code 3685: *The Opera Quarterly* (ISSN 0736-0053) is published quarterly (4 times a year) by Oxford University Press, a nonprofit, educational organization, located at 2001 Evans Road, Cary, North Carolina 27513-2009. The Editor is E. Thomas Glasow, 197 Oaklawn Drive, Rochester, New York 14617-1813. There are no known bondholders, mortgagees, or other security holders owning or holding 1 percent or more of total amount of bonds, mortgages or other securities. The purpose, function, and nonprofit status of this organization and the exempt status for federal income tax purposes have not changed during the preceding 12 months. The annual subscription price is $42 for individuals and $110 for institutions. During the preceding 12 months, the average number of copies printed for each issue was 3,900, the average paid circulation 3,011, the average free distribution 11, the average number of copies distributed 3,022. Corresponding figures for the last issue before filing: total number of copies printed 4,100, total paid circulation 3,387, total free copies distributed 11, total distribution 3,398. Average percent paid 99%; actual percent paid 99%.

I certify that the statements made by me above are correct and complete.

Gloria Bruno
Manager, Journals Customer Service
Oxford University Press

(This statement is for 1999.)

Musical Studies Journals by Oxford University Press

THE OPERA QUARTERLY
Editor: E. THOMAS GLASOW

Volume 16, 2000 (4 issues)
http://www.oq.oupjournals.org
Institutions: $119   Individuals: $42
Students: $25

For over a decade, *The Opera Quarterly* has earned enthusiastic praise from opera lovers and professionals for its presentation of stimulating, enlightening, and enjoyable reading on all aspects of opera. Each issue contains original articles and incisive reviews of books, recordings and videotapes. Rare and beautiful photographs, some never before published, typically accompany the articles and reviews. *The Opera Quarterly* offers opera enthusiasts an in-depth look at every element of this richest of art forms.

THE MUSICAL QUARTERLY
Editor: LEON BOTSTEIN

Volume 84, 2000 (4 issues)
http://www.mq.oupjournals.org
Institutions:$99   Individuals: $44
Students: $29
FIRST TIME SUBSCRIBERS RECEIVE 20% OFF

Look no further than *The Musical Quarterly* to find imaginative, pathbreaking ideas, by both young and well-known composers, critics, and scholars from across the whole spectrum of musical thought and practice. *MQ* is the richest and most vibrant American voice in the field today, shaping new forms of musicological inquiry. The journal is packed with the latest work from the field—every issue features these lively sections: "American Musics"; "Music and Culture"; "The Twentieth Century"; "Institutions, Industries, Technologies"; and "Primary Sources".

EARLY MUSIC
Editor: TESS KNIGHTON

Volume 28, 2000 (4 issues)
http://www.em.oupjournals.org
Institutions: $354   Individuals: $81
Students: $45

Over the last few years performances on period instruments have played an ever larger role in concert programs and record catalogs. This fast-growing interest is underscored by the high attendance at early music festivals across the United States. At the center is *Early Music*. Beautifully produced, it is one of the most articulate and widely read magazines to cover the field of historical performance. In each issue of *Early Music* leading specialists from all over the world review in detail the latest publications and recordings.

JOURNAL OF THE ROYAL MUSICAL ASSOCIATION
Volume 125, 2000 (2 issues)
http://www.jrma.oupjournals.org
Institutions: $117 Individuals: $71

The *Journal of the Royal Musical Association* was established in 1986 and is now one of the major refereed musicological journals in Britain. It publishes high-quality articles and extended reviews in all areas of musicology, including music analysis and ethnomusicology.

MUSIC & LETTERS
Volume 81, 2000 (4 issues)
http://www.ml.oupjournals.org
Institutions: $133   Individuals: $77

Founded in 1920 *Music & Letters* is long established as the leading British journal of musical scholarship. Its coverage embraces all fields of musical inquiry, from the earliest times to the present day, and its authorship is international. A particularly valued feature is the range and number of reviews covering books (not only in English), scholarly editions of music of the past, and new music.

Oxford University Press, 2001 Evans Road, Cary NC 27513 Tel: (919) 677- 0977
Fax: (919) 677-1714 E-mail: jnlorders@oup-usa.org **Outside the Americas:**
Great Clarendon Street, Oxford OX2 6DP, UK Tel: +44 (0) 1865 267907
Fax: +44 (0) 1865 267485 E-mail: jnl.orders@oup.co.uk

MUSFILY2K

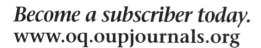

Countertenor David Daniels (whose Handel aria CD is reviewed in the next issue of The Opera Quarterly, *as Arsace in the 1998 Glimmerglass Opera production of Handel's* Partenope. *(Photo by George Mott. Courtesy of Glimmerglass Opera.)*